MW01092802

ACQUIRING WISDOM

Adhering to the Word of God from Zeal to Reveal

TED FREEMAN

ISBN 978-1-64003-929-2 (Paperback)
ISBN 978-1-64003-930-8 (Digital)

Copyright © 2018 Ted Freeman
All rights reserved
First Edition

All rights reserved. No part of this publication may be reproduced, distributed, or transmitted in any form or by any means, including photocopying, recording, or other electronic or mechanical methods without the prior written permission of the publisher. For permission requests, solicit the publisher via the address below.

Covenant Books, Inc.
11661 Hwy 707
Murrells Inlet, SC 29576
www.covenantbooks.com

This book is the Father's work. I worked only as his scribe (writer), so that what God wanted is made abundantly known and would be done at this time. I humbly, with great servitude to our Father, present God's work for us.

—Pastor Ted

Contents

Information to Help

Wisdom can only come from our heavenly Father. So "acquiring" it can only be ascertained from God's words and the teachings of his Son, Jesus the Christ. To achieve our goal of "acquiring more wisdom," we have attained the help of the following Holy Bible translations. Their abbreviations will appear throughout this work:

- English Standard Version (ESV)
- The Message (MSG) Bible
- New International Version (NIV)
- New Living Translation (NLT)
- New King James Version (NKJV)
- King James Version (KJV)
- Christian Standard Bible (CSB)
- New American Standard Bible (NASB)
- The Interlinear Bible
- International Standard Version (ISV)

Author's Notes

Welcome to the beginning of a personal journey with your "First Love" of your life, the "Creator of all," the great "I AM that I AM," "our heavenly Father."

Enjoy getting reacquainted or acquainted with aspects of God's love for us and our commitments to God, which may have been pushed to the back burners of our lives. Reestablish or create the relationship with your God that will bring you "peace of mind" no matter what you are going through.

This journey is your journey. I have kept my flavoring to a minimum, as instructed by the Father. If you know me and find it hard to find me in this writing, then I've done my job through obedience to the Father, through the teachings of his Son, Jesus the Christ, and adherence to the guidance of the Holy Spirit.

Take your time and enjoy reinforcing, rebuilding, and fortifying your relationship with the God of your life.

Remember:

"The proof of desire is in the pursuit!!!"

Be blessed.

—Ted

Preface

ANCIENT OF DAYS

Psalm 32

Blessed is the one whose transgression is forgiven, whose sin is covered.

Blessed is the man against whom the LORD counts no iniquity, and in whose spirit there is no deceit.

For when I kept silent, my bones wasted away through my groaning all day long.

For day and night your hand was heavy upon me; my strength was dried up as by the heat of summer. Selah

I acknowledged my sin to you, and I did not cover my iniquity; I said, "I will confess my transgressions to the LORD," and you forgave the iniquity of my sin. Selah

Therefore let everyone who is godly offer prayer to you at a time when you may be found; surely in the rush of great waters, they shall not reach him. You are a hiding place for me; you preserve me from trouble; you surround me with shouts of deliverance. Selah

I will instruct you in the way you should go; I will counsel you with my eye upon you. Be not like a horse or a mule, without understanding, which must be curbed with a bit and bridle, or it will not stay near you.

Many are the sorrows of the wicked, but steadfast love surrounds the one who trusts in the LORD. Be glad in the LORD, and rejoice, O righteous, and shout for joy, all you upright in heart! (Psalm 32:1–11, ESV)

[Selah = Pause]

—David

Current of Days

As you sit down to read this book, do not let your mind race ahead of your eyes. Each sentence, paragraph, and page builds to the next. This book is a bridge, or a pathway, and God's pathways are always revealed one step at a time.

If you try to run ahead, you will become confused and want to give up. However, you must remember the purpose for scripture.

> *Every part of Scripture is God-breathed and useful one way or another—showing us truth, exposing our rebellion, correcting our mistakes, training us to live God's way. Through the Word we are put together and shaped up for the tasks God has for us. (2 Timothy 3:16 and 17, MSG)*

Read and learn, question, and search for the answers. Every question you have, you can receive the answer if you read and think and learn. God has a plan and a purpose for every one of us, and if we study his word and adhere to it, all will be revealed.

—Rhonda L. Freeman

Introduction

I was going to have someone else write the Introduction. Then the Father said to me, "I will write my own Introduction." Enough said.

> *Don't worry about anything; instead, pray about everything. Tell God what you need, and thank him for all he has done. Then you will experience God's peace, which exceeds anything we can understand. His peace will guard your hearts and minds as you live in Christ Jesus.*
>
> *And now, dear brothers and sisters, one final thing. Fix your thoughts on what is true, and honorable, and right, and pure, and lovely, and admirable. Think about things that are excellent and worthy of praise. Keep putting into practice all you learned and received from me—everything you heard from me and saw me doing. Then the God of peace will be with you. (Philippians 4:6—9, NLT)*

Section 1

WHAT MUST I DO?

Chapter 1

ADHERENCE

On the fourth day of the ninth month, in the fourth year of the reign of King Darius, GOD's Message again came to Zechariah.

The town of Bethel had sent a delegation headed by Sarezer and Regem-Melech to pray for GOD's blessing and to confer with the priests of the Temple of GOD-of the Angel-Armies, and also with the prophets. They posed this question: "Should we plan for a day of mourning and abstinence next August, the seventieth anniversary of Jerusalem's fall, as we have been doing all these years?"

GOD-of the Angel-Armies gave me this Message for them, for all the people and for the priests: "When you held days of fasting every fifth and seventh month all these seventy years, were you doing it for me? And when you held feasts, was that for me? Hardly. You're interested in religion, I'm interested in people."

"There's nothing new to say on this subject. Don't you still have the message of the earlier prophets from the time when Jerusalem was still a thriving, bustling city and the outlying country-

side, the Negev and Shephelah, was populated?"
[This is the message that GOD gave Zechariah.]
Well, the message hasn't changed. GOD-of-the-
Angel-Armies said then and says now:

"Treat one another justly. Love your neighbors. Be compassionate with each other. Don't
take advantage of widows, orphans, visitors, and
the poor. Don't plot and scheme against one
another—that's evil."

"But did your ancestors listen? No, they set
their jaws in defiance. They shut their ears. They
steeled themselves against GOD's revelation and
the Spirit-filled sermons preached by the earlier
prophets by order of GOD-of-the-Angel-Armies.
And GOD became angry, really angry, because he
told them everything plainly and they wouldn't
listen to a word he said."

"So [this is what GOD-of-the-Angel-Armies
said] if they won't listen to me, I won't listen to
them. I scattered them to the four winds. They
ended up strangers wherever they were. Their
'promised land' became a vacant lot—weeds
and tin cans and thistles. Not a sign of life. They
turned a dreamland into a wasteland." (Zechariah
7:1–14, MSG)

Why is it so difficult for us to have the wisdom and understanding necessary to follow the directives that our Father has abundantly laid out for us? We have very little difficulty following the laws
established for our day-to-day existence, but the spiritual directives
of God alter our wisdom and confuse our understanding. Clearly,
that is because of our day-to-day existence and our determination of
what we must do from moment to moment. We place major importance on the earthly hierarchy of what is important and valuable,
which does not leave much room for understanding the value of or
the wisdom of God's spiritual directives.

Every aspect of our earthly world is designed to be in total conflict with how God wants us to proceed on this earth.

> When all the people heard of Jesus' arrival, they flocked to see him and also to see Lazarus, the man Jesus had raised from the dead. Then the leading priests decided to kill Lazarus, too, for it was because of him that many of the people had deserted them and believed in Jesus. (John 12:9–11, NLT)
>
> If the world hates you, remember that it hated me first. The world would love you as one of its own if you belonged to it, but you are no longer part of the world. I chose you to come out of the world, so it hates you. (John 15:18 and 19, NLT)
>
> Then they began to argue among themselves about who would be the greatest among them. Jesus told them, "In this world the king and great men lord it over their people, yet they are called 'friends of the people.' But among you it will be different. Those who are the greatest among you should take the lowest rank, and the leader should be like a servant. Who is more important, the one who sits at the table or the one who serves? The one who sits at the table, of course. But not here! For I am among you as one who serves." (Luke 22:24–30, NLT)

There is conflict, a life of conflict because adhering to the Father's wisdom and his understanding clashes with our existence, our wisdom, and our understanding, an existence that spawns death and destruction, an existence that fosters, particularly in men, a concept that a reason to live becomes a difficult adventure.

Men, in particular but not exclusively, have historically found noble and not so noble reasons to end their existence. The biggest problem is finding a reason to live. The world will provide us endless opportunities to die, harm ourselves, and destroy and harm others, but will never offer us the formula for life. Until we choose life, the blessings of God cannot overtake us, only the curses. God has told us to choose life.

> "Now listen! Today I am giving you a choice between life and death, between prosperity and disaster. For I command you this day to love the LORD your God and keep his commands, decrees, and regulations by walking in his ways. If you do this, you will live and multiply, and the LORD your God will bless you and the land you are about to enter and occupy." (Deuteronomy 30:15 and 16, NLT)

> "Today I have given you the choice between life and death, between blessings and curses. Now I call on heaven and earth to witness the choice you make. Oh, that you would choose life, so that you and your descendants might live! You can make this choice by loving the LORD your God, obeying him, and committing yourself firmly to him. This is the key to your life. And if you love and obey the LORD, you will live long in the land the LORD swore to give your ancestors Abraham, Isaac, and Jacob." (Deuteronomy 30:19 and 20, NLT)

> Those who heard Jesus use this illustration didn't understand what he meant, so he explained it to them: "I tell you the truth, I am the gate for the sheep. All who came before me were thieves and robbers. But the true sheep did not listen to them. Yes, I am the gate. Those who come in through me will be saved. They will come and go freely and will find good pastures. The thief's purpose is to steal and kill and destroy. My pur-

pose is to give them a rich and satisfying life."
(John 10:6–10, NLT)

"Don't imagine that I came to bring peace to the earth! I came not to bring peace, but a sword."

"I have come to set a man against his father, a daughter against her mother, and a daughter-in-law against her mother-in-law. Your enemies will be right in your own household!"

"If you love your father or mother more than you love me, you are not worthy of being mine; or if you love your son or daughter more than me, you are not worthy of being mine. If you refuse to take up your cross and follow me, you are not worthy of being mine. If you cling to your life, you will lose it; but if you give up your life for me, you will find it." (Matthew 10:34–39, NLT)

"A brother will betray his brother to death, a father will betray his own child, and children will rebel against their parents and cause them to be killed. And all nations will hate you because you are my followers. But everyone who endures to the end will be saved." (Matthew 10:21 and 22, NLT)

And this is what God has testified: He has given us eternal life, and this life is in his Son. Whoever has the Son has life; whoever does not have God's Son does not have life. (1 John 5:11 and 12, NLT)

No matter how we look at life, God's approach to it does not coincide with the world's approach to life. A friend asked me, "What is the difference between confidence and arrogance?" I gave him a response that was constructed and generated on my own spiritual base. I had forgotten to ask the Holy Spirit (a human frailty that I am too often guilty of). Ten hours later, the Holy Spirit told me to tell him that the difference was "confidence is based on faith and arrogance is based on self-reliance."

A life in Christ that guides you and helps fulfill our mandate to help others and let our little light shine is our goal.

> Do to others whatever you would like them to do to you. This is the essence of all that is taught in the law and the prophets. (Matthew 7:12, NLT)
>
> You are the light of the world—like a city on a hilltop that cannot be hidden. No one lights a lamp and then puts it under a basket. Instead, a lamp is placed on a stand, where it gives light to everyone in the house. In the same way, let your good deeds shine out for all to see, so that everyone will praise your heavenly Father. (Matthew 5:14–16, NLT)

Unfortunately, when we do not adhere to God's wisdom and understanding for our existence, we are enrolled in a secret society that has us running around incanting slogans similar to but not limited to these:

- God knows my heart.
- What God has done for me is between God and me.
- It doesn't take all that.
- I go to church.
- God blesses me for me.
- I can't find a church home I like.
- I can do it at home.
- I don't like….
- Those people in the choir are mean.
- I think they're all that.
- I saw him trying to….
- I don't have time.

Leaning on our own understanding and earthly wisdom creates a dangerous society of undercover followers of Christ. This grouping is known as the Society of Undercover Christians (SUC.), making their members secret agents of Jesus Christ.

There is one major problem with this Society of Undercover Christians that does not conform to adherence with the Father's wisdom and understanding for our lives. He doesn't need undercover agents. This approach and membership in this group could have very dire consequences.

> "I tell you the truth, everyone who acknowledges me publicly here on earth, the Son of Man will also acknowledge in the presence of God's angels. But anyone who denies me here on earth will be denied before God's angels." (Luke 12:8–9, NLT)
>
> When he finally arrives, blazing in beauty and all his angels with him, the Son of Man will take his place on his glorious throne. Then all the nations will be arranged before him and he will sort the people out, much as a shepherd sorts out sheep and goats, putting sheep to his right and goats to his left.
>
> Then the King will say to those on his right, "Enter, you who are blessed by my Father! Take what's coming to you in this kingdom. It's been ready for you since the world's foundation. And here's why:
>
> - I was hungry and you fed me,
> - I was thirsty and you gave me a drink,
> - I was homeless and you gave me a room,
> - I was shivering and you gave me clothes,
> - I was sick and you stopped to visit,
> - I was in prison and you came to me."

Then those "sheep" are going to say, "Master, what are you talking about? When did we see you hungry and feed you, thirsty and give you a drink? And when did we ever see you sick or in prison and come to you?" Then the King will say, "I'm telling the solemn truth: Whenever you did one of these things to someone overlooked or ignored, that was me—you did it to me."

Then he will turn to the "goats," the ones on his left, and say, "Get out, worthless goats! You're good for nothing but the fires of hell. And why? Because—

- I was hungry and you gave me no meal;
- I was thirsty and you gave me no drink;
- I was homeless and you gave me no bed;
- I was shivering and you gave me no clothes;
- Sick and in prison, and you never visited."

Then those "goats" are going to say, "Master, what are you talking about? When did we ever see you hungry or thirsty or shivering or sick or in prison and didn't help?"

He will answer them, "I'm telling the solemn truth: Whenever you failed to do one of these things to someone who was being overlooked or ignored, that was me—you failed to do it to me."

Then those "goats" will be herded to their eternal doom, but the "sheep" to their eternal reward. (Matthew 25:31–46, MSG)

Members of the Society of Undercover Christians are jeopardizing their eternal life by leaning on their own understanding and relying on their earthly wisdom. They end up being too concerned about themselves or the way the world may think about them letting the light of Christ shine in them. They go along with all sorts of things just to be accepted or gain favor in this world. They deny directions and guidance, given by the word of God. They hide their talents, forsake their families, abandon their communities, and reject their commission given to them, by not adhering to God's wisdom and understanding for their lives.

They find themselves lost in the wilderness of life wondering why they are still lost, frustrated, and with no peace of mind. It's time to get a clue. Adherence to the will of God for your life will bring the peace of mind so needed.

Chapter 2

WISDOM CALLS

We've been taught that adherence to God's will is an either/or proposition. You either do it or you don't, but we still attempt to make it a blended situation of what God wants and what we want or think; that just won't work in our lives.

No one can serve two masters. For you will hate one and love the other; you will be devoted to one and despise the other. You cannot serve both God and money.

> That is why I tell you not to worry about everyday life—whether you have enough food and drink, or enough clothes to wear. Isn't life more than food, and your body more than clothing? Look at the birds. They don't plant or harvest or store food in barns, for your heavenly Father feeds them. And aren't you far more valuable to him than they are? Can all your worries add a single moment to your life? (Matthew 6:24–27, NLT)

Our heavenly Father has made it abundantly clear to us the importance of wisdom and the importance of "getting understanding."

> And this is what he says to all humanity: "The fear of the Lord is true wisdom; to forsake evil is real understanding." (Job 28:28, NLT)

Fear of the LORD is the foundation of true knowledge, but fools despise wisdom and discipline. (Proverbs 1:7, NLT)

Trust in the LORD with all your heart; do not depend on your own understanding. Seek his will in all you do, and he will show you the path to take. (Proverbs 3:5 and 6, NLT)

Don't be impressed with your own wisdom. Instead, fear the LORD and turn away from evil. Then you will have healing for your body and strength for your bones. (Proverbs 3:7 and 8, NLT)

Blessed is the one who finds wisdom, and the one who gets understanding, for the gain from her is better than gain from silver and her profit better than gold. She is more precious than jewels, and nothing you desire can compare with her. Long life is in her right hand; in her left hand are riches and honor. Her ways are ways of pleasantness, and all her paths are peace. (Proverbs 3:13–17, ESV)

Wisdom is a tree of life to those who embrace her; happy are those who hold her tightly. By wisdom the LORD founded the earth; by understanding he created the heavens. (Proverbs 3:18 and 19, NLT)

Getting wisdom is the wisest thing you can do! And whatever else you do, develop good judgment. If you prize wisdom, she will make you great. Embrace her, and she will honor you. (Proverbs 4:7 and 8, NLT)

Fear of the LORD is the foundation of wisdom. Knowledge of the Holy One results in good judgement. (Proverbs 9:10, NLT)

Wisdom will multiply your days and add years to your life. If you become wise, you will be the one to benefit. If you scorn wisdom, you will be the one to suffer. (Proverbs 9:11 and 12, NLT)

Fear of the LORD teaches wisdom; humility precedes honor. (Proverbs 15: 33, NLT)

Sensible people keep their eyes glued on wisdom, but a fool's eyes wander to the ends of the earth. (Proverbs 17:24, NLT)

To acquire wisdom is to love oneself; people who cherish understanding will prosper. (Proverbs 19:8, NLT)

No human wisdom or understanding or plan can stand against the LORD. (Proverbs 21:30, NLT)

A house is built by wisdom and becomes strong through good sense. Through knowledge its rooms are filled with all sorts of precious riches and valuables. The wise are mightier than the strong, and those with knowledge grow stronger and stronger. (Proverbs 24:3–5, NLT)

Wisdom is too lofty for fools. Among leaders at the city gate, they have nothing to say. (Proverbs 24:7, NLT)

The man who loves wisdom brings joy to his father, but if he hangs around with prostitutes, his wealth is wasted. (Proverbs 29:3, NLT)

"I am weary, O God; I am weary and worn out, O God. I am too stupid to be human, and I lack common sense. I have not mastered human wisdom, nor do I know the Holy One." (Proverbs 30:1–3, NLT)

Wisdom and understanding, understanding and wisdom—why is it so difficult for us to accept these theories? Why do we debate, mitigate, and dilute these concepts? Why do we spend our entire lives searching for something that is constantly in front of us our entire lives? God has made it perfectly clear in Job 28:28 (NLT) that "*fear* and *forsake*" are rudimentary qualities we must have for "true wisdom" and "real understanding."

We are taught not to be afraid because God is with us.

> For God has not given us a spirit of fear and timidity, but of power, love, and self-discipline. (2 Timothy 1:7, NLT)

Then we're told.

> Fear of the LORD is the foundation of true knowledge. (Proverbs 1:7a, NLT)

Leaning on our own understanding will allow us to become confused and will lead to us making wrong choses in life. We do know one thing for sure that God is not the author of confusion.

> But the wisdom from above is first of all pure. It is also peace loving, gentle at all times, and willing to yield to others. It is full of mercy and good deeds. It shows no favoritism and is always sincere. And those who are peacemakers will plant seeds of peace and reap a harvest of righteousness. (James 3:17–18, NLT)
>
> For God is not a God of disorder but of peace, as in all the meetings of God's holy people. (1 Corinthians 14:33, NLT)

Chapter 3

THE INTRODUCTION OF PRIDE (ORIGINAL SIN)

We used to have it way back in the garden of Eden, and now it's time for us to recapture what we had, as much as it's humanly possible and always striving toward coming closer to what God wants from us.

Since God is not the author of confusion, then there must be something in us that creates confusion and keeps us from "fearing God in thought, action, and deeds" and "forsaking and abandoning anything that's displeasing to God." It is something that every human being has been confronted with. It's been passed down from Adam and Eve and has been identified as the "original sin."

> Now the serpent was more crafty than any other beast of the field that the LORD God had made.
>
> He said to the woman, "Did God actually say, 'You shall not eat of any tree in the garden'?" And the women said to the serpent, "We may eat of the fruit of the trees in the garden, but God said, 'You shall not eat of the fruit of the tree that is in the midst of the garden, neither shall you touch it, lest you die.'" But the serpent said to the woman, "You will not surely die. For God knows that when you eat of it your eyes will be

opened, and you will be like God, knowing good and evil." So when the woman saw that the tree was good for food, and that it was a delight to the eyes, and that the tree was to be desired to make one wise, she took of its fruit and ate, and she gave some to her husband who was with her, and he ate. Then the eyes of both were opened, and they knew that they were naked. And they sewed fig leaves together and made themselves loincloths. (Genesis 3:1–7, ESV)

The infusion of the original sin into our spiritual DNA has caused every human being to waiver in their fear of God (wisdom and understanding) and their forsaking of those things that displease God (sin). That original sin has a name, and that name is pride.

"And if, in spite of all this, you still disobey me, I will punish you seven times over for your sins. I will break your proud spirit by making the skies as unyielding as iron and the earth as hard as bronze. All your work will be for nothing, for your land will yield no crops, and your trees will bear no fruit." (Leviticus 26:18–20, NLT)

But when David's oldest brother, Eliab, heard David talking to the men, he was angry. "What are you doing around here anyway?" he demanded. "What about those few sheep you're supposed to be taking care of? I know about your pride and deceit. You just want to see the battle!" (1 Samuel 17:28, NLT)

About that time Hezekiah became deathly ill. He prayed to the LORD, who healed him and gave him a miraculous sign. But Hezekiah did not respond appropriately to the kindness shown him, and he became proud. So the LORD's anger came against him and against Judah and

Jerusalem. Then Hezekiah humbled himself and repented of his pride, as did the people of Jerusalem. So the LORD's anger did not fall on them during Hezekiah's lifetime. (2 Chronicles 32:24–26, NLT)

He makes them turn from doing wrong; he keeps them from pride. (Job 33:17, NLT)

People cry out when they are oppressed. They groan beneath the power of the mighty.

Yet they don't ask, "Where is God my Creator, the one who gives songs in the night?

Where is the one who makes us smarter than the animals and wiser than the birds of the sky?"

And when they cry out, God does not answer because of their pride. (Job 35:9–12, NLT)

The wicked are too proud to seek God. They seem to think that God is dead. Yet they succeed in everything they do. They do not see your punishment awaiting them. (Psalms 10:4 and 5, NLT)

Thou shalt hide them in the secret of thy presence from the pride of man: thou shalt keep them secretly in a pavilion from the strife of tongues. (Psalm 31:20, KJV)

He beholdeth all high things: he is a king over all the children of pride. (Job 41:34, KJV)

Pride goeth before destruction, and an haughty spirit before a fall.

Better it is to be of an humble spirit with the lowly than to divide the spoil with the proud. (Proverbs 16:18 and 19, KJV)

All who fear the LORD will hate evil. Therefore, I hate pride and arrogance, corruption and perverse speech. (Proverbs 8:13, NLT)

Pride leads to disgrace, but with humility comes wisdom. (Proverbs 11:2, NLT)

Pride leads to conflict; those who take advice are wise. (Proverbs 13:10, NLT)

Pride ends in humiliation, while humility brings honor. (Proverbs 29:23, NLT)

The LORD of Heaven's Armies has done it to destroy your pride and bring low all earth's nobility. (Isaiah 23:9, NLT)

Then I received this message from the LORD: "This is what the LORD says: This shows how I will rot away the pride of Judah and Jerusalem. These wicked people refuse to listen to me. They stubbornly follow their own desires and worship other gods. Therefore, they will become like this loincloth—good for nothing! As a loincloth clings to a man's waist, so I created Judah and Israel to cling to me, says the LORD. They were to be my people my pride, my glory—an honor to my name. But they would not listen to me." (Jeremiah 13:8–11, NLT)

"You have been deceived by the fear you inspire in others and by your own pride. You live in a rock fortress and control the mountain heights. But even if you make your nest among the peaks with the eagles, I will bring you crashing down," says the LORD. (Jeremiah 49:16, NLT)

Scripture after scripture guiding our paths, but we continue to find it difficult to acquire the wisdom that God wants us to have. Clearly our pride, the original sin, is at its root. Just look at Adam and Eve and Cain and Abel. Their inner need to be like God caused them to violate the only commandment they had:

The LORD God placed the man in the Garden of Eden to tend and watch over it. But the

LORD God warned him, "You may freely eat the fruit of every tree in the garden—except the tree of the knowledge of good and evil. If you eat its fruit, you are sure to die." (Genesis 2:15–17, NLT)

Even after Adam's and Eve's unleashing of the main destroyer of wisdom and understanding, in all human beings' lives, "pride," even after their expulsion from the garden of Eden, God was readily available to participate in their daily lives and activities. God moved among us. He was available to converse with us. God walked among people talking and guiding them.

He continued to impart wisdom and understanding according to our needs, but the wisdom of God was fading fast because of the false desires and wants that the original sin, "pride," had introduced. Understanding of what was demanded of us by God was rapidly disintegrating in our hearts and being replaced with our desire and ability to turn from God, because of sin.

Now I, Nebuchadnezzar, praise and glorify and honor the King of heaven. All his acts are just and true, and he is able to humble the proud. (Daniel 4: 37, NLT)

But when his heart was lifted up, and his mind hardened in pride, he was deposed from his kingly throne, and they took his glory from him:

And he was driven from the sons of men; and his heart was made like the beasts, and his dwelling was with the wild asses: they fed him with grass like oxen, and his body was wet with the dew of heaven; till he knew that the most high God ruled in the kingdom of men, and that he appointeth over it whomsoever he will.

And thou his son, O Belshazzar, hast not humbled thine heart, though thou knewest all this;

But has lifted up thyself against the Lord of heaven; and they have brought the vessels of his house before thee, and thou, and thy lords, thy wives, and thy concubines, have drunk wine in them; and thou hast praised the gods of silver, and gold, of brass, iron, wood and stone, which see not, nor hear, nor know: and the God in whose hand thy breath is, and whose are all thy ways, hast thou not glorifies. (Daniel 5:20–23, KJV)

And the pride of Israel doth testify to his face: therefore shall Israel and Ephraim fall in their iniquity; Judah also shall fall with them.

They shall go with their flocks and with their herds to seek the LORD; but they shall not find him; he hath withdrawn himself from them. (Hosea 5:5 and 6, KJV)

You have been deceived by your own pride because you live in a rock fortress and make your home high in the mountains. "Who can ever reach us way up here?" you ask boastfully. But even if you soared as high as eagles and built your nest among the stars, I would bring you crashing down, says the LORD. (Obadiah 1:3–4, NLT)

And then he added, "It is what comes from inside that defiles you. For from within, out of a person's heart, come evil thoughts, sexual immorality, theft, murder, adultery, greed, wickedness, deceit, lustful desires, envy, slander, pride, and foolishness. All these vile things come from within; they are what defile you." (Mark 7:20–23, NLT)

Not a novice, lest being lifted up with pride he fall into the condemnation of the devil. (1 Timothy 3:6, KJV)

For the world offers only a craving for physical pleasure, a craving for everything we see, and pride in our achievements and possessions. These are not from the Father, but from the world." (1 John 2:16, NLT)

But he did not accept Cain and his gift. This made Cain very angry, and he looked dejected.

"Why are you so angry?" the LORD asked Cain. "Why do you look so dejected? You will be accepted if you do what is right. But if you refuse to do what is right, then watch out! Sin is crouching at the door, eager to control you. But you must subdue it and be its master."

One day Cain suggested to his brother, "Let's go out into the fields." And while they were in the field, Cain attacked his brother, Abel, and killed him.

Afterward the LORD asked Cain, "Where is your brother? Where is Abel?"

"I don't know," Cain responded. "Am I my brother's guardian?" (Genesis 4:5–9, NLT)

Cain replied to the LORD, "My punishment is too great for me to bear! You have banished me from the land and your presence; you have made me a homeless wanderer. Anyone who finds me will kill me!" (Genesis 4:13 and 14, NLT)

The LORD replied, "No, for I will give a sevenfold punishment to anyone who kills you." Then the LORD put a mark on Cain to warn anyone who might try to kill him. So Cain left the LORD's presence and settled in the land of Nod, east of Eden. (Genesis 4:15 and 16, NLT)

Dwelling in the presence of God is the goal that we have to work toward. Cain was given it at birth and could not appreciate it. [I know you have always had a curiosity about Nod and where Cain's wife came from. Concentrate on the *presence of the Lord* as a constant 24/7. Then the relevancy of dwelling in Nod loses its importance to you.]

I tell the story of Cain and Abel to show God's presence and interaction among human beings (Gen. 4:1–16). The actual translation of Hebrew verse 14 reads:

> Lo, You have driven me out from the face of the earth today. And I shall be hidden from Your face. And I shall be a vagabond and a fugitive on the earth. And it will be that anyone who finds me shall kill me. (Genesis 4:14, The Interlinear Bible)

God walked among us and then withdrew himself because of our sin nature brought on by the absence of wisdom and the leaning on our own understanding.

What the Lord shows us is that a lot of what we use today, to get into the presence of God (worship), are things that Cain, his family, and the people of Nod invented to get into God's presence—all things made necessary by our inability to acquire wisdom and understanding, causing us to be out of the presence of God.

> Cain had sexual relations with his wife, and she became pregnant and gave birth to Enoch. Than Cain founded a city, which was named Enoch, after his son. Enoch had a son named Irad. Irad became the father of Mehujael. Mehujael became the father of Methushael. Methushael became the father of Lamech.
>
> Lamech married two women. The first was named Adah, and the second was Zillah. Adah gave birth to Jabal, who was the first of those who raise livestock and live in tents. His brother's name was Jubal, the first of all who play the harp and flute. Lamech's other wife, Zillah, gave birth to a son named Tubal-cain. He became an expert

in forging tools of bronze and iron. Tubal-cain had a sister named Naamah. One day Lamech said to his wives,

"Adah and Zillah, hear my voice; listen to me, you wives of Lamech. I have killed a man who attacked me, a young man who wounded me. If someone who kills Cain is punished seven times, then the one who kills me will be punished seventy-seven times!" (Genesis 4:17–24, NLT)

Six generations from Cain, Lamech changed God's marriage policy, of one man and one woman (verse 19), which would eventually become the foundation for multiple relationships in marriages for royalty like David and Solomon; for common people, it became adultery and fornication. Lamech also justified the murder he committed based on God's mandate that pertained only to Cain. So he became the first murderer to justify murder in his mind with his own rationalization (Genesis 4:23 and 24). Murder wasn't new. Cain attested to that in verse 14 when he said he would be killed.

God could no longer walk among his humans who were in open defiance of his will, by sinning. His love for his creations permitted the creation of Nod, for when they exercised their free will, but more and more humans were finding comfort in their free will instead of God's will.

God walking among us and then withdrawing himself because of our sin nature was inevitable because our sin nature was spawned by pride, the original sin. The Father will not look upon sin which caused the most agonizing moment in Jesus Christ's walk on this planet, having to be separated from the Father while carrying our sins on the cross.

He went on a little farther and fell to the ground. He prayed that, if it were possible, the awful hour awaiting him might pass him by.

"Abba, Father," he cried out, "everything is possible for you. Please take this cup of suffering away from me. Yet I want your will to be done, not mine." (Mark 14:35 and 36, NLT)

At noon, darkness fell across the whole land until three o'clock. Then at three o'clock Jesus called out with a loud voice, "Eloi, Eloi, lema sabachthani?" which means "My God, my God, why have you abandoned me?" (Mark 15:33 and 34, NLT)

God kicked Adam and Eve out of the garden of Eden, but he did not stop walking among them. God has hidden so many huge nuggets, in plain sight, in the Bible that he will not reveal until we enter and submit to his wisdom and understanding.

Because of Enoch's willingness to grow into God's wisdom and understanding, God showed us how he had planned to translate all three components of our existence to heaven (flesh, soul, and spirit) before the introduction of sin by Adam and Eve. Now we have to leave our sinful flesh here on earth, until Christ's second coming. It's a lot like when Momma would tell you to leave those muddy shoes outside on the porch, until they get cleaned. God also told Enoch, who was born while Adam was still alive, about the second coming of Christ.

When Enoch was 65 years old, he became the father of Methuselah. After the birth of Methuselah, Enoch lived in close fellowship with God for another 300 years, and he had other sons and daughters. Enoch lived 365 years, walking in close fellowship with God. Then one day he disappeared, because God took him. (Genesis 5:21–24, NLT)

Enoch, who lived in the seventh generation after Adam, prophesied about these people. He said, "Listen! The Lord is coming with countless thousands of his holy ones to execute judgment on the people of the world. He will convict every

person of all the ungodly things they have done
and for all the insults that ungodly sinners have
spoken against him." (Jude 1:14 and 15, NLT)

We had it but lost it, in the presence of God without having
to utilize prayer, intercessory prayer, personal guidance meditation
(the kind of relationship Enoch had with God), music, singing, and
preaching or having to suppress posturing and human delicacies.
Human delicacies are covert and overt presentations of "pride" in our
relationship with God, usually amplified in God's houses of worship.

Walking and talking with God day and night, what peace of
mind!

Blessed is the man that walketh not in the
counsel of the ungodly, nor standeth in the way
of sinners, nor sitteth in the seat of the scornful.

But his delight is in the law of the LORD;
and in his law doth he meditate day and night.

And he shall be like a tree planted by the
rivers of water, that bringeth forth his fruit in his
season; his leaf also shall not wither; and whatsoever he doeth shall prosper.

The ungodly are not so: but are like the
chaff which the wind driveth away.

Therefore the ungodly shall not stand in the
judgment, nor sinners in the congregation of the
righteous.

For the LORD knoweth the way of the
righteous: but the way of the ungodly shall perish. (Psalm 1:1–6, KJV)

The old folks had a saying: "Familiarity breeds contempt."

It is quite apparent in Cain's actions that reverence to the will
of God was secondary to what Cain wanted. Cain found it easy to
develop this type of attitude in the "presence of the *Lord*." It wasn't

until he realized that he would no longer be in the "presence of the Lord" that he realized the consequences of his actions.

God got tired of walking among us in the midst of all our sins. So the *Lord* decided to remove himself from our company and force us to "seek his presence" through prayer, intercessory prayer, personal guidance meditation, music, singing, assembling ourselves, and preaching.

The story of Cain and Abel shows us that individual worship of God had been going on through offerings (Genesis 4:3 and 4) because God was literally in their presence, like he was later with Enoch, seventh generation from Adam (Genesis 5:23). Our sins forced God to readjust how we communicate with him. This readjustment requires individual and group efforts in order to accomplish the goal of "being in the presence of God" and reacquiring God's wisdom.

"Nod" means a place of wandering, vagrancy, fleeing, disappearing, and wavering—all things associated with not being obedient to the will of God. As more and more of his beloved creations accepted a "Nod mentality," God decided he would treat all his humans like they were in "Nod" and force them to cry out to him, "worship." **We just "Nodded out."**

> **When Seth grew up, he had a son and named him Enosh. At that time people first began to worship the LORD by name. (Genesis 4:26, NLT)**

We, human beings, have to call on the Father (praise) in order to be in his presence (worship), in order to acquire the wisdom and understanding that God has for you.

Chapter 4

NODDING OUT

He that getteth wisdom loveth his own soul: he that keepeth understanding shall find good.

—(Proverbs 19:8, KJV)

"Nodding out" transfers dependency for acquiring wisdom and understanding from God to earthly things, thoughts, and desires that motivate our senses and our belief in self-determination and a "right to something."

We have a hard time believing and understanding how Satan, the devil, has manipulated the earth. Satan's action causes human beings to be misguided by earthly wisdom and lean on their own understanding.

> When the seventy-two disciples returned, they joyfully reported to him, "Lord, even the demons obey us when we use your name!"
>
> "Yes," he told them, "I saw Satan fall from heaven like lightning! Look, I have given you authority over all the power of the enemy, and you can walk among snakes and scorpions and crush them. Nothing will injure you. But don't rejoice because evil spirits obey you; rejoice

because your names are registered in heaven." (Luke 10:17–20, NLT)

"But I will continue doing what I have always done. This will undercut those who are looking for an opportunity to boast that their work is just like ours. These people are false apostles. They are deceitful workers who disguise themselves as apostles of Christ. But I am not surprised! **Even Satan disguises himself as an angel of light. So it is no wonder his servants also disguise themselves as servants of righteousness. In the end they will get the punishment their wicked deeds deserve." (2 Corinthians 11:12–15, NLT)**

"And so I insist—and God backs me up on this—that there be no going along with the crowd, the empty-headed, mindless crowd. They've refused for so long to deal with God that they've lost touch not only with God but with reality itself. They can't think straight anymore. Feeling no pain, they let themselves go in sexual obsession, addicted to every sort of perversion.

But that's no life for you. You learned Christ! My assumption is that you have paid careful attention to him, been well instructed in the truth precisely as we have it in Jesus. Since, then, we do not have the excuse of ignorance, everything—and I do mean everything—connected with that old way of life has to go. It's rotten through and through. Get rid of it! And then take on an entirely new way of life—a God fashioned life, a life renewed from the inside and working itself into your conduct as God accurately reproduces his character in you.

What this adds up to, then, is this: no more lies, no more pretense. Tell your neighbor the truth. In Christ's body we're all connected to each other, after all. When you lie to others, you end up lying to yourself.

Go ahead and be angry. You do well to be angry—but don't use your anger as fuel for revenge. And don't stay angry. Don't go to bed angry. Don't give the Devil that kind of foothold in your life." (Ephesian 4:17–27, MSG)

A final word: Be strong in the Lord and in his mighty power. Put on all of God's armor so that you will be able to stand firm against all strategies of the devil. For we are not fighting against flesh-and-blood enemies, but against evil rulers and authorities of the unseen world, against mighty powers in this dark world, and against evil spirits in the heavenly places. (Ephesians 6:10–12, NLT)

So humble yourselves before God. Resist the devil, and he will flee from you. Come close to God, and God will come close to you. Wash your hands, you sinners; purify your hearts, for your loyalty is divided between God and the world. (James 4:7 and 8, NLT)

So humble yourselves under the mighty power of God, and at the right time he will lift you up in honor. Give all your worries and cares to God, for he cares about you.

Stay alert! Watch out for your great enemy, the devil. He prowls around like a roaring lion, looking for someone to devour. Stand firm against him, and be strong in your faith. Remember that your Christian brothers and sisters all over the world are going through the same kind of suffering you are. (1 Peter 5:6–9, NLT)

Everyone who sins is breaking God's law, for all sin is contrary to the law of God. And you know that Jesus came to take away our sins, and there is no sin in him. Anyone who continues to live in him will not sin. But anyone who keeps on sinning does not know him or understand who he is.

Dear children, don't let anyone deceive you about this: When people do what is right, it shows that they are righteous, even as Christ is righteous. But when people keep on sinning, it shows that they belong to the devil, who has been sinning since the beginning. But the Son of God came to destroy the works of the devil. (1 John 3:4–8, NLT)

And the dragon lost the battle, and he and his angels were forced out of heaven. This great dragon—the ancient serpent called the devil, or Satan, the one deceiving the whole world—was thrown down to the earth with all his angels. (Revelation 12:8 and 9, NLT)

Our "spirit's" interest in God has been hindered by things of the flesh. Our flesh is centered on our five (5) senses, seeing, touching, hearing, smelling, and tasting. If human existence revolves around these five areas, as foundation of our wisdom and understanding, it becomes extremely difficult to accept God's wisdom and understanding as the basis of life.

Triviality is the epicenter of our senses, and our senses are the command center for our flesh. Something as temporary as this house of dirt cannot help but be shallow and unstable.

And the LORD God formed man of the dust of the ground, and breathed into his nostrils the breath of life; and man became a living soul. (Genesis 2:7, KJV)

There is nothing but a castle on the beach, if left in our hands, a temporary home which, if dealt with correctly, is here to carry out

God's will. All the confusion, all the deceit, all the loneliness, and all the wrong erupts in our lives from this hub of destruction called flesh.

> Anyone who listens to my teaching and follows it is wise, like a person who builds a house on solid rock. Though the rain comes in torrents and the floodwaters rise and the winds beat against that house, it won't collapse because it is built on bedrock. But anyone who hears my teaching and ignores it is foolish, like a person who builds a house on sand. When the rains and floods come and the winds beat against the house, it will collapse with a mighty crash.
>
> When Jesus had finished saying these things, the crowds were amazed at his teaching, for he taught with real authority—quite unlike their teachers of religious law. (Matthew 7:24–29, NLT)

While all five senses are inhibitors to our walk with God, the most dangerous of the senses is hearing. Christ stated:

> Then Jesus called to the crowd to come and hear. "Listen," he said, "and try to understand. It's not what goes into your mouth that defiles you; you are defiled by the words that come out of your mouth." (Matthew 15:10 and 11, NLT)
>
> "So why do you keep calling me 'Lord, Lord!' when you don't do what I say? I will show you what it's like when someone comes to me, listens to my teaching, and then follows it. It is like a person building a house who digs deep and lays the foundation on solid rock. When the floodwaters rise and break against the house, it stands firm because it is well built. But anyone

who hears and doesn't obey is like a person who builds a house without a foundation. When the floods sweep down against that house, it will collapse into a heap of ruins." (Luke 6:46–49, NLT)

The vehicle utilized to embed items and imprint thoughts, in our soul, as to what comes out our mouth is hearing.

A good tree can't produce bad fruit, and a bad tree can't produce good fruit. A tree is identified by its fruit. Figs never grow on thornbushes, nor grapes on bramble bushes. A good person produces good things from the treasury of a good heart, and an evil person produces evil things from the treasury of an evil heart. What you say flows from what is in your heart. (Luke 6:43–45, NLT)

Hearing is the tool used by God to deposit wisdom and understanding into our existence.

But how can they call on him to save them unless they believe him? And how can they believe in him if they have never heard about him? And how can they hear about him unless someone tells them? And how will anyone go and tell them without being sent? That is why the Scriptures say, "How beautiful are the feet of messengers who bring good news!" (Romans 10:14 and 15, NLT)

Hearing is the method, chosen by God, to build up and strengthen our spiritual being.

So faith comes from hearing, that is, hearing the Good News about Christ. (Romans 10:17, NLT)

Hearing is God's pipeline to the soul.

> For Christ didn't send me to baptize, but to preach the Good News—and not with clever speech, for fear that the cross of Christ would lose its power.
> The message of the cross is foolish to those who are headed for destruction! But we who are being saved know it is the very power of God. As the Scriptures say, "I will destroy the wisdom of the wise and discard the intelligence of the intelligent."
> So where does this leave the philosophers, the scholars, and the world's brilliant debaters? God has made the wisdom of this world look foolish. Since God in his wisdom saw to it that the world would never know him through human wisdom, he has used our foolish preaching to save those who believe. (1 Corinthians 1:17–21, NLT)

More than gold, more than earthly possessions, hearing is the most valuable asset we can acquire.

We are not the only ones who realize this fact. Satan has worked overtime to create stumbling blocks to impede our hearing. Satan has employed very subtle techniques, which govern our world and reduce our ability to acquire God's wisdom and the understanding we need.

These techniques have been devised to impede our acceptance of God's wisdom and understanding. These "devil"-inspired concepts have been devised to:

➤ **Create a dependency on self-reliance.**
➤ **Do something over hearing from God (listening).**
➤ **Make rebellion from God's word look right.**

➢ **Make changing to follow God's wisdom look unsuited for your situation.**

➢ **Promote the concept of a futile God.**

• **Create a dependency on self-reliance.**

Trust in the LORD with all your heart; do not depend on your own understanding.

Seek his will in all you do, and he will show you which path to take.

Don't be impressed with your own wisdom. Instead, fear the LORD and turn away from evil.

Then you will have healing for your body and strength for your bones. (Proverbs 3:5–8, NLT)

You simple people, use good judgement. You foolish people, show some understanding. (Proverbs 8:5, NLT)

"How can I know all the sins lurking in my heart? Cleanse me from these hidden faults." (Psalm 19:12, NLT)

• **Do something over hearing from God (listening).**

The LORD gave this message to Jonah son of Amittai:

"Get up and go to the great city of Nineveh. Announce my judgement against it because I have seen how wicked its people are."

But Jonah got up and went in the opposite direction to get away from the LORD. He went down to the port of Joppa, where he found a ship leaving for Tarshish. He bought a ticket and went on board, hoping to escape from the LORD by sailing to Tarshish. (Jonah 1:1 and 2, NLT)

In the first month, the entire company of the People of Israel arrived in the Wilderness of Zin. The people stayed in Kadesh.

Miriam died there, and she was buried.

There was no water there for the community, so they ganged up on Moses and Aaron. They attacked Moses: "We wish we'd died when the rest of our brothers died before GOD. Why did you haul this congregation of GOD out here into the wilderness to die, people and cattle alike? And why did you take us out of Egypt in the first place, dragging us into this miserable country? No grains, no figs, no grapevines, no pomegranates—and now not even water!"

Moses and Aaron walked from the assembled congregation to the Tent of Meeting and threw themselves facedown on the ground. And they saw the Glory of God.

God spoke to Moses: "Take the staff. Assemble the community, you and your brother Aaron. Speak to that rock that's right in front of them and it will give water. You will bring water out of the rock for them; congregation and cattle will both drink."

Moses took the staff away from GOD's presence, as commanded. He and Aaron rounded up the whole congregation in front of the rock. Moses spoke: "Listen, rebels! Do we have to bring water out of this rock for you?"

With that Moses raised his arm and slammed his staff against the rock—once, twice. Water poured out. Congregation and cattle drank.

GOD said to Moses and Aaron, "Because you didn't trust me, didn't treat me with holy reverence in front of the People of Israel, you two aren't going to lead this company into the land that I am giving them."

These were the Waters of Meribah (Bickering) where the People of Israel bickered with GOD, and he revealed himself as holy. (Numbers 20:1–13, MSG)

This behavior continues even in the New Testament.

Then Simon Peter drew a sword and slashed off the right ear of Malchus, the high priest's slave.

But Jesus said to Peter, "Put your sword back into its sheath. Shall I not drink from the cup of suffering the Father has given me?" (John 18:10 and 11, NLT)

When the other disciples saw what was about to happen, they exclaimed, "Lord, should we fight? We brought the swords!" And one of them struck at the high priest's slave, slashing off his right ear.

But Jesus said, "No more of this." And he touched the man's ear and healed him." (Luke 22:49–51, NLT)

Jesus said, "My friend, go ahead and do what you have come for."

Than the others grabbed Jesus and arrested him. But one of the men with Jesus pulled out his sword and struck the high priest's slave, slashing off his ear.

"Put away the sword," Jesus told them. "Those who use the sword will die by the sword. Don't you realize that I could ask my Father for thousands of angels to protect us, and he would send them instantly? But if I did, how would the

Scriptures be fulfilled that describe what must happen now?" (Matthew 26:50–54, NLT)

"And so, my children, listen to me, for all who follow my ways are joyful.

Listen to my instruction and be wise. Don't ignore it." (Proverbs 8:32 and 33, NLT)

"Blessed is the man that heareth me, watching daily at my gates, waiting at the posts of my doors.

For whoso findeth me findeth life, and shall obtain favour of the LORD." (Proverbs 8:34 and 35, KJV)

- **Make rebellion from God's word look right.**

"The time has come for Aaron to join his ancestors in death. He will not enter the land I am giving the people of Israel, because the two of you rebelled against my instructions concerning the water at Meribah." (Numbers 20:24, NLT)

"For I know how rebellious and stubborn you are. Even now, while I am still alive and am here with you, you have rebelled against the LORD. How much more rebellious will you be after my death!

Now summon all the elders and officials of your tribes, so that I can speak to them directly and call heaven and earth to witness against them. I know that after my death you will become utterly corrupt and will turn from the way I have commanded you to follow. In the days to come, disaster will come down on you, for you will do what is evil in the LORD's sight, making him very angry with your actions." (Deuteronomy 31:27–29, NLT)

The tribes of Reuben and Gad owned vast numbers of livestock. So when they saw that the lands of Jazer and Gilead were ideally suited for their flocks and herds, they came to Moses, Eleazar the priest, and the other leaders of the community. They said, "Notice the towns of Ataroth, Dibon, Jazer, Nimrah, Heshbon, Elealeh, Sibmah, Nebo, and Beon. The LORD has conquered this whole area for the community of Israel, and it is ideally suited for all our livestock. If we have found favor with you, please let us have this land as our property instead of giving us land across the Jordan River." (Numbers 32:1–5, NLT)

"And when the time comes"—GOD's Decree!—"I'll see to it that they dig up the bones of the kings of Judah, the bones of the princes and priests and prophets, and yes, even the bones of the common people. They'll dig them up and spread them out like a congregation at worship before sun, moon, and stars, all those sky gods they've been so infatuated with all these years, following their 'lucky stars' in doglike devotion. The bones will be left scattered and exposed, to reenter the soil as fertilizer, like manure."

"Everyone left—all from this evil generation unlucky enough to still be alive in whatever godforsaken place I will have driven them to—will wish they were dead." Decree of GOD-of-the-Angel-Armies.

Tell them this, GOD's Message:

"Do people fall down and not get up? Or take the wrong road and then just keep going? So why does this people go backward, and just keep on going—backward! They stubbornly hold on to their illusions, refuse to change direction.

I listened carefully but heard not so much as a whisper. No one expressed one word of regret. Not a single 'I'm sorry' did I hear. They just kept at it, blindly and stupidly banging their heads against a brick wall. Cranes know when it's time to move south for winter. And robins, warblers, and bluebirds know when it's time to come back again. But my people? My people know nothing, not the first thing of GOD and his rule."

"How can you say, 'We know the score. We're the proud owners of GOD's revelation'? Look where it's gotten you—stuck in illusion. Your religion experts have taken you for a ride! Your know-it alls will be unmasked, caught and shown up for what they are. Look at them! They know everything but GOD's Word. Do you call that 'knowing'?"

"So here's what will happen to the know-it-alls: I'll make them wifeless and homeless. Everyone's after the dishonest dollar, little people and big people alike. Prophets and priests and everyone in between twist words and doctor truth. My dear Daughter—my people—broken, shattered, and yet they put on Band-Aids, saying, 'It's not so bad. You'll be just fine.' But things are not 'just fine'! Do you suppose they are embarrassed over this outrage? Not really. They have no shame. They don't even know how to blush. There's no hope for them. They've hit bottom and there's no getting up. As far as I'm concerned, they're finished." GOD has spoken.

"I went out to see if I could salvage anything"—GOD's Decree—"but found nothing: Not a grape, not a fig, just a few withered leaves. I'm taking back everything I gave them."

So why are we sitting here, doing nothing? Let's get organized. Let's go to the big city and at least die fighting. We've gotten GOD's ultimatum: We're damned if we do and damned if we don't—damned because of our sin against him. We hoped things would turn out for the best, but it didn't happen that way. We were waiting around for healing—and terror showed up! From Dan at the northern borders we hear the hooves of horses, horses galloping, horses neighing. The ground shudders and quakes. They're going to swallow up the whole country. Towns and people alike—fodder for war.

"What's more, I'm dispatching poisonous snakes among you, snakes that can't be charmed, snakes that will bite you and kill you." GOD's Decree!

"I drown in grief. I'm heartsick. Oh, listen! Please listen! It's the cry of my dear people reverberating through the country. Is GOD no longer in Zion? Has the King gone away? Can you tell me why they flaunt their plaything-gods, their silly, imported no-gods before me? The crops are in, the summer is over, but for us nothing's changed. We're still waiting to be rescued. For my dear broken people, I'm heartbroken. I weep, seized by grief. Are there no healing ointments in Gilead? Isn't there a doctor in the house? So why can't something be done to heal and save my dear, dear people?" (Jeremiah 8:1–22, MSG)

Now the angel of the LORD went up from Gilgal to Bochim. And he said, "I brought you up from Egypt and brought you into the land that I swore to give to your fathers. I said, 'I will never break my covenant with you, and you shall make no covenant with the inhabitants of this land; you shall break down their altars.' But you have not obeyed my voice. What is this you have done? So now I say, I will not drive them out before you, but they shall become thorns in your sides, and their gods shall be a snare to you." As soon as the angel of the LORD spoke these words to all the people of Israel, the people lifted up their voices and wept. And they called the name of that place Bochim. And they sacrificed there to the LORD. (Judges 2:1–5, ESV)

In those days Israel had no king; all the people did whatever seemed right in their own eyes. (Judges 21:25, NLT)

And when these went into Micah's house and took the carved image, the ephod, the household gods, and the metal image, the priest said to them, "What are you doing?" And they said to him, "Keep quiet; put your hand on your mouth and come with us and be to us a father and a priest. Is it better for you to be priest to the house of one man, or to be priest to a tribe and clan in Israel?" And the priest's heart was glad. He took the ephod and the household gods and the carved image and went along with the people.

So they turned and departed, putting the little ones and the livestock and the goods in front of them. When they had gone a distance from the home of Micah, the men who were in the houses near Micah's house were called out, and they overtook the people of Dan. And they shouted to the people of Dan, who turned around and said to Micah, "What is the matter with you, that you come with such a company?" And he said, "You take my gods that I made and the priest, and go away, and what have I left? How then do you ask me, 'What is the matter with you?'" And the people of Dan said to him, "Do not let your voice be heard among us, lest angry fellows fall upon you, and you lose your life with the lives of your household." Then the people of Dan went their way. And when Micah saw that they were too strong for him, he turned and went back to his home. (Judges 18:18–26, ESV)

Then, with Micah's idols and his priest, the men of Dan came to the town of Laish, whose people were peaceful and secure. They attacked with swords and burned the town to the ground. There was no one to rescue the people, for they lived a great distance from Sidon and had no allies nearby. This happened in the valley near Beth-rehob.

Then the people of the tribe of Dan rebuilt the town and lived there. They renamed the town Dan after their ancestor, Israel's son, but it had originally been called Laish.

Then they set up the carved image, and they appointed Jonathan son of Gershom, son of Moses, as their priest. This family continued as priests for the tribe of Dan until the Exile. So Micah's carved image was worshiped by the tribe of Dan as long as the Tabernacle of God was in Shiloh. (Judges 18:27–31, NLT)

Now in those days Israel had no king. There was a man from the tribe of Levi living in a remote area of the hill country of Ephraim. One day he brought home a woman from Bethlehem in Judah to be his concubine. But she became angry with him and returned to her father's home in Bethlehem.

After about four months, her husband set out for Bethlehem to speak personally to her and persuade her to come back. He took with him a servant and a pair of donkeys. When he arrived at her father's house, her father saw him and welcomed him. (Judges 19:1–3, NLT)

But this time the man wasn't willing to spend another night. He got things ready, left, and went as far as Jebus (Jerusalem) with his pair of saddled donkeys, his concubine, and his servant. At Jebus, though, the day was nearly gone. The servant said to his master, "It's late; let's go into this Jebusite city and spend the night."

But his master said, "We're not going into any city of foreigners. We'll go on to Gibeah." He directed his servant, "Keep going. Let's go ahead. We'll spend the night either at Gibeah or Ramah."

So they kept going. As they pressed on, the sun finally left them in the vicinity of Gibeah, which belongs to Benjamin. They left the road there to spend the night at Gibeah.

The Levite went and sat down in the town square, but no one invited them in to spend the night. Then, late in the evening, an old man came in from his day's work in the fields. He was from the hill country of Ephraim and lived temporarily in Gibeah where all the local citizens were Benjamites. When the old man looked up and saw the traveler in the town square, he said, "Where are you going? And where are you from?"

The Levite said, "We're just passing through. We're coming from Bethlehem on our way to a remote spot in the hills of Ephraim. I come from there. I've just made a trip to Bethlehem in Judah and I'm on my way back home, but no one has invited us in for the night. We wouldn't be any trouble: We have food and straw for the donkeys, and bread and wine for the woman, the young man and me—we don't need anything."

The old man said, "It's going to be all right; I'll take care of you. You aren't going to spend the night in the town square." He took them home and fed the donkeys. They washed up and sat down to a good meal. (Judges 19:10–21, MSG)

While they were enjoying themselves, some of the wicked men of the city surrounded the house. Pounding on the door, they shouted to the old man who owned the house, "Bring out the man who came to your house so we can have sex with him."

The owner of the house went outside and said to them, "No, my friends, don't be so vile. Since this man is my guest, don't' do this outrageous thing. Look, here is my virgin daughter, and his concubine. I will bring them out to you now, and you can use them and do to them whatever you wish. But as for this man, don't do such an outrageous thing."

But the men would not listen to him. So the man took his concubine and sent her outside to them, and they raped her and abused her throughout the night, and at dawn they let her go. At daybreak the woman went back to the house where her master was staying, fell down at the door and lay there until daylight.

When her master got up in the morning and opened the door of the house and stepped out to continue on his way, there lay his concubine, fallen in the doorway of the house, with her hands on the threshold. He said to her, "Get up; let's go." But there was no answer. Then the man put her on his donkey and set out for home.

When he reached home, he took a knife and cut up his concubine, limb by limb, into twelve parts and sent them into all the areas of Israel. Everyone who saw it was saying to one another, "Such a thing has never been seen or done, not since the day the Israelites came up out of Egypt. Just imagine! We must do something! So speak up!" (Judges 19:22–30, NIV)

Then all the Israelites were united as one man, from Dan in the north to Beersheba in the south, including those from across the Jordan in the land of Gilead. The entire community assembled in the presence of the LORD at Mizpah. (Judges 20:1, NLT)

The leaders of all the people of the tribes of Israel took their places in the assembly of God's people, four hundred thousand men armed with swords. (The Benjamites heard that the Israelites had gone to Mizpah.) Then the Israelites said, "Tell us how this awful thing happened."

So the Levite, the husband of the murdered woman, said, "I and my concubine came to Gibeah in Benjamin to spend the night. During the night the men of Gibeah came after me and surrounded the house, intending to kill me. They raped my concubine, and she died. I took my concubine, cut her into pieces and sent one piece to each region of Israel's inheritance, because they committed this lewd and outrageous act in Israel. Now, all you Israelites, speak up and tell me what you have decided to do."

All the men rose up together as one saying, "None of us will go home. No not one of us will return to his house. But now this is what we'll do to Gibeah: We'll go up against it in the order decided by casting lots. We'll take ten men out of every hundred from all the tribes of Israel, and a hundred from a thousand, and a thousand from ten thousand, to get provisions for the army. Then, when the army arrives at Gibeah in Benjamin, it can give them what they deserve for this outrageous act done in Israel." So all the Israelites got together and united as one against the city.

The tribes of Israel sent messengers throughout the tribe of Benjamin, saying, "What about this awful crime that was committed among you? Now turn those wicked men of Gibeah over to us so that we may put them to death and purge the evil from Israel."

But the Benjamites would not listen to their fellow Israelites. From their towns they came together at Gibeah to fight against the Israelites. At once the Benjamites mobilized twenty-six thousand swordsmen from their towns, in addition to seven hundred able young men from those living in Gibeah. Among all these soldiers there were seven hundred select troops who were left-handed, each of whom could sling a stone at a hair and not miss.

Israel, apart from Benjamin, mustered four hundred thousand swordsmen, all of them fit for battle.

The Israelites went up to Bethel and inquire of God. They said, "Who of us is to go up first to fight against the Benjamites?"

The LORD replied, "Judah shall go first."

The next morning the Israelites got up and pitched camp near Gibeah. The Benjamites came out of Gibeah and cut down twenty-two thousand Israelites on the battlefield that day. But the Israelites encouraged one another and again took up their positions where they had stationed themselves the first day. The Israelites went up and wept before the LORD until evening, and they inquired of the LORD. They said, 'Shall we go up again to fight against the Benjamites, our fellow Israelites?"

The LORD answered, "Go up against them."

Then the Israelites drew near to Benjamin the second day. This time, when the Benjamites came out from Gibeah to oppose them, they cut down another eighteen thousand Israelites, all of them armed with swords. (Judges 20:2–25, NIV)

Then all the Israelites, the whole army, went up to Bethel, and there they sat weeping before the LORD. They fasted that day until evening and presented burnt offerings and fellowship offerings to the LORD. And the Israelites inquired of the LORD. (In those days the ark of the covenant of God was there, with Phinehas son of Eleazar, the son of Aaron, ministering before it.) They asked, "Shall we go up again to fight against the Benjamites, our fellow Israelites, or not?"

The LORD responded, "Go, for tomorrow I will give them into your hands."

Then Israel set an ambush around Gibeah. They went up against the Benjamites on the third day and took up positions against Gibeah as they had done before. The Benjamites came out to meet them and were drawn away from the city. They began to inflict casualties on the Israelites as before, so that about thirty men fell in the open field and on the roads—the one leading to Bethel and the other to Gibeah. While the Benjamites were saying, "We are defeating them as before," the Israelites were saying, "Let's retreat and draw them away from the city to the roads." (Judges 20:26–32, NIV)

All the men of Israel moved from their places and took up positions at Baal Tamar, and the Israelite ambush charged out of its place on the west of Gibeah. Then ten thousand of Israel's able young men made a frontal attack on Gibeah. The fighting was so heavy that the Benjamites did not realize how near disaster was. The LORD defeated Benjamin before Israel, and on that day the Israelites struck down 25,100 Benjamites, all armed with swords. Then the Benjamites saw that they were beaten.

Now the men of Israel had given way before Benjamin, because they relied on the ambush they had set near Gibeah. Those who had been in ambush made a sudden dash into Gibeah, spread out and put the whole city to the sword. The Israelites had arranged with the ambush that they should send up a great cloud of smoke from the city, and then the Israelites would counterattack.

The Benjamites had begun to inflict casualties on the Israelites (about thirty), and they said, "We are defeating them as in the first battle." But when the column of smoke began to rise from the city, the Benjamites turned and saw the whole city going up in smoke. Then the Israelites counterattacked, and the Benjamites were terrified, because they realized disaster had come to them. So they fled before the Israelites in the direction of the wilderness, but they could not escape the battle. And the Israelites who came out of the towns cut them down there. They surrounded the Benjamites, chased them and easily overran them in the vicinity of Gibeah on the east. Eighteen thousand Benjamites fell, all of them valiant fighters. As they turned and fled toward the wilderness to the rock of Rimmon, the Israelites cut down five thousand men along the roads. They kept pressing after the Benjamites as far as Gidom and struck down two thousand more.

On that day twenty-five thousand Benjamites swordsmen fell, all of them valiant fighters. But six hundred of them turned and fled into the wilderness to the rock of Rimmon, where they stayed four months. The men of Israel went back to Benjamin and put all the towns to the sword, including the animals and everything else they found. All the towns they came across they set on fire. (Judges 20:33–48, NIV)

The men of Israel had taken an oath at Mizpah: "Not one of us will give his daughter in marriage to a Benjamite."

The people went to Bethel, where they sat before God until evening, raising their voices and weeping bitterly. "LORD, God of Israel," they cried, "why has this happened to Israel? Why should one tribe be missing from Israel today?"

Early the next day the people built an altar and presented burnt offerings and fellowship offerings.

Then the Israelites asked, "Who from all the tribes of Israel has failed to assemble before the LORD?" For they had taken a solemn oath that anyone who failed to assemble before the LORD at Mizpah was to be put to death.

Now the Israelites grieved for the tribe of Benjamin, their fellow Israelites. "Today one tribe is cut off from Israel," they said. "How can we provide wives for those who are left, since we have taken an oath by the LORD not to give them any of our daughters in marriage?" Then they asked, "Which one of the tribes of Israel failed to assemble before the LORD at Mizpah?" They discovered that no one from Jabesh Gilead had come to the camp for the assembly. For when they counted the people, they found that none of the people of Jabesh Gilead were there.

So the assembly sent twelve thousand fighting men with instructions to go to Jabesh Gilead and put to the sword those living there, including the women and children. "This is what you are to do," they said. "Kill every male and every woman who is not a virgin." They found among the people living in Jabesh Gilead four hundred young women who had never slept with a man, and they took them to the camp at Shiloh in Canaan.

Then the whole assembly sent an offer of peace to the Benjamites at the rock of Rimmon. So the Benjamites returned at that time and were given the women of Jabesh Gilead who had been spared. But there were not enough for all of them.

The people grieved for Benjamin, because the LORD had made a gap in the tribes of Israel. And the elders of the assembly said, "With the women of Benjamin destroyed, how shall we provide wives for the men who are left? The Benjamite survivors must have heirs," they said, "so that a tribe of Israel will not be wiped out. We can't give them our daughters as wives, since we Israelites have taken this oath: 'Cursed be anyone who gives a wife to a Benjamite.' But look, there is the annual festival of the LORD in Shiloh, which lies north of Bethel, east of the road that goes from Bethel to Shechem, and south of Lebonah."

So they instructed the Benjamites, saying, "Go and hide in the vineyards and watch. When the young women of Shiloh come out to join in the dancing, rush from the vineyards and each of you seize one of them to be your wife. Then return to the land of Benjamin. When their fathers or brothers complain to us, we will say to them, 'Do us the favor of helping them, because we did not get wives for them during the war. You will not be guilty of breaking your oath because you did not give your daughters to them.'"

So that is what the Benjamites did. While the young women were dancing, each man caught one and carried her off to be his wife. Then they returned to their inheritance and rebuilt the towns and settled in them.

At that time the Israelites left that place and went home to their tribes and clans, each to his own inheritance. (Judges 21:1–24, NIV)

In those days Israel had no king; all the people did whatever seemed right in their own eyes. (Judges 21:25, NLT)

- **Make changing to follow God's wisdom look unsuited for your situation.**

While the Israelites were camped at Acacia Grove, some of the men defiled themselves by having sexual relations with local Moabite women. These women invited them to attend sacrifices to their gods, so the Israelites feasted with them and worshiped the gods of Moab. In this way, Israel joined in the worship of Baal of Peor, causing the LORD's anger to blaze against his people. (Numbers 25:1–3, NLT)

After that generation died, another generation grew up who did not acknowledge the LORD or remember the mighty things he had done for Israel.

The Israelites did evil in the LORD's sight and served the images of Baal. They abandoned the LORD, the God of their ancestors, who had brought them out of Egypt. They went after other gods, worshiping the gods of the people around them. And they angered the LORD. They abandoned the LORD to serve Baal and the images of Ashtoreth. This made the LORD burn with anger against Israel, so he handed them over to raiders who stole their possessions. He turned them over to their enemies all around, and they were no longer able to resist them. Every time Israel went out to battle, the LORD fought against them, causing them to be defeated, just as he had warned. And people were in great distress. (Judges 2:10–15, NLT)

Then the LORD raised up judges to rescue the Israelites from their attackers. Yet Israel did not listen to the judges but prostituted themselves by worshipping other gods. How quickly they turned away from the path of their ancestors, who had walked in obedience to the LORD's commands. (Judges 2:16 and 17, NLT)

So the LORD burned with anger against Israel. He said, "Because these people have violated my covenant, which I made with their ancestors, and have ignored my commands. I will no longer drive out the nations that Joshua left unconquered when he died. I did this to test Israel—to see whether or not they would follow the ways of the LORD as their ancestors did." That is why the LORD left those nations in place. He did not quickly drive them out or allow Joshua to conquer them all. (Judges 2:20–23, NLT)

- **Promote the idea that words are harmless and powerless.**

Don't trap yourself by making a rash promise to God and only later counting the cost. (Proverbs 20:25, NLT)

When you make a promise to God, don't delay in following through, for God takes no pleasure in fools. Keep all the promises you make to him. It is better to say nothing than to make a promise and not keep it. Don't let your mouth make you sin. And don't defend yourself by telling the Temple messenger that the promise you made was a mistake. That would make God angry, and he might wipe out everything you have achieved. (Ecclesiastes 5:4–6, NLT)

Or suppose you make a foolish vow of any kind, whether its purpose is for good or for bad. When you realize its foolishness, you must admit your guilt. (Leviticus 5:4, NLT)

At that time the Spirit of the LORD came upon Jephthah, and he went throughout the land of Gilead and Manasseh, including Mizpah in Gilead, and from there he led an army against the Ammonites. And Jephthah made a vow to the LORD. He said, "If you give me victory over the Ammonites,

I will give to the LORD whatever comes out of my house to meet me when I return in triumph. I will sacrifice it as a burnt offering." (Judges 11:29–31, NLT)

Then Jephthah went over to fight the Ammonites, and the LORD gave them into his hands. He devastated twenty towns from Aroer to the vicinity of Minnith, as far as Abel Keramim. Thus Israel subdued Ammon.

When Jephthah returned to his home in Mizpah, who should come out to meet him but his daughter, dancing to the sound of timbrels! She was an only child. Except for her he had neither son nor daughter. When he saw her, he tore his clothes and cried, "Oh no, my daughter! You have brought me down and I am devastated. I have made a vow to the LORD that I cannot break."

"My father," she replied, "you have given your word to the LORD. Do to me just as you promised, now that the LORD has avenged you of your enemies, the Ammonites. But grant me this one request," she said. "Give me two months to roam the hills and weep with my friends, because I will never marry."

"You may go," he said. And he let her go for two months. She and her friends went into the hills and wept because she would never marry. After the two months, she returned to her father, and he did to her as he had vowed. And she was a virgin.

From this comes the Israelite tradition that each year the young women of Israel go out for four days to commemorate the daughter of Jephthah the Gileadite. (Judges 11:32–40, NIV)

- **Promote the concept of a futile God.**

When the Israelites saw that their situation was critical and that their army was hard pressed, they hid in caves and thickets, among the rocks, and in pits and cisterns. Some Hebrews even crossed the Jordan to the land of Gad and Gilead.

Saul remained at Gilgal, and all the troops with him were quaking with fear. He waited seven days, the time set by Samuel; but Samuel did not come to Gilgal, and Saul's men began to scatter. So he said, "Bring me the burnt offering and the fellowship offerings." And Saul offered up the burnt offering. Just as he finished making the offering, Samuel arrived, and Saul went out to greet him.

"What have you done?" asked Samuel.

Saul replied, "When I saw that the men were scattering, and that you did not come at the set time, and that the Philistines were assembling at Mikmash, I thought, 'Now the Philistines will come down against me at Gilgal, and I have not sought the LORD's favor.' So I felt compelled to offer the burnt offering."

"You have done a foolish thing," Samuel said. "You have not kept the command the LORD your God gave you; if you had, he would have established your kingdom over Israel for all time. But now your kingdom will not endure; the LORD has sought out a man after his own heart and appointed him ruler of his people, because you have not kept the LORD's command." (1 Samuel 13:6–14, NIV)

Another example is:

Then Eliakim, Shebna and Joah said to the field commander, "Please speak to your servants in Aramaic, since we understand it. Don't speak to us in Hebrew in the hearing of the people on the wall."

But the commander replied, "Was it only to your master and you that my master sent me to say these things, and not to the people sitting on the wall—who, like you, will have to eat their own excrement and drink their own urine?"

Then the commander stood and called out in Hebrew, "Hear the words of the great king, the king of Assyria! This is what the king says: Do not let Hezekiah deceive you. He cannot deliver you! Do not let Hezekiah persuade you to trust in the LORD when he says, 'The LORD will surely deliver us; this city will not be given into the hand of the king of Assyria.'

Do not listen to Hezekiah. This is what the king of Assyria says: Make peace with me and come out to me. Then each of you will eat fruit from your own vine and fig tree and drink water from your own cistern, until I come and take you to a land like your own—a land of grain and new wine, a land of bread and vineyards.

Do not let Hezekiah mislead you when he says, 'The LORD will deliver us.' Have the gods of any nations ever delivered their lands from the hand of the king of Assyria? Where are the gods of Hamath and Arpad? Where are the gods of Sepharvaim? Have they rescued Samaria from my hand? Who of all the gods of these countries have been able to save their lands from me? How then can the LORD deliver Jerusalem from my hand?"

But the people remained silent and said nothing in reply, because the king had commanded, "Do not answer him."

Then Eliakim son of Hilkiah the palace administrator, Shebna the secretary and Joah son of Asaph the recorder went to Hezekiah, with their clothes torn, and told him what the field commander had said. (Isaiah 36:11–20, NIV)

And it came to pass, when king Hezekiah heard it, that he rent his clothes, and covered himself with sackcloth, and went into the house of the LORD.

And he sent Eliakim, who was over the household, and Shebna the scribe, and the elders of the priests covered in sackcloth, unto Isaiah the prophet the son of Amoz. (Isaiah 37:1 and 2, KJV)

After King Hezekiah's officials delivered the king's message to Isaiah, the prophet replied, "Say to your master, 'This is what the LORD says: Do not be disturbed by this blasphemous speech against me from the Assyrian king's messengers. Listen! I myself will move against him, and the king will receive a message that he is needed at home. So he will return to his land, where I will have him killed with a sword.'" (Isaiah 37:5–7, NLT)

Soon afterward King Sennacherib received word that King Tirhakah of Ethiopia was leading an army to fight against him. Before leaving to meet the attack, he sent messengers back to Hezekiah in Jerusalem with this message:

"This message is for King Hezekiah of Judah. Don't let your God, in whom you trust, deceive you with promises that Jerusalem will not be captured by the king of Assyria. You know perfectly well what the kings of Assyria have done wherever they have gone. They have completely destroyed everyone who stood in their way! Why should you be any different? Have the gods of other nations rescued them—such nations as Gozan, Haran, Rezeph, and the people of Eden who were in Tel-assar? My predecessors destroyed them all! What happened to the king of Hamath and the king of Arpad? What happened to the kings of Sepharvaim, Hena, and Ivvah?" (Isaiah 37:9–13, NLT)

After Hezekiah received the letter from the messengers and read it, he went up to the LORD's Temple and spread it out before the LORD. (Isaiah 37:14, NLT)

That night the angel of the LORD went out to the Assyrian camp and killed 185,000 Assyrian soldiers. When the surviving Assyrians woke up the next morning, they found corpses everywhere. Then King Sennacherib of Assyria broke camp and returned to his own land. He went home to his capital of Nineveh and stayed there.

One day while he was worshiping in the temple of his god Nisroch, his sons Adrammelech and Sharezer killed him with their swords. They then escaped to the land of Ararat, and another son, Esarhaddon, became the next king of Assyria. (Isaiah 37:36–38, NLT)

Even in the New Testament, it continued:

They traveled through the whole island until they came to Paphos. There they met a Jewish sorcerer and false prophet named Bar-Jesus, who was an attendant of the proconsul, Sergius Paulus. The proconsul, an intelligent man, sent for Barnabas and Saul because he wanted to hear the word of God. But Elymas the sorcerer (for that is what his name means) opposed them and tried to turn the proconsul from the faith. Then Saul, who was also called Paul, filled with the Holy Spirit, looked straight at Elymas and said, "You are a child of the devil and an enemy of everything that is right! You are full of all kinds of deceit and trickery. Will you never stop perverting the right ways of the Lord? Now the hand of the Lord is against you. You are going to be blind for a time, not even able to see the light of the sun."

Immediately mist and darkness came over him, and he groped about, seeking someone to lead him by the hand. When the proconsul saw what had happened, he believed, for he was amazed at the teaching about the Lord. (Acts 13:6–12, NIV)

God did extraordinary miracles through Paul, so that even handkerchiefs and aprons that had touched him were taken to the sick, and their illnesses were cured and the evil spirits left them.

Some Jews who went around driving out evil spirits tried to invoke the name of the Lord Jesus over those who were demon-possessed. They would say, "In the name of Jesus whom Paul preaches, I command you to come out." Seven sons of Sceva, a Jewish chief priest, were doing this. One day the evil spirit answered them, "Jesus I know, and Paul I know about, but who are you?" Then the man who had the evil spirit jumped on them and overpowered them all. He gave them such a beating that they ran out of the house naked and bleeding.

When this became known to the Jews and Greeks living in Ephesus, they were all seized with fear, and the name of the Lord Jesus was held in high honor. (Acts 19:11–17, NIV)

Confusion, deceit, murder, and harm are all brought about by not maintaining a hearing life, centered on the edicts of God. We just "nod out," losing focus on the reality of God, drifting into a stupor, taking on the appearance of the walking dead.

The people of God know what is expected from them but have a difficult time hearing the *Lord* when our senses, emotions, feelings, desires, attitudes, and a "right to…" persona speak louder to us than the word of God.

They create "itchy ears" that make accepting false idols, the pursuit of stuff, and hatred or dislike of other human beings fashionable. They cause temples devoted to strengthening God's word to compromise and dilute their mandate because of day-to-day existence. Temples of love are converted into houses of stupor just "nodding out."

We are "Old Testament" people by nature and "pride," under a "new complete covenant" by "spirit," through the "teachings and sacrifice" of the Christ. Yet we try to live in the Book of Judges with our knowledge of Christ, a complete oxymoron, still trying to lean on Judges 21:25—"In those days Israel had no king; everyone did as they saw fit" (NIV). "Who is the king of your life?"

In order to combat this stupor and malaise that impedes our mandate to keep God first in everything and to love our neighbor as ourselves, we must improve and gain a better understanding of our hearing life and the tools that the Father has provided us to keep from nodding out.

Those tools and a better hearing life will also help us to fulfill our directive from Christ.

> Then the eleven disciples left for Galilee, going to the mountain where Jesus had told them to go. When they saw him, they worshiped him—but some of them doubted!
>
> Jesus came and told his disciples, "I have been given all authority in heaven and on earth. Therefore, go and make disciples of all the nations, baptizing them in the name of the Father and the Son and the Holy Spirit. Teach these new disciples to obey all commands I have given you.

And be sure of this: I am with you always, even to the end of the age." (Matthew 28:16–20, NLT)

To acquire wisdom is to love oneself; people who cherish understanding will prosper. (Proverbs 19:8, NLT)

Chapter 5

A HEARING LIFE

Come to me with your ears wide open. Listen, and you will find life.

—Isaiah 55:3, NLT

A "hearing life" is the goal that God wants us to achieve in order to realize maximum benefit from our communication with God. A "hearing life" is composed of three components:

1. **Hearing (paying attention)** – being able to delineate that voice that requires you to respond to it (paying attention). When I was growing up, we would spend all day playing baseball, basketball, or football. Each one of us could distinguish our mother's voice and immediately "pay attention." Our mothers were shouting because of the distance, but God speaks to us in "a still small voice."

    "Go out and stand before me on the mountain," the LORD told him. And as Elijah stood there, the LORD passed by, and a mighty windstorm hit the mountain. It was such a terrible blast that the rocks were torn loose, but the LORD was not in the wind. After the wind there was an earthquake, but the LORD was not in the earthquake. And after the earthquake there was a fire, but the LORD was not in the fire. And after the fire there was the sound of a gentle whisper. When Elijah heard it, he wrapped his face in his cloak and went out and stood at the entrance of the cave.

And a voice said, "What are you doing here, Elijah?" (1 Kings 19:11–13, NLT)

God still speaks to us in that whisper amid the confusion and concerns of our daily lives. Hearing from God requires us to eliminate the attention we give to the storms and concerns around us and "pay attention" to his still small voice.

The problem is that we are trying to figure out how to "hear God" while being bombarded by the noises of the world. Everyone is talking to us, and we talk back. Some talk is essential to us and others, some talk is important to us and others, some talk is distracting, some talk has no relevancy, and some talk is just additional noise destroying our ability to hear God and other human beings.

This ends up introducing a posture of overtalking everything in our lives. We, in a redundant style, end up applying the tenants of the "talking triad": message sent, message received, and message understood.

It's the third component of the "talking triad" that damages our listening and hearing abilities in our relationship with God.

You trying to make God understand what you are saying is an impossibility. Accept the premises that you know about God and stop talking so much in your prayer life.

Anyone with children or grandchildren is well versed in this dilemma. Your child comes home and exclaims that they need to bring cookies to the school for the class party, at the end of the month. For three weeks at every waking opportunity, you hear "When are we going to get the cookies?" or "You know we haven't got the cookies yet." God knows what you have need of. He knows what he has promised you. Spend more time listening and hearing.

2. **Listening (willingness to accept)** – being able to accept
    and give authority to what you have heard. Four times a
    year, Mom would require us to engage in a thorough clean-
    ing of the house (baseboards, venetian blinds, air vents,
    walls, windows, appliances, etc.). While we would have
    other thoughts and plans that were more enticing to our
    personal desires (playing with our friends), our willingness
    to accept what we "heard" was based on the recognized
    authority my mother and father had over our lives. We
    knew there were benefits and consequences based on our
    "willingness to accept" what we heard.

    If you fully obey the LORD your God and
    carefully follow all his commands I give you
    today, the LORD your God will set you high
    above all the nations on earth. All these blessings
    will come on you and accompany you if you obey
    the LORD your God:
    You will be blessed in the city and blessed
    in the country.
    The fruit of your womb will be blessed, and
    the crops of your land and the young of your live-
    stock—the calves of your herds and the lambs of
    your flocks.
    Your basket and your kneading trough will
    be blessed.
    You will be blessed when you come in and
    blessed when you go out.
    The LORD will grant that the enemies who
    rise up against you will be defeated before you.
    They will come at you from one direction but
    flee from you in seven.
    The LORD will send a blessing on your
    barns and on everything you put your hand to.
    The LORD your God will bless you in the land
    he is giving you.

The LORD will establish you as his holy people, as he promised you on oath, if you keep the commands of the LORD your God and walk in obedience to him. Then all peoples on earth will see that you are called by the name of the LORD, and they will fear you. The LORD will grant you abundant prosperity—in the fruit of your womb, the young of your livestock and the crops of your ground—in the land he swore to your ancestors to give you.

The LORD will open the heavens, the storehouse of his bounty, to send rain on your land in season and to bless all the work of your hands. You will lend to many nations but will borrow from none. The LORD will make you the head, not the tail. If you pay attention to the commands of the LORD your God, that I give you this day and carefully follow them, you will always be at the top, never at the bottom. Do not turn aside from any of the commands I give you today, to the right or to the left, following other gods and serving them. (Deuteronomy 28:1–14, NIV)

However, if you do not obey the LORD your God and do not carefully follow all his commands and decrees I am giving you today, all these curses will come on you and overtake you:

You will be cursed in the city and cursed in the country.

Your basket and your kneading trough will be cursed.

The fruit of your womb will be cursed, and the crops of your land, and the calves of your herds and the lambs of your flocks.

You will be cursed when you come in and cursed when you go out.

The LORD will send on you curses, confusion and rebuke in everything you put your hand to, until you are destroyed and come to sudden ruin because of the evil you have done in forsaking him. The LORD will plague you with diseases until he has destroyed you from the land you are entering to possess. The LORD will strike you with wasting disease, with fever and inflammation, with scorching heat and drought, with blight and mildew, which will plague you until you perish. The sky over your head will be bronze, the ground beneath you iron. The LORD will turn the rain of your country into dust and powder; it will come down from the skies until you are destroyed.

The LORD will cause you to be defeated before your enemies. You will come at them from one direction but flee from them in seven, and you will become a thing of horror to all the kingdoms on earth. Your carcasses will be food for all the birds and the wild animals, and there will be no one to frighten them away. The LORD will afflict you with the boils of Egypt and with tumors, festering sores and the itch, from which you cannot be cured. The LORD will afflict you with madness, blindness and confusion of mind. At midday you will grope about like a blind person in the dark. You will be unsuccessful in everything you do; day after day you will be oppressed and robbed, with no one to rescue you.

You will be pledged to be married to a woman, but another will take her and rape her. You will build a house, but you will not live in it. You will plant a vineyard, but you will not even begin to enjoy its fruit. Your ox will be slaughtered before your eyes, but you will eat none of

it. Your donkey will be forcibly taken from you
and will not be returned. Your sheep will be given
to your enemies, and no one will rescue them.
Your sons and daughters will be given to another
nation, and you will wear out your eyes watching
for them day after day, powerless to lift a hand.
A people that you do not know will eat what
your land and labor produced, and you will have
nothing but cruel oppression all your days. The
sights you see will drive you mad. The LORD
will afflict your knees and legs with painful boils
that cannot be cured, spreading from the soles of
your feet to the top of your head. (Deuteronomy
28:15–35, NIV)

These are the terms of the covenant the
LORD commanded Moses to make with the
Israelites in Moab, in addition to the covenant he
had made with them at Horeb. (Deuteronomy
29:1, NIV)

3. **Responding (doing, completing the inquiry, request, or
    task)** – it is our responsibility to respond to what we have
    heard and accepted, in the time frame of the authority pre-
    senting it. My mother and her very capable enforcer, my
    father, did not set their clock according to my watch, and
    neither does God.

At that time the kingdom of heaven will be
like ten virgins who took their lamps and went
out to meet the bridegroom. Five of them were
foolish and five were wise. The foolish ones took
their lamps but did not take any oil with them.
The wise ones, however, took oil in jars along
with their lamps. The bridegroom was a long
time in coming, and they all became drowsy and
fell asleep.

At midnight the cry rang out: "Here's the bridegroom! Come out to meet him!"

Then all the virgins woke up and trimmed their lamps. The foolish ones said to the wise, "Give us some of your oil; our lamps are going out."

"No," they replied, "there may not be enough for both us and you. Instead, go to those who sell oil and buy some for yourselves."

But while they were on their way to buy oil, the bridegroom arrived. The virgins who were ready went in with him to the wedding banquet. And the door was shut.

Later the others also came. "Lord, Lord," they said, "open the door for us!"

But he replied, "Truly I tell you, I don't know you."

Therefore keep watch, because you do not know the day or the hour. (Matthew 25:1–13, NIV)

If you heard the word from God and you accepted the word from God, then do what God wants, the way God wants it! Stop turning the pure juice of God into your brand of Kool-Aid.

Hearing from God makes us realize how naked we are spiritually, emotionally, physically, and mentally, in God's presence.

You may need to fine-tune your hearing; but denying hearing from God is an impossibility.

The wrath of God is being revealed from heaven against all the godlessness and wickedness of people, who suppress the truth by their wickedness, since what may be known about God is plain to them, because God has made it plain to them. For since the creation of the world God's invisible qualities—his eternal power and divine nature—have been clearly seen, being understood from what has been made, so that people are without excuse.

For although they knew God, they neither glorified him as God nor gave thanks to him, but their thinking became futile and their foolish hearts were darkened. Although they claimed to be wise, they became fools and exchanged the glory of the immortal God for images made to look like a mortal human being and birds and animals and reptiles. (Romans 1:18–23, NIV)

Refusing to adhere to hearing from the Creator will guarantee no "peace of mind" and could lead to missing out on eternal life with the *Lord*.

When the Son of Man comes in his glory, and all the angels with him, he will sit on his glorious throne. All the nations will be gathered before him, and he will separate the people one from another as a shepherd separates the sheep from the goats. He will put the sheep on his right and the goats on his left.

Then the King will say to those on his right, "Come you who are blessed by my Father; take your inheritance, the kingdom prepared for you since the creation of the world. For I was hungry and you gave me something to eat, I was thirsty and you gave me something to drink, I was a stranger and you invited me in, I needed clothes and you clothed me, I was sick and you looked after me, I was in prison and you came to visit me."

Then the righteous will answer him, "Lord, when did we see you hungry and feed you, or thirsty and give you something to drink? When did we see you a stranger and invite you in or needing clothes and clothe you? When did we see you sick or in prison and go to visit you?"

The King will reply, "Truly I tell you, whatever you did for one of the least of these brothers and sisters of mine, you did for me."

Then he will say to those on his left, "Depart from me, you who are cursed, into the eternal fire prepared for the devil and his angels. For I was hungry and you gave me nothing to eat, I was thirsty and you gave me nothing to drink, I was a stranger and you did not invite me in, I needed clothes and you did not clothe me, I was sick and in prison and you did not look after me."

They also will answer, "Lord, when did we see you hungry or thirsty or a stranger or needing clothes or sick or in prison, and did not help you?"

He will reply, "Truly I tell you, whatever you did not do for one of the least of these, you did not do for me."

Then they will go away to eternal punishment, but the righteous to eternal life. (Matthew 25:31–46, NIV)

Not everyone who says to me, "Lord, Lord," will enter the kingdom of heaven, but only the one who does the will of my Father who is in heaven. Many will say to me on that day, "Lord, Lord, did we not prophesy in your name and in your name drive out demons and in your name perform miracles?" Then I will tell them plainly, "I never knew you. Away from me, you evildoers!" (Matthew 7:21–23, NIV)

Somebody has skimmed over this part because you think you are fully exempt. I would advise all individuals who are still in need of help with their "hearing life" to be very careful. Continue to check with the Holy Spirit until you receive the right response. The good thing is this: A negative condition of ending up thinking you are going to heaven but you end up in hell is reversible, until the moment of death.

Hearing from God can be a very scary thing, depending on your level of obedience to the will of God. To be completely exposed in the presence of the Creator has caused many an individual to forgo the completeness that God has for their life.

> On the first day of the third month after the Israelites left Egypt—on that very day—they came to the Desert of Sinai. After they set out from Rephidim, they entered the Desert of Sinai, and Israel camped there in the desert in front of the mountain.
>
> Then Moses went up to God, and the LORD called to him from the mountain and said, "This is what you are to say to the descendants of Jacob and what you are to tell the people of Israel: 'You yourselves have seen what I did to Egypt, and how I carried you on eagles' wings and brought you to myself. Now if you obey me fully and keep my covenant, then out of all nations you will be my treasured possession. Although the whole earth is mine, you will be for me a kingdom of priests and a holy nation.' These are the words you are to speak to the Israelites."
>
> So Moses went back and summoned the elders of the people and set before them all the words the LORD had commanded him to speak. The people all responded together, "We will do everything the LORD has said." So Moses brought their answer back to the LORD. (Exodus 19:1–8, NIV)

The Israelites are about to turn an eleven-day journey to the promise land into a forty-year odyssey.

> (It takes eleven days to go from Horeb to Kadesh Barnea by the Mount Seir road.)
> In the fortieth year, on the first day of the eleventh month, Moses proclaimed to the Israelites all that the LORD had commanded him concerning them. This was after he had defeated Sihon king of the Amorites, who reigned in Heshbon, and at Edrei had defeated Og king of Bashan, who reigned in Ashtaroth.
> East of the Jordan in the territory of Moab, Moses began to expound this law, saying: (Deuteronomy 1:2–5, NIV)
> The LORD said to Moses, "I am going to come to you in a dense cloud, so that the people will hear me speaking with you and will always put their trust in you." Then Moses told the LORD what the people had said.
> And the LORD said to Moses, "Go to the people and consecrate them today and tomorrow. Have them wash their clothes and be ready by the third day, because on that day the LORD will come down on Mount Sinai in the sight of all the people. Put limits for the people around the mountain and tell them, 'Be careful that you do not approach the mountain or touch the foot of it. Whoever touches the mountain is to be put to death. They are to be stoned or shot with arrows; not a hand is to be laid on them. No person or animal shall be permitted to live.' Only when the ram's horn sounds a long blast may they approach the mountain."
> After Moses had gone down the mountain to the people, he consecrated them, and they

washed their clothes. Then he said to the people, "Prepare yourselves for the third day. Abstain from sexual relations."

On the morning of the third day there was thunder and lightning, with a thick cloud over the mountain, and a very loud trumpet blast. Everyone in the camp trembled. Then Moses led the people out of the camp to meet with God, and they stood at the foot of the mountain. Mount Sinai was covered with smoke, because the LORD descended on it in fire. The smoke billowed up from it like smoke from a furnace, and the whole mountain trembled violently. As the sound of the trumpet grew louder and louder, Moses spoke and the voice of God answered him.

The LORD descended to the top of Mount Sinai and called Moses to the top of the mountain. So Moses went up and the LORD said to him, "Go down and warn the people so they do not force their way through to see the LORD and many of them perish. Even the priests, who approach the LORD, must consecrate themselves, or the LORD will break out against them."

Moses said to the LORD, "The people cannot come up Mount Sinai, because you yourself warned us, 'Put limits around the mountain and set it apart as holy.'"

The LORD replied, "Go down and bring Aaron up with you. But the priests and the people must not force their way through to come up to the LORD, or he will break out against them."

So Moses went down to the people and told them. (Exodus 19:9–25, NIV)

When the people saw the thunder and lightning and heard the trumpet and saw the mountain in smoke, they trembled with fear. They stayed at a distance and said to Moses, "Speak to us yourself and we will listen. But do not have God speak to us or we will die."

Moses said to the people, "Do not be afraid. God has come to test you, so that the fear of God will be with you to keep you from sinning."

The people remained at a distance, while Moses approached the thick darkness where God was.

Then the LORD said to Moses, "Tell the Israelites this: 'You have seen for yourselves that I have spoken to you from heaven: Do not make any gods to be alongside me; do not make for yourselves gods of silver or gods of gold.

Make an altar of earth for me and sacrifice on it your burnt offerings and fellowship offerings, your sheep and goats and your cattle. Wherever I cause my name to be honored, I will come to you and bless you. If you make an altar of stones for me, do not build it with dressed stones, for you will defile it if you use a tool on it. And do not go up to my altar on steps, or your private parts may be exposed.'" (Exodus 20:18–26, NIV)

Their desire to develop a "hearing life" with God would only be sparked by tragedy, deceit, and loss, because of their inability to stay in the presence of God and acquire his wisdom and understanding.

Your "pride" is scared of the "presence of God." Your "pride" does not want to be a priest of the *Lord*. Your "pride" does not want to be in the "presence of the *Lord*." Your "pride" does not want to hear or listen to the mandates of God. Your "pride" hates God; it wants to be like God! Your "pride" wants to follow its wisdom, and it wants to lean on its own understanding.

Being in the presence of God at Mount Sinai, a church service, your car, a public place, or the privacy of your home can be a scary proposition. Clearly the concern of a physical death is not appropriate, since God clearly expressed that he had work for them and for us to do. The scary death is the death of "self" (what we think, what we want, how we want it, and when we want it). Your "pride" must ultimately die. Without this death, it is impossible to hear, listen, and accomplish the work that God has for you.

> Pride precedes destruction; an arrogant spirit appears before a fall. (Proverbs 16:18, ISV)
>
> Then he said to the crowd, "If any of you wants to be my follower, you must turn from your selfish ways, take up your cross daily, and follow me. If you try to hang on to your life, you will lose it. But if you give up your life for my sake, you will save it. And what do you benefit if you gain the whole world but are yourself lost or destroyed?" (Luke 9:23–25, NLT)

The closeness that God desires to have with all human beings can only be obtained by learning to achieve a better "hearing life" with God. This "hearing life" is known as meditation. Meditation is a process of growth, in stages, of communicating and hearing God better.

We have attempted to dissect God's approach to meditation to the point where we endeavor to segregate the components from each other. This dissecting creates a wide schism between each component. This rupture makes it difficult to understand each component and transition between the components and utilize each component effectively.

Our "hearing life" with God also includes our ability to seek clarification from the Creator on the logistical matters of our lives (the whats, the hows, the wheres, and the whens). All too often our "hearing life" is replaced with a "talking life."

A "talking life" is counterproductive to learning our purpose for our existence and getting answers, from God, that bring "peace of mind." We spend a great deal of time telling and asking God about things he already knows about. We end up leaning on our own understanding, based on the world around us.

No one can serve two masters. Either you will hate the one and love the other, or you will be devoted to the one and despise the other. You cannot serve both God and money.

"Therefore I tell you, do not worry about your life, what you will eat or drink; or about your body, what you will wear. Is not life more than food, and the body more than clothes? Look at the birds of the air; they do not sow or reap or store away in barns, and yet your heavenly Father feeds them. Are you not much more valuable than they? Can any one of you by worrying add a single hour to your life?

And why do you worry about clothes? See how the flowers of the field grow. They do not labor or spin. Yet I tell you that not even Solomon in all his splendor was dressed like one of these. If that is how God clothes the grass of the field, which is here today and tomorrow is thrown into the fire, will he not much more clothe you—you of little faith? So do not worry, saying, 'What shall we eat?' or 'What shall we drink?' or 'What shall we wear?' For the pagans run after all these things, and your heavenly Father knows that you need them. But seek first his kingdom and his righteousness, and all these things will be given to you as well. Therefore do not worry about tomorrow, for tomorrow will worry about itself. Each day has enough trouble of its own." (Matthew 6:24–34, NIV)

A dominant "talking life" (more talking than listening) with God creates a worldly importance that supersedes God's desires for your life. God wants to provide for you so you can provide for others, but you can't lean on your own understanding and wisdom.

And he told them this parable: "The ground of a certain rich man yielded an abundant harvest. He thought to himself, 'What shall I do? I have no place to store my crops.'

Then he said, 'This is what I'll do. I will tear down my barns and build bigger ones, and there I will store my surplus grain. And I'll say to myself, "You have plenty of grain laid up for many years. Take life easy; eat drink and be merry."'

But God said to him, 'You fool! This very night your life will be demanded from you. Then who will get what you have prepared for yourself?'

This is how it will be with whoever stores up things for themselves but is not rich toward God." (Luke 12:16–21, NIV)

A "talking life" inhibits spiritual growth. We feel the need to orient God with our cares of everyday life. We stand to pray when we should be making ourselves as small and humble as possible. I know this is contrary to tradition in many sectors, but it does not follow the rules for prayer.

"And when you pray, do not be like the hypocrites, for they love to pray standing in the synagogues and on the street corners to be seen by others. Truly I tell you, they have received their reward in full. But when you pray, go into your room, close the door and pray to your Father, who is unseen. Then your Father, who sees what is done in secret, will reward you. And when you pray, do not keep on babbling like pagans, for they think they will be heard because of their many words. Do not be like them, for your Father knows what you need before you ask him.

This, then, is how you should pray:

'Our Father in heaven, hallowed be your name, your kingdom come, your will be done, on earth as it is in heaven. Give us today our daily bread. And forgive us our debts, as we also have forgiven our debtors. And lead us not into temptation, but deliver us from the evil one.'

For if you forgive other people when they sin against you, your heavenly Father will also forgive you. But if you do not forgive others their sins, your Father will not forgive your sins." (Matthew 6:5–15, NIV)

Standing to pray was an initial way to identify yourself as a Christian, when asked during persecution. It is a custom that was initiated in honor of those individuals, like the early persecuted followers of Christ in the Roman arena, who stood up and lost their lives because they were Christians (followers of Christ). The irony of the situation is that we will stand to pray but find it difficult to stand for Christ when it matters or could be detrimental to our perceived existence, desires, and position in our everyday lives.

Developing our "hearing life" requires us to first realize that its primary purpose is spiritual and pertains primarily to learning and strengthening God's "purpose for our existence." We often get this distorted by being forced to reside in a world that we are not destined to stay in.

"If the world hates you, keep in mind that it hated me first. If you belonged to the world, it would love you as its own. As it is, you do not belong to the world, but I have chosen you out of the world. That is why the world hates you. Remember what I told you: 'A servant is not greater than his master.' If they persecuted me, they will persecute you also. If they obeyed my teaching, they will obey yours also. They will treat you this way because of my name, for they do not know the one who sent me. If I had not come and spoken to them, they would not be guilty of sin; but now they have no excuse for their sin. Whoever hates me hates my Father as well." (John 15:18–23, NIV)

Every human being from Mother Theresa to Adolph Hitler was born to this world with a specific purpose, designated by God, for the uplifting of God's kingdom. God decided which seed of your father, out of millions of candidates, would join with your mother's egg and produce you! Whether we learn and accept the purpose God has for our lives through God's wisdom and understanding, like Mother Theresa, or lean on our own wisdom and understanding we have for our lives, like Adolph Hitler, is a matter of personal preference (free will). Free will is our manifestation of our original sin of pride. It is our attempt to be like God.

Then Balak's anger burned against Balaam. He struck his hands together and said to him, "I summoned you to curse my enemies, but you have blessed them these three times. Now leave at once and go home! I said I would reward you handsomely, but the LORD has kept you from being rewarded." (Numbers 24:10 and 11, NIV)

Balaam had been summoned to curse the Israelites, who had camped in Moab. God informed him that he could not curse the Israelites. So he didn't; he blessed them. Then leaning on his own understanding and wisdom, he told King Balak to make their women available to destroy the Israelites' worship and resolve, costing twenty-four thousand Israelite lives.

While Israel was staying in Shittim, the men began to indulge in sexual immorality with Moabite women, who invited them to the sacrifices to their gods. The people ate the sacrificial meal and bowed down before these gods. So Israel yoked themselves to the Baal of Peor. And the LORD's anger burned against them.

The LORD said to Moses, "Take all the leaders of these people, kill them and expose them in broad daylight before the LORD, so that the LORD's fierce anger may turn away from Israel."

So Moses said to Israel's judges, "Each of you must put to death those of your people who have yoked themselves to the Baal of Peor."

Then an Israelite man brought into the camp a Midianite woman right before the eyes of Moses and the whole assembly of Israel while they were weeping at the entrance to the tent of meeting. When Phinehas son of Eleazar, the son of Aaron, the priest, saw this, he left the assembly, took a spear in his hand and followed the Israelite into the tent. He drove the spear into both of them, right through the Israelite man and into the woman's stomach. Then the plague against the Israelites was stopped; but those who died in the plague numbered 24,000.

The LORD said to Moses, "Phinehas son of Eleazar, the son of Aaron, the priest, has turned my anger away from the Israelites. Since he was as zealous for my honor among them as I am, I did not put an end to them in my zeal. Therefore tell him I am making my covenant of peace with him. He and his descendants will have a covenant of a lasting priesthood, because he was zealous for the honor of his God and made atonement for the Israelites."

The name of the Israelite who was killed with the Midianite woman was Zimri son of Salu, the leader of a Simeonite family. And the name of the Midianite woman who was put to death was Kozbi daughter of Zur, a tribal chief of a Midianite Family.

The LORD said to Moses, "Treat the Midianites as enemies and kill them. They treated you as enemies when they deceived you in the Peor incident involving their sister Kozbi, the daughter of a Midianite leader, the woman who was killed when the plague came as a result of the incident." (Numbers 25:1–18, NIV)

They fought against Midian, as the LORD commanded Moses, and killed every man. Among their victims were Evi, Rekem, Zur, Hur and Reba—the five kings of Midian. They also killed Balaam son of Beor with the sword. The Israelites captured the Midianite women and children and took all the Midianite herds, flocks and goods as plunder. (Numbers 31:7–9, NIV)

"Have you allowed all the women to live?" he asked them. "They were the ones who followed Balaam's advice and enticed the Israelites to be unfaithful to the LORD in the Peor incident, so that a plague struck the LORD's people. Now kill all the boys. And kill every woman who has slept with a man, but save for yourselves every girl who has never slept with a man." (Numbers 31:15–18, NIV)

This world continuously attempts to keep us confused and agitated. It tries and often succeeds in turning our attentions away from our "hearing life" to a "talking life" with God. The ploy, to keep us from developing an effective "hearing life," depends on us not being able to constantly remember and accept these facts. We "nodded out" from moments to decades making us susceptible to stand in our own wisdom, thinking we are acceptable to God.

We must stand diligent in God's wisdom and understanding to stay conscious of what we are doing to ourselves. For most of us, it's not the lack of knowledge to stay focused on the wisdom and understanding offered to us by our heavenly Father, but the lapse of remembrance that causes us to forget:

1. That we sin daily

"So the trouble is not with the law, for it is spiritual and good. The trouble is with me, for I am all too human, a slave to sin. I don't really understand myself, for I want to do what is right, but I don't do it. Instead, I do what I hate. But if I know that what I'm doing is wrong, this shows that I agree that the law is good. So I am not the one doing wrong; it is sin living in me that does it.

And I know that nothing good lives in me, that is, in my sinful nature. I want to do what is right, but I can't. I want to do what is good, but I don't. I don't want to do what is wrong, but I do it anyway. But if I do what I don't want to do, I am not really the one doing wrong; it is sin living in me that does it.

I have discovered this principle of life—that when I want to do what is right, I inevitably do what is wrong. I love God's law with all my heart.

But there is another power within me that is at war with my mind. This power makes me a slave to the sin that is still within me. Oh, what a miserable person I am! Who will free me from this life that is dominated by sin and death? Thank God! The answer is in Jesus Christ our Lord. So you see how it is: In my mind I really want to obey God's law, but because of my sinful nature I am a slave to sin." (Romans 7:14–25, NLT)

This scripture may require more attention, in order to develop a better understanding. So we will use the translation in the Message (MSG) Bible, starting at verse 13, to magnify the word of God:

"I can already hear your next question: 'Does that mean I can't even trust what is good [that is, the law]? Is good just as dangerous as evil?' No again! Sin simply did what sin is so famous for doing: using the good as a cover to tempt me to do what would finally destroy me. By hiding within God's good commandment, sin did far more mischief than it could ever have accomplished on its own.

I can anticipate the response that is coming: 'I know that all God's commands are spiritual, but I'm not. Isn't this also your experience?' Yes. I'm full of myself—after all, I've spent a long time in sin's prison. What I don't understand about myself is that I decide one way, but then I act another, doing things I absolutely despise. So if I can't be trusted to figure out what is best for myself and then do it, it becomes obvious that God's command is necessary.

But I need something more! For if I know the law but still can't kept it, and if the power of sin within me keeps sabotaging my best intentions, I obviously need help! I realize that I don't have what it takes. I can will it, but I can't do it. I decide to do good, but I don't really do it; I decide not to do bad, but then I do it anyway. My decisions, such as they are, don't result in actions. Something has gone wrong deep within me and gets the better of me every time.

It happens so regularly that it's predictable. The moment I decide to do good, sin is there to trip me up. I truly delight in God's commands, but it's pretty obvious that not all of me joins in that delight. Parts of me covertly rebel, and just when I least expect it, they take charge.

I've tried everything and nothing helps. I'm at the end of my rope. Is there no one who can do anything for me? Isn't that the real question?

The answer, thank God, is that Jesus Christ can and does. He acted to set things right in this life of contradictions where I want to serve God with all my heart and mind, but am pulled by the influence of sin to do something totally different." (Romans 7:13–25, MSG)

So don't lose a minute in building on what you've been given, complementing your basic faith with good character, spiritual understanding, alert discipline, passionate patience, reverent wonder, warm friendliness, and generous love, each dimension fitting into and developing the others. With these qualities active and growing in your lives, no grass will grow under your feet, no day will pass without its reward as you mature in your experience of our Master Jesus. Without these qualities you can't see what's right before you, oblivious that your old sinful life has been wiped off the books. (2 Peter 1:5–9, MSG)

Yes, we sin daily and often because of our human nature. We can reduce the frequency and types of sin by staying in tune with what God requires of us. Sinning is like ice-skating: The more you practice the principles that keep you upright, the less you fall.

What then? are we better than they? No, in no wise: for we have before proved both Jews and Gentiles, that they are all under sin;

As it is written, There is none righteous, no, not one: There is none that understandeth, there is none that seeketh after God.

They are all gone out of the way, they are together become unprofitable; there is none that doeth good, no not one.

Their throat is an open sepulcher; with their tongues they have deceit; the poison of asps is under their lips:

Whose mouth is full of cursing and bitterness:

Their feet are swift to shed blood:

Destruction and misery are in their ways:

And the way of peace have they not known:

There is no fear of God before their eyes.

Now we know that what things soever the law saith, it saith to them who are under the law: that every mouth may be stopped, and all the world may become guilty before God.

Therefore by the deeds of the law there shall no flesh be justified in his sight: for by law is the knowledge of sin. (Romans 3:9–20, KJV)

Yes, we all have sinned and have come short of the glory of God. When we accept God's wisdom and learn his understanding of how we should live our lives and conduct ourselves, on this planet, then the Father makes provisions for our lives on earth and eternally.

But now apart from the law the righteousness of God has been made known, to which the Law and the Prophets testify. This righteousness is given through faith in Jesus Christ to all who believe. There is no difference between Jew and Gentile, for all have sinned and fall short of the glory of God, and all are justified freely by his grace through the redemption that came by

Christ Jesus. God presented Christ as a sacrifice of atonement, through the shedding of his blood—to be received by faith. He did this to demonstrate his righteousness, because in his forbearance he had left the sins committed beforehand unpunished—he did it to demonstrate his righteousness at the present time, so as to be just and the one who justifies those who have faith in Jesus.

Where, then is boasting? It is excluded. Because of what law? The law that requires works? No, because of the law that requires faith. For we maintain that a person is justified by faith apart from the works of the law. (Romans 3:21–28, NIV)

Human beings for millenniums have enjoyed debating between law and faith. In an attempt to reduce confusion in our lives, I asked the Holy Spirit how do the two come together. The Holy Spirit said to me, "The sole purpose of the law is to identify, to you, what is sinful to God. Once the law has done that, it has completed its job. Faith takes over after that—faith that God knows what is better for us than we do."

Spiritually God opposes our earthly beliefs, that one sin is worse than another sin, by saying all sins are the same. There are neither big sins nor little sins. Sin is sin!

They kept demanding an answer, so he stood up again and said, "All right, but let the one who has never sinned throw the first stone!" (John 8:7, NLT)

All sin is a foul smell in the nostrils of God. Yet, we can end up thinking either my sins are not as bad as his or her sins or my sins and/or lifestyle is so terrible I can't be forgiven. This is absolutely wrong on both accounts.

The only sin that cannot be forgiven is blasphemy against the Holy Spirit.

Whoever is not with me is against me, and whoever does not gather with me scatters. And so I tell you, every kind of sin and slander can be forgiven, but blasphemy against the Spirit will not be forgiven. Anyone who speaks a word against the Son of Man will be forgiven, but anyone who speaks against the Holy Spirit will not be forgiven, either in this age or the age to come. (Matthew 12:30–32, NIV)

In order to commit this sin, you must be a spirit that knows the Holy Spirit and denies the Holy Spirit's authority; that is why Lucifer and his demons can never be forgiven. We are flesh, and we walk by "faith."

Faith is the confidence that what we hope for will actually happen; it gives us assurance about things we cannot see. (Hebrew 11:1, NLT)

We will not know the Holy Spirit as spirit until death or the second coming of Christ. Faith is what we utilize to trust in God's wisdom and understanding.

2. **That "going along to get along" is contrary to being a disciple of Christ, a follower of Christ's teachings, a Christian**

Large crowds were traveling with Jesus, and turning to them he said: "If anyone comes to me and does not hate father and mother, wife and children, brothers and sisters—yes, even their own life—such a person cannot be my disciple. And whoever does not carry their cross and follow me cannot be my disciple.

Suppose one of you wants to build a tower. Won't you first sit down and estimate the cost to see if you have enough money to complete it? For if you lay the foundation and are not able to finish it, everyone who sees it will ridicule you, saying, 'This person began to build and wasn't able to finish.'

Or suppose a king is about to go to war against another king. Won't he first sit down and consider whether he is able with ten thousand men to oppose the one coming against him with twenty thousand? If he is not able, he will send a delegation while the other is still a long way off and will ask for terms of peace. In the same way, those of you who do not give up everything you have cannot be my disciples.

Salt is good, but if it loses its saltiness, how can it be made salty again? It is fit neither for the soil nor for the manure pile; it is thrown out.

Whoever has ears to hear, let them hear."
(Luke 14:25–35, NIV)

"Going along to get along" is a virus that has inundated those who have put their hands on the plow. This virus is more devastating than cancer, Ebola, and the bubonic plague rolled into one. While these maladies wreak havoc in our earthly existence, "going along to get along" impacts the eternal spiritual lives of individuals who come to us, the men and women of God, to provide proper direction not according to the world but according to the word of God.

As they were walking along the road, a man said to him, "I will follow you wherever you go."

Jesus replied, "Foxes have dens and birds have nests, but the Son of Man has no place to lay his head."

He said to another man, "Follow me."

But he replied, "Lord, first let me go and bury my father."

Jesus said to him, "Let the dead bury their own dead, but you go and proclaim the kingdom of God."

Still another said, "I will follow you, Lord; but first let me go back and say goodbye to my family."

Jesus replied, "No one who puts a hand to the plow and looks back is fit for service in the kingdom of God." (Luke 9:57–62, NIV)

The subtle measures of traditional behavior ease into and eventually distort our view of God's wisdom and understanding, for our lives. We need to adhere to God's mandate for our lives without the inclusion of habit or routine.

God had laid out a whole procedure to the Israelites of how they were to present their sacrifices to him.

When the altar was anointed, the leaders brought their offerings for its dedication and presented them before the altar. For the LORD had said to Moses, "Each day one leader is to bring his offering for the dedication of the altar."

The one who brought his offering on the first day was Nahshon son of Amminadab of the tribe of Judah.

His offering was one silver plate weighing a hundred and thirty shekels and one silver sprinkling bowl weighing seventy shekels, both according to the sanctuary shekel, each filled with the finest flour mixed with olive oil as a grain offering; one gold dish weighing ten shekels, filled with incense; one young bull, one ram and one male lamb a year old for a burnt offering; one male goat for a sin offering; and two oxen, five rams, five male goats and five male lambs a year old to be sacrificed as a fellowship offering. This was the offering of Nahshon son of Amminadab. (Numbers 7:10–17, NIV)

Yes, you were to bring your offerings to the altar—offerings that belonged to you, that traveled with you, which were truly a sacrifice for you and your family. Leaning on their own earthly wisdom and understanding and incorporating "going along to get along," they, the leadership, started to allow people to buy their offerings at the temple. It made it convenient, no more lugging heavy items from home and corralling animals all the way to the temple.

Such compromising on the dictate of the Father ignited this response from Christ Jesus:

> On reaching Jerusalem, Jesus entered the temple courts and began driving out those who were buying and selling there. He overturned the tables of the money changers and the benches of those selling doves, and would not allow anyone to carry merchandise through the temple courts. And as he taught them, he said, "Is it not written: 'My house will be called a house of prayer for all nations'? But you have made it 'a den of robbers.'"
>
> The chief priests and the teachers of the law heard this and began looking for a way to kill him, for they feared him, because the whole crowd was amazed at his teaching. (Mark 11:15–18, NIV)

"Going along to get along" could cause you to have to take the same test over and over, till you get it right. It could also cause you to lose out on opportunities of growth that God has for you.

> Now it was the governor's custom at the festival to release a prisoner chosen by the crowd. At that time they had a well-known prisoner whose

name was Jesus Barabbas. So when the crowd had gathered, Pilate asked them, "Which one do you want me to release to you: Jesus Barabbas, or Jesus who is called the Messiah?" For he knew it was out of self-interest that they had handed Jesus over to him.

While Pilate was sitting on the judge's seat, his wife sent him this message: "Don't have anything to do with that innocent man, for I have suffered a great deal today in a dream because of him." (Matthew 27:15–19, NIV)

3. That the "golden rule" must be followed in totality

Don't pick on people, jump on their failures, criticize their faults—unless, of course, you want the same treatment. That critical spirit has a way of boomeranging. It's easy to see a smudge on your neighbor's face and be oblivious to the ugly sneer on your own. Do you have the nerve to say, "Let me wash your face for you," when your own face is distorted by contempt? It's this whole traveling road-show mentality all over again, playing a holier-than-thou part instead of just living your part. Wipe that ugly sneer off your own face, and you might be fit to offer a washcloth to your neighbor. (Matthew 7:1–5, MSG)

We learned this as children, and our experiences in the world began to erode this tenant. We learned to become selective in whom we are willing to accept according to the "golden rule." Even though Christ has made it abundantly clear that every human being is entitled to having the "golden rule" applied to them, too many of us attempt to introduce our own selective criteria to God's golden rule. We use such things as religious preference in worshiping the Father, denominational difference within the same worship orientation to the Father, sex, race, ethnicity, sexual orientation, where you reside on the globe, and on and on and on. Christ addressed all these issues. Our unwillingness to accept Jesus Christ's teachings on these matters is only because we depend on our earthly wisdom, which causes us to lean on our own understanding as if it was the crutch needed to stay upright and correct in our own minds and eyes.

> "You have heard that it was said, 'Love your neighbor and hate your enemy.' But I tell you, love your enemies and pray for those who perse-cute you, that you may be children of your Father in heaven. He causes his sun to rise on the evil and the good, and sends rain on the righteous and the unrighteous. If you love those who love you, what reward will you get? Are not even the tax collectors doing that? And if you greet only your own people, what are you doing more than others? Do not even pagans do that? Be perfect, therefore, as your heavenly Father is perfect." (Matthew 5:43–48, NIV)

Human beings love a pecking order. We have listings for every-thing. We list and prioritize everything that is earthly and spiritual alike. If you have any doubt about this, take a look at the *Guinness Book of Records.*

Our obsessive need to categorize leads us to categorize every-thing in our lives. We argue about who's the greatest running back in football or the greatest basketball player or the greatest boxer or singer or general. The list goes on and on. Our obsession with rank-ing everything and anything even leads us to try and rank sin. Again, all sins are on the same level of separation from God. They are all poisoned Kool-Aid. The only difference is flavoring, some like grape, some like cherry, and some like orange. Sin will provide you with whatever flavor of death you prefer.

Our need to rank and categorize will even cause the best of us to lean on our own understanding and attempt to determine our value to God. Categorizing often occurs when challenging emotional decisions, based on our earthly wisdom, are sprung on us. It becomes more prevalent right after we have done something right in the eyes of the Father. Even a man as committed to God as Elijah succumbed to this problem of magnifying our importance.

Elijah could confront a king, his soldiers, all the people of Israel, 450 prophets of Baal, and 400 prophets of Asherah, by himself. Elijah killed all 450 prophets of Baal, ended the drought, and outran the king's chariot back to Jezreel.

But when confronted with a threat from Jezebel, Elijah got scared and ran into the wilderness and hid in a cave, because he had determined that he was the last prophet working for God—a great man of God overemphasizing his position in God's plan for his people.

Now Elijah the Tishbite, from Tishbe in Gilead, said to Ahab, "As the LORD, the God of Israel, lives, whom I serve, there will be neither dew nor rain in the next few years except at my word."

Then the word of the LORD came to Elijah: "Leave here, turn eastward and hide in the Kerith Ravine, east of the Jordan. You will drink from the brook, and I have directed the ravens to supply you with food there."

So he did what the LORD had told him. He went to the Kerith Ravine, east of the Jordan, and stayed there. The ravens brought him bread and meat in the morning and bread and meat in the evening, and he drank from the brook. (1 Kings 17:1–6, NIV)

After a long time, in the third year, the word of the LORD came to Elijah: "Go and present yourself to Ahab, and I will send rain on the land." So Elijah went to present himself to Ahab.

Now the famine was severe in Samaria, and Ahab had summoned Obadiah, his palace administrator. (Obadiah was a devout believer in the LORD. While Jezebel was killing off the LORD's prophets, Obadiah had taken a hundred prophets and hidden them in two caves, fifty in each, and had supplied them with food and water.) (1 Kings 18:1–4, NIV)

As Obadiah was walking along, Elijah met him. Obadiah recognized him, bowed down to the ground, and said, "Is it really you, my lord Elijah?"

"Yes," he replied. "Go tell your master, 'Elijah is here.'"

"What have I done wrong," asked Obadiah, "that you are handing your servant over to Ahab to be put to death? As surely as the LORD your God lives, there is not a nation or kingdom where my master has not sent someone to look for you. And whenever a nation or kingdom claimed you were not there, he made them swear they could not find you. But now you tell me to go to my master and say, 'Elijah is here.' I don't know where the Spirit of the LORD may carry you when I leave you. If I go and tell Ahab and he doesn't find you, he will kill me. Yet I your servant have worshiped the LORD since my youth. Haven't you heard, my lord, what I did while Jezebel was killing the prophets of the LORD? I hid a hundred of the LORD's prophets in two caves, fifty in each, and supplied them with food and water. And now you tell me to go to my master and say, 'Elijah is here.' He will kill me!"

Elijah said, "As the LORD Almighty lives, whom I serve, I will surely present myself to Ahab today."

So Obadiah went to meet Ahab and told him, and Ahab went to meet Elijah. When he saw Elijah, he said to him, "Is that you, you troubler of Israel?"

"I have not made trouble for Israel," Elijah replied. "But you and your father's family have. You have abandoned the LORD's commands and have followed the Baals. Now summon the people from all over Israel to meet me on Mount Carmel. And bring the four hundred and fifty prophets of Baal and the four hundred prophets of Asherah, who eat at Jezebel's table."

So Ahab sent word throughout all Israel and assembled the prophets on Mount Carmel. Elijah went before the people and said, "How long will you waver between two opinions? If the LORD is God, follow him; but if Baal is God, follow him."

But the people said nothing.

Then Elijah said to them, "I am the only one of the LORD's prophets left, but Baal has four hundred and fifty prophets. Get two bulls for us. Let Baal's prophets choose one for themselves, and let them cut it into pieces and put it on wood but not set fire to it. I will prepare the other bull and put it on wood but not set fire to it. Then you call on the name of your god, and I will call on the name of the LORD. The god who answers by fire—he is God."

Then all the people said, "What you say is good." (1 Kings 18:7–24, NIV)

Elijah said to the prophets of Baal, "Choose one of the bulls and prepare it first, since there are so many of you. Call on the name of your god, but do not light the fire." So they took the bull given them and prepared it.

Then they called on the name of Baal from morning till noon. "Baal, answer us!" they shouted. But there was no response; no one answered. And they danced around the altar they had made.

At noon Elijah began to taunt them. "Shout louder!" he said. "Surely he is a god! Perhaps he is deep in thought, or busy, or traveling. Maybe he is sleeping and must be awakened." So they shouted louder and slashed themselves with swords and spears, as was their custom, until the blood flowed. Midday passed, and they continued their frantic prophesying until the time for the evening sacrifice. But there was no response, no one answered, no one paid attention. (1 Kings 18:25–29, NIV)

Then Elijah said to all the people, "Come her to me." They came to him, and he repaired the altar of the LORD, which had been torn down. Elijah took twelve stones, one for each of the tribes descended from Jacob, to whom the word of the LORD had come, saying, "Your name shall be Israel." With the stones he built an altar in the name of the LORD, and he dug a trench around it large enough to hold two seahs of seeds. He arranged the wood, cut the bull into pieces and laid it on the wood. Then he said to them, "Fill four large jars with water and pour it on the offering and on the wood."

"Do it again," he said, and they did it again.

"Do it a third time," he ordered, and they did it the third time. The water ran down around the altar and filled the trench.

At the time of sacrifice, the prophet Elijah stepped forward and prayed: "LORD, the God of Abraham, Isaac and Israel, let it be known today that you are God in Israel and that I am your servant and have done all these things at your command. Answer me, LORD, answer me, so these people will know that you, LORD, are God, and that you are turning their hearts back again."

Then the fire of the LORD fell and burned up the sacrifice, the wood, the stones and the soil, and also licked up the water in the trench.

When all the people saw this, they fell prostrate and cried, "The LORD—he is God! The LORD—he is God!"

Then Elijah commanded them, "Seize the prophets of Baal. Don't let anyone get away!" They seized them, and Elijah had them brought down to the Kishon Valley and slaughtered there. (1 Kings 18:30–40, NIV)

And Elijah said to Ahab, "Go, eat and drink, for there is the sound of a heavy rain." So Ahab went off to eat and drink, but Elijah climbed to the top of Carmel, bent down to the ground and put his face between his knees.

"Go and look toward the sea," he told his servant. And he went up and looked.

"There is nothing there," he said.

Seven times Elijah said, "Go back."

The seventh time the servant reported, "A cloud as small as a man's hand is rising from the sea."

So Elijah said, "Go and tell Ahab, 'Hitch up your chariot and go down before the rain stops you,'"

Meanwhile, the sky grew black with clouds, the wind rose, a heavy rain started falling and Ahab rode off to Jezreel. The power of the LORD came on Elijah and, tucking his cloak into his belt, he ran ahead of Ahab all the way to Jezreel. (1 Kings 18:41–46, NIV)

Now Ahab told Jezebel everything Elijah had done and how he had killed all the prophets with the sword. So Jezebel sent a messenger to Elijah to say, "May the gods deal with me, be it ever so severely, if by this time tomorrow I do not make your life like that of one of them."

Elijah was afraid and ran for his life. When he came to Beersheba in Judah, he left his servant there, while he himself went a day's journey into the wilderness. He came to a broom bush, sat down under it and prayed that he might die. "I have had enough, LORD," he said. "Take my life; I am no better than my ancestors." Then he lay down under the bush and fell asleep.

All at once an angel touched him and said, "Get up and eat." He looked around, and there by his head was some bread baked over hot coals, and a jar of water. He ate and drank and then lay down again.

The angel of the LORD came back a second time and touched him and said, "Get up and eat, for the journey is too much for you." So he got up and ate and drank. Strengthened by that food, he traveled forty days and forty nights until he reached Horeb, the mountain of God. There he went into a cave and spent the night. And the word of the LORD came to him: "What are you doing here, Elijah?" (1 Kings 19:1–9, NIV)

He replied, "I have been very zealous for the LORD God Almighty. The Israelites have rejected your covenant, torn down your altars, and put your prophets to death with the sword. I am the only one left, and now they are trying to kill me too."

The LORD said, "Go out and stand on the mountain in the presence of the LORD, for the LORD is about to pass by."

Then a great and powerful wind tore the mountains apart and shattered the rocks before the LORD, but the LORD was not in the wind. After the wind there was an earthquake, but the LORD was not in the earthquake. After the earthquake came a fire, but the LORD was not in the fire. And after the fire came a gentle whisper. When Elijah heard it, he pulled his cloak over his face and went out and stood at the mouth of the cave.

Then a voice said to him, "What are you doing here, Elijah?"

He replied, "I have been very zealous for the LORD God Almighty. The Israelites have rejected your covenant, torn down your altars, and put your prophets to death with the sword. I am the only one left, and now they are trying to kill me too."

The LORD said to him, "Go back the way you came, and go to the Desert of Damascus. When you get there, anoint Hazael king over Aram. Also, anoint Jehu son of Nimshi king over Israel, and anoint Elisha son of Shaphat from Abel Meholah to succeed you as prophet. Jehu will put to death any who escape the sword of Hazael, and Elisha will put to death any who escape the sword of Jehu. Yet I reserve seven thousand in Israel—all whose knees have not bowed down to Baal and whose mouths have not kissed him." (1 Kings 19:10–18, NIV)

Confusion in the midst of the world can not only cause us to forget the "golden rule" but, even more devastating, cause us to forget that God is in charge of everything! Disruptive situations, obtrusive events, and uncontrollable happenings cause us and even those with a greater sensitivity to the presence of the *Lord* to forget. This causes us to forget God's wisdom and the understanding that the

Father is in charge of every breath, at all times. This can cause us to go running from a "shadow" and panicking from a "boo."

> "The LORD is my shepherd; I shall not want.
>
> He maketh me to lie down in green pastures: he leadeth me beside the still waters.
>
> He restoreth my soul: he leadeth me in the paths of righteousness for his name's sake.
>
> Yea, though I walk through the valley of the shadow of death, I will fear no evil: for thou art with me; thy rod and thy staff they comfort me."
> (Psalm 23:1–4, KJV)

It's difficult to remember the "golden rule" when you can't remember the "first rule" in the midst of the windstorms, earthquake, and fires in our daily existence. The "first rule" is: **Keep God first in everything.**

> Hearing that Jesus had silenced the Sadducees, the Pharisees got together. One of them, an expert in the law, tested him with this question: "Teacher, which is the greatest commandment in the Law?"
>
> Jesus replied: "'Love the Lord your God with all your heart and with all your soul and with all your mind.' This is the first and greatest commandment. And the second is like it: 'Love your neighbor as yourself.' All the Law and the Prophets hang on these two commandments."
> (Matthew 22:3440, NIV)

It was hard for a focused and devoted man like Elijah, and it is tough for us! When we stay mindful of the teachings of Jesus Christ, we are able to stay above the turmoil of the world. We find it easier to stay in the wisdom that God has for us instead of sinking into our own wisdom and understanding. A perfect example of focus versus the lack of focus follows:

> Immediately Jesus made the disciples get into the boat and go on ahead of him to the other side, while he dismissed the crowd. After he had dismissed them, he went up on a mountainside by himself to pray. Later that night, he was there alone, and the boat was already a considerable distance from land, buffeted by the waves because the wind was against it.
>
> Shortly before dawn Jesus went out to them, walking on the lake. When the disciples saw him walking on the lake, they were terrified. "It's a ghost," they said, and cried out in fear.
>
> But Jesus immediately said to them: "Take courage! It is I. Don't be afraid."
>
> "Lord, if it's you," Peter replied, "tell me to come to you on the water."
>
> "Come," he said.
>
> Then Peter got down out of the boat, walked on the water and came toward Jesus. But when he saw the wind, he was afraid and, beginning to sink, cried out, "Lord, save me!"
>
> Immediately Jesus reached out his hand and caught him. "You of little faith," he said, "why did you doubt?"
>
> And when they climbed into the boat, the wind died down. Then those who were in the boat worshiped him, saying, "Truly you are the Son of God." (Matthew 14:22–33, NIV)

For Elijah, Peter, you, and myself, it all comes down to "being still" in the midst of turmoil and knowing God is God all by himself.

He says, "Be still, and know that I am God;
I will be exalted among the nations,
I will be exalted in the earth."
The LORD Almighty is with us; the God of
Jacob is our fortress." (Psalm 46:10 and 11, NIV)

4. That your God purpose must be put into action

It's not about your health, your likes or dislikes, nor your perceived wants and desires. It is about accepting and completing your God-given task. God's love for us is patient. Even when we fall headlong into our wisdom and attempt to reside in our understanding, the Father never gives up on us. Three perfect examples are Peter's mother-in-law, Jonah, and Manasseh.

Peter's mother-in-law was ill, and Jesus healed her. Her healing was to help spread Christ's work, not for her to lean on her own understanding.

And when Jesus was come into Peter's house,
he saw his wife's mother laid and sick with fever.
And he touched her hand, and the fever left
her: and she arose and ministered unto them.
(Matthew 8:14 and 15, KJV)

Jonah was in service to the Father as a prophet. Using his own wisdom and leaning on his own understanding, Jonah thought what his opinion was and what he wanted to do could trump God's dictate.

The word of the LORD came to Jonah
son of Amittai: "Go to the great city of Nineveh
and preach against it, because its wickedness has
come up before me."
But Jonah ran away from the LORD and
headed for Tarshish. He went down to Joppa,
where he found a ship bound for that port. After

paying the fare, he went aboard and sailed for Tarshish to flee from the LORD.

Then the LORD sent a great wind on the sea, and such a violent storm arose that the ship threatened to break up. All the sailors were afraid and each cried out to his own god. And they threw the cargo into the sea to lighten the ship.

But Jonah had gone below deck, where he lay down and feel into a deep sleep. The captain went to him and said, "How can you sleep? Get up and call on your god! Maybe he will take notice of us so that we will not perish."

Then the sailors said to each other, "Come, let us cast lots to find out who is responsible for this calamity." They cast lots and the lot fell on Jonah. So they asked him, "Tell us, who is responsible for making all this trouble for us? What kind of work do you do? Where do you come from? What is your country? From what people are you?"

He answered, "I am a Hebrew and I worship the LORD, the God of heaven, who made the sea and the dry land."

This terrified them and they asked, "What have you done?" (They knew he was running away from the LORD, because he had already told them so.)

The sea was getting rougher and rougher. So they asked him, "What should we do to you to make the sea calm down for us?"

"Pick me up and throw me into the sea," he replied, "and it will become calm. I know that it is my fault that this great storm has come upon you."

Instead, the men did their best to row back to land. But they could not, for the sea grew even

wilder than before. Then they cried out to the
LORD, "Please, LORD, do not let us die for
taking this man's life. Do not hold us accountable for killing an innocent man, for you, LORD
have done as you pleased." Then they took Jonah
and threw him overboard, and the raging sea
grew calm. At this the men greatly feared the
LORD, and they offered a sacrifice to the LORD
and made vows to him.

Now the LORD provided a huge fish to swallow Jonah, and Jonah was in the belly of the fish
three days and three nights. (Jonah 1:1–17, NIV)

Jonah rectified his relationship with the *Lord* while in the belly
of the great fish, and the *Lord* ordered the fish to spit him onto the
beach. Just like us, Jonah became a little more obedient based on
what the *Lord* brought him through but still thought his opinion
(leaning on his own wisdom and understanding) meant something.

Then the word of the LORD came to Jonah
a second time: "Go to the great city of Nineveh
and proclaim to it the message I give you."

Jonah obeyed the word of the LORD and
went to Nineveh. Now Nineveh was a very large
city; it took three days to go through it. Jonah
began by going a day's journey into the city, proclaiming, "Forty more days and Nineveh will be
overthrown." The Ninevites believed God. A fast
was proclaimed, and all of them, from the greatest to the least, put on sackcloth.

When Jonah's warning reached the king of
Nineveh, he rose from his throne, took off his
royal robes, covered himself with sackcloth and
sat down in the dust. This is the proclamation he
issued in Nineveh:

"By the decree of the king and his nobles:

Do not let people or animals, herds or flocks, taste anything; do not let them eat or drink. But let people and animals be covered with sackcloth. Let everyone call urgently on God. Let them give up their evil ways and their violence. Who knows? God may yet relent and with compassion turn from his fierce anger so that we will not perish."

When God saw what they did and how they turned from their evil ways, he relented and did not bring on them the destruction he had threatened." (Jonah 3:1–10, NIV)

But to Jonah this seemed very wrong, and he became angry. He prayed to the LORD, "Isn't this what I said, LORD, when I was still at home? That is what I tried to forestall by fleeing to Tarshish. I knew that you are a gracious and compassionate God, slow to anger and abounding in love, a God who relents from sending calamity. Now, LORD, take away my life, for it is better for me to die than to live."

But the LORD replied, "Is it right for you to be angry?"

Jonah had gone out and sat down at a place east of the city. There he made himself a shelter, sat in its shade and waited to see what would happen to the city. Then the LORD God provided a leafy plant and made it grow up over Jonah to give shade for his head to ease his discomfort, and Jonah was very happy about the plant. But at dawn the next day God provided a worm, which chewed the plant so that it withered. When the sun rose, God provided a scorching east wind, and the sun blazed on Jonah's head so that he grew faint. He wanted to die, and said, "It would be better for me to die than to live."

But God said to Jonah, "Is it right for you to be angry about the plant?"

"It is," he said. "And I'm so angry I wish I were dead."

But God said, "You have been concerned about this plant, though you did not tend it or make it grow. It sprang up overnight and died overnight. And should I not have concern for the great city of Nineveh, in which there are more than a hundred and twenty thousand people who cannot tell their right hand from their left—and also many animals?" (Jonah 4:1–11, NIV)

Even when you're working for God, you can be like Jonah where you are still attempting to acquire God's wisdom and understanding for your life and what the Father requires of you.

A king we will talk about later in greater detail is King Manasseh of Judah. Manasseh was in a totally different situation than Jonah.

King Manasseh of Judah had no God on his mind and committed some of the greatest abominations in the history of the Israelite kings. Manasseh sacrificed "God's children" to false gods by fire. He placed statues of false gods, in the *Lord*'s Temple. King Manasseh was a terrible man until he acquired the *Lord*'s wisdom and understanding.

Manasseh was a lot like some of us. We needed **an awakening** to appreciate God's wisdom and understanding in our lives.

> *Better is the end of a thing than the beginning thereof: and the patient in spirit is better than the proud in spirit. (Ecclesiates 7:8, KJV)*

5. That your spiritual life is not ruled by "tradition and habit"

Human beings are creatures of habit. How many times has someone lost their connection with God because a fellow worshiper is sitting in their seat or the new pastor wants to take down the drapes that Grandma had bought for the church? "Tradition and habit," if tempered with God's wisdom and understanding, are beneficial to our growth in learning God's purpose for our lives, but are easily manipulated if our eyes come off of the teachings of Jesus Christ.

> So the Pharisees and teachers of the law asked Jesus, "Why don't your disciples live according to the tradition of the elders instead of eating their food with defiled hands?"
> He replied, "Isaiah was right when he prophesied about you hypocrites; as it is written:
> 'These people honor me with their lips, but their hearts are far from me. They worship me in vain; their teachings are merely human rules.' You have let go of the commands of God and are holding on to human traditions."
> And he continued, "You have a fine way of setting aside the commands of God in order to observe your own traditions! For Moses said, 'Honor your father and mother,' and, 'Anyone who curses their father or mother is to be put to death.' But you say that if anyone declares that what might have been used to help their father or mother is Corban (that is, devoted to God)— then you no longer let them do anything for their father or mother. Thus you nullify the word of God by your tradition that you have handed down. And you do many things like that." (Mark 7:5–13, NIV)

The apostle Paul showed us how a zeal for "tradition and habit" caused him to be a major contributor to the death and persecution of followers of Jesus Christ, Christians—his participation in the death of one of the first deacons of the Church, Stephen, in particular.

Paul, also called Saul (Saul is Paul's name in Hebrew; Paul is his name in Greek), became a devoted follower of the teachings of Christ (a Christian), after **an awakening** and time to acquire the wisdom of God and gain the understanding of God to make it the mainstay of his life.

> In those days when the number of disciples was increasing, the Hellenistic Jews among them complained against the Hebraic Jews because their widows were being overlooked in the daily distribution of food. So the Twelve gathered all the disciples together and said, "It would not be right for us to neglect the ministry of the word of God in order to wait on tables. Brothers and sisters, choose seven men from among you who are known to be full of the Spirit and wisdom. We will turn this responsibility over to them and will give our attention to prayer and the ministry of the word."
>
> This proposal pleased the whole group. They chose Stephen, a man full of faith and of the Holy Spirit; also Philip, Procorus, Nicanor, Timon, Parmenas, and Nicolas from Antioch, a convert to Judaism. They presented these men to the apostles, who prayed and laid their hands on them.
>
> So the word of God spread. The number of disciples in Jerusalem increased rapidly, and a large number of priests became obedient to the faith. (Acts 6:1–7, NIV)
>
> Now Stephen, a man full of God's grace and power, performed great wonders and signs among the people. Opposition arose, however, from members of the Synagogue of the Freedmen (as it was called)—Jews of Cyrene and Alexandria as well as the provinces of Cilicia and Asia—who began to argue with Stephen. But they could not

stand up against the wisdom the Spirit gave him as he spoke.

Then they secretly persuaded some men to say, "We have heard Stephen speak blasphemous words against Moses and against God."

So they stirred up the people and the elders and the teachers of the law. They seized Stephen and brought him before the Sanhedrin. They produced false witnesses, who testified, "This fellow never stops speaking against this holy place and against the law. For we have heard him say that this Jesus of Nazareth will destroy this place and change the customs Moses handed down to us."

All who were sitting in the Sanhedrin looked intently at Stephen, and they saw that his face was like the face of an angel. (Acts 6:8–15, NIV)

Stephen spent the majority of Acts chapter 7 reciting Jewish history from Abraham in Mesopotamia, before he settled in Haran, to Solomon building the temple. Then he turned his attention to the people there.

"You stiff-necked people, uncircumcised in heart and ears, you always resist the Holy Spirit. As your fathers did, so do you. Which of the prophets did your fathers not persecute? And they killed those who announced beforehand the coming of the Righteous One, whom you have now betrayed and murdered, you who received the law as delivered by angels and did not keep it."

Now when they heard these things they were enraged, and they ground their teeth at him. But he, full of the Holy Spirit, gazed into heaven and saw the glory of God. And he said,

"Behold, I see the heavens opened, and the Son of Man standing at the right hand of God." But they cried out with a loud voice and stopped their ears and rushed together at him. Then they cast him out of the city and stoned him. And the witnesses laid down their garments at the feet of a young man named Saul. And as they were stoning Stephen, he called out, "Lord Jesus, receive my spirit." And falling to his knees he cried with a loud voice, "Lord, do not hold this sin against them." And when he had said this, he fell asleep. (Acts 7:51–60, ESV)

And Saul approved of his execution.

And there arose on that day a great persecution against the church in Jerusalem, and they were all scattered throughout the regions of Judea and Samaria, except the apostles. Devout men buried Stephen and made great lamentation over him. But Saul was ravaging the church, and entering house after house, he dragged off men and women and committed them to prison. (Acts 8:1–3, ESV)

But Saul, still breathing threats and murder against the disciples of the Lord, went to the high priest and asked him for letters to the synagogues at Damascus, so that if he found any belonging to the Way, men or women, he might bring them bound to Jerusalem." (Acts 9:1 and 2, ESV)

Paul (Saul name is officially changed to the Greek form Paul in Acts 13:9) was a real zealot to his wisdom and understanding of God's directives, but this was about to come to an end, based on God's timing. It was time for Paul to have an "awakening" to the wisdom and understanding of the Father.

Now as he went on his way, he approached Damascus, and suddenly a light from heaven shone around him. And falling to the ground, he heard a voice saying to him, "Saul, Saul, why are you persecuting me?" And he said, "Who are you, Lord?" And he said, "I am Jesus, whom you are persecuting. But rise and enter the city, and you will be told what you are to do." (Acts 9:3–6, ESV)

Paul's "awakening" was difficult not only on him but also on the followers of Christ. Paul had to change from what had identified him for his entire life into a man governed by the will of God. He was learning how to become more and more obedient to what God wanted for his life, by accepting God's wisdom and gaining God's understanding. Conversely, followers of Christ, Christians, had to readjust their perceptions. They had to accept the fact that God can and will use anyone he chooses whenever he chooses. This was an "awakening" for Christians to grow in God's wisdom and increase their understanding of the Father's understanding.

The men who were traveling with him stood speechless, hearing the voice but seeing no one. Saul rose from the ground, and although his eyes were opened, he saw nothing. So they led him by the hand and brought him into Damascus. And for three days he was without sight, and neither ate nor drank.

Now there was a disciple at Damascus named Ananias. The Lord said to him in a vision, "Ananias." And he said, "Here I am, Lord." And the Lord said to him, "Rise and go to the street called Straight, and at the house of Judas look for a man of Tarsus named Saul, for behold, he is praying, and he has seen in a vision a man named Ananias come in and lay his hands on him so that he might regain his sight." But Ananias answered, "Lord, I have heard from many about this man, how much evil he has done to your saints at Jerusalem. And here he has authority from the chief priests to bind all who call on your name." But the Lord said to him, "Go, for he is a chosen instrument of mine to carry my name before the Gentiles and kings and the children of Israel. For I will show him how much he must suffer for the sake of my name." So Ananias departed and entered the house. And laying his hands on him he said, "Brother Saul, the Lord Jesus who appeared to you on the road by which you came has sent me so that you may regain your sight and be filled with the Holy Spirit." And immediately something like scales fell from his eyes, and he regained his sight. Then he rose and was baptized; and taking food, he was strengthened.

For some days he was with the disciples at Damascus. And immediately he proclaimed Jesus in the synagogues, saying, "He is the Son of God." And all who heard him were amazed and said, "Is not this the man who made havoc in Jerusalem of those who called upon this name? And has he not come here for this purpose, to bring them bound before the chief priests?" But Saul increased all the more in strength, and confounded the Jews who lived in Damascus by proving that Jesus was the Christ.

When many days had passed, the Jews plotted to kill him, but their plot became known to Saul. They were watching the gates day and night in order to kill him, but his disciples took him by night and let him down through an opening in the wall, lowering him in a basket.

And when he had come to Jerusalem, he attempted to join the disciples. And they were all afraid of him, for they did not believe that he was a disciple. But Barnabas took him and brought him to the apostles and declared to them how on the road he had seen the Lord, who spoke to him, and how at Damascus he had preached boldly in the name of Jesus. So he went in and out among them at Jerusalem, preaching boldly in the name of the Lord. And he spoke and disputed against the Hellenists. But they were seeking to kill him. And when the brothers learned this, they brought him down to Caesarea and sent him off to Tarsus.

So the church throughout all Judea and Galilee and Samaria had peace and was being built up. And walking in the fear of the Lord and in the comfort of the Holy Spirit, it multiplied. (Acts 9:7–31, ESV)

A major contributor to our inability to become more obedient to the will of God for our lives is "zeal." We must move from "zeal" to "reveal."

"Brothers, my heart's desire and prayer to God for them is that they may be saved. For, I bear them witness that they have a zeal for God, but not according to knowledge. For, being ignorant of the righteousness of God, and seeking to establish their own, they did not submit to God's righteousness. For Christ is the end of the law for righteousness to everyone who believes." (Romans 10:1–4, ESV)

We must allow the Lord to prepare us to carry out our "purpose(s)," on his time schedule. Our task is to be prepared when we are called to enact our "purpose(s)" according to God.

Mark Twain said, "The two most important days in your life are the day you are born and the day you find out why you were born." It's our task to spend the time like Paul did to be ready for our "reveal." Acquiring God's wisdom will allow us to abandon "zeal," move into "reveal," and gain the understanding of God to effectuate our purpose as defined by God, instead of just going through the motions.

> "For I would have you know, brothers, that the gospel that was preached by me is not man's gospel. For I did not receive it from any man, nor was I taught it, but I received it through a revelation of Jesus Christ. For you have heard of my former life in Judaism, how I persecuted the church of God violently and tried to destroy it. And I was advancing in Judaism beyond many of my own age among my people, so extremely zealous was I for the traditions of my fathers. But when he who had set me apart before I was born, and who called me by his grace, was pleased to reveal his Son to me, in order that I might preach him among the Gentiles, I did not immediately consult with anyone, nor did I go up to Jerusalem to those who were apostles before me, but I went away into Arabia, and returned again to Damascus.
>
> Then after three years I went up to Jerusalem to visit Cephas and remained with him fifteen days. But I saw none of the other apostles except James the Lord's brother. (In what I am writing to you, before God, I do not lie!) Then I went into the regions of Syria and Cilicia. And I was still unknown in person to the churches of Judea that are in Christ. They only were hearing it said, 'He who used to persecute us is now preaching the faith he once tried to destroy.' And they glo-

rified God because of me." (Galatians 1:11–24, ESV)

"Then after fourteen years I went up again to Jerusalem with Barnabas, taking Titus along with me. I went up because of a revelation and set before them (though privately before those who seemed influential) the gospel that I proclaim among the Gentiles, in order to make sure I was not running or had not run in vain. But even Titus, who was with me, was not forced to be circumcised, though he was a Greek. Yet because of false brothers secretly brought in—who slipped in to spy out our freedom that we have in Christ Jesus, so that they might bring us into slavery—to them we did not yield in submission even for a moment, so that the truth of the gospel might be preserved for you. And from those who seemed to be influential (what they were makes no difference to me; God shows no partiality)—those, I say, who seemed influential added nothing to me. On the contrary, when they saw that I had been entrusted with the gospel to the uncircumcised, just as Peter had been entrusted with the gospel to the circumcised (for he who worked through Peter for his apostolic ministry to the circumcised worked also through me for mine to the Gentiles), and when James and Cephas and John, who seemed to be pillars, perceived the grace that was given to me, they gave the right hand of fellowship to Barnabas and me, that we should go to the Gentiles and they to the circumcised. Only, they asked us to remember the poor, the very thing I was eager to do." (Galatains 2:1–10, ESV)

Look beneath the surface so you can judge correctly. (John 7:24, NLT)

Section 2

THE TOOLS YOU NEED

Chapter 6

MOVING FROM ZEAL TO REVEAL

Now great crowds accompanied him, and he turned and said to them, "If anyone comes to me and does not hate his own father and mother and wife and children and brothers and sisters, yes, and even his own life, he cannot be my disciple. Whoever does not bear his own cross and come after me cannot be my disciple. For which of you, desiring to build a tower, does not first sit down and count the cost, whether he has enough to complete it? Otherwise, when he has laid a foundation and is not able to finish, all who see it begin to mock him, saying, 'This man began to build and was not able to finish.' Or what king, going out to encounter another king in war, will not sit down first and deliberate whether he is able with ten thousand to meet him who comes against him with twenty thousand? And if not, while the other is yet a great way off, he sends a delegation and asks for terms of peace. So therefore, any one of you who does not renounce all that he has cannot be my disciple."

—(Luke 14:25–33, ESV)

The first great "reveal" is the revelation, for most of us, that God has never forsaken us, in spite of our relationship with sin. He loves, forgives, and provides for us in spite of us trying to use our earthly wisdom while leaning on our own understanding. After that "reveal," we find ourselves euphoric with joy and consumed with "zeal."

Webster defines "zeal" as a fervor for a person, cause, or object. It continues to define a "zealot" as an excessively zealous person, fanatic. A "fan" is short for fanatic. While this has been deemed acceptable, in the world, for sports, politics, and other areas of human involvement, it can and will allow our "two cents" to creep into our efforts for the Father and Christ.

Yes, "zeal" is appropriate for when we come together, in fellowship, under our belief and devotion to God; but we have to be very careful as it relates to other human beings.

> Behold, how good and how pleasant it is for brethren to dwell together in unity!
>
> It is like the precious ointment upon the head, that ran down upon the beard, even Aaron's beard: that went down to the skirts of his garments;
>
> As the dew of Hermon, and as the dew that descended upon the mountains of Zion: for there the LORD commanded the blessing, even life for evermore. (Psalm 133, KJV)
>
> "I will bless the LORD at all times; his praise shall continually be in my mouth. My soul makes its boast in the LORD; let the humble hear and be glad. Oh, magnify the LORD with me, and let us exalt his name together!" (Psalm 34:1–3, ESV)

"Zeal" should be reserved for when we assemble, like minds in worship, prayer, and any activity where we are on "one accord" and "like-minded" discussing, praying, praising, and worshiping God.

So if there is any encouragement in Christ, any comfort from love, any participation in the Spirit, any affection and sympathy, complete my joy by being of the same mind, having the same love, being in full accord and of one mind. Do nothing from selfish ambition or conceit, but in humility count others more significant than yourselves. Let each of you look not only to his own interests, but also to the interest of others. Have this mind among yourselves, which is yours in Christ Jesus, who, though he was in the form of God, did not count equality with God a thing to be grasped, but emptied himself, by taking the form of a servant, being born in the likeness of men. And being found in human form, he humbled himself by becoming obedient to the point of death, even death on a cross. Therefore God has highly exalted him and bestowed on him the name that is above every name, so that at the name of Jesus every knee should bow, in heaven and on earth and under the earth, and every tongue confess that Jesus Christ is Lord, to the glory of God the Father.

Therefore, my beloved, as you have always obeyed, so now, not only as in my presence but much more in my absence, work out your own salvation with fear and trembling, for it is God who works in you, both to will and to work for his good pleasure.

Do all things without grumbling or disputing, that you may be blameless and innocent, children of God without blemish in the midst of a crooked and twisted generation, among whom you shine as lights in the world, holding fast to the word of life, so that in the day of Christ I may be proud that I did not run in vain or labor in vain. (Philippians 2:1–16, ESV)

The caution about "zeal" is necessary because of our human tendencies to judge, dislike, abandon, ignore, and avoid individuals whose beliefs, appearance, customs, language, ethnicity, race, etc. are different from what we are used to or like.

Therefore be imitators of God, as beloved children. And walk in love, as Christ loved us and gave himself up for us, a fragrant offering and sacrifice to God.

But sexual immorality and all impurity or covetousness must not even be named among you, as is proper among saints. Let there be no filthiness nor foolish talk nor crude joking, which are out of place, but instead let there be thanksgiving. For you may be sure of this, that everyone who is sexually immoral or impure, or who is covetous (that is, an idolater), has no inheritance in the kingdom of Christ and God. Let no one deceive you with empty words, for because of these things the wrath of God comes upon the sons of disobedience. Therefore do not become partners with them; for at one time you were darkness, but now you are light in the Lord. Walk as children of light (for the fruit of light is found in all that is good and right and true), and try to discern what is pleasing to the Lord. Take no part in the unfruitful works of darkness, but instead expose them. For it is shameful even to speak of the things that they do in secret. But when anything is exposed by the light, it becomes visible, for anything that becomes visible is light. Therefore it says,

"Awake, O sleeper, and arise from the dead, and Christ will shine on you."

Look carefully then how you walk, not as unwise but as wise, making the best use of the time, because the days are evil. Therefore do not be foolish, but understand what the will of the Lord is. And do not get drunk with wine, for that is debauchery, but be filled with the Spirit, addressing one another in psalms and hymns and spiritual songs, singing and making melody to the Lord with your heart, giving thanks always and for everything to God the Father in the name of our Lord Jesus Christ, submitting to one another out of reverence for Christ. (Ephesians 5:1–21, ESV)

Truly our purpose, in general, on this planet is "to keep God first in everything," "love our neighbor as our self," *go* and share the "good news of the gospel," and make "disciples" for Christ.

Jesus sent his twelve harvest hands out with this charge:

"Don't begin by traveling to some far-off place to convert unbelievers. And don't try to be dramatic by tackling some public enemy. Go to the lost, confused people right here in the neighborhood. Tell them that the kingdom is here. Bring health to the sick. Raise the dead. Touch the untouchables. Kick out the demons. You have been treated generously, so live generously.

Don't think you have to put on a fund-raising campaign before you start. You don't need a lot of equipment. You are the equipment, and all you need to keep that going is three meals a day. Travel light.

When you enter a town or village, don't insist on staying in a luxury inn. Get a modest place with some modest people, and be content there until you leave.

When you knock on a door, be courteous in your greeting. If they welcome you, be gentle in your conversation. If they don't welcome you, quietly withdraw. Don't make a scene. Shrug your shoulders and be on your way. You can be sure that on Judgement Day they'll be mighty sorry—but it's no concern of yours now.

Stay alert. This is hazardous work I'm assigning you. You're going to be like sheep running through a wolf pack, so don't call attention to yourselves. Be as cunning as a snake, inoffensive as a dove.

Don't be naïve. Some people will impugn your motives, others will smear your reputation—just because you believe in me. Don't be upset when they haul you before the civil authorities. Without knowing it, they've done you—and me—a favor, given you a platform for preaching the kingdom news! And don't worry about what you'll say or how you'll say it. The right words will be there; the Spirit of your Father will supply the words.

When people realize it is the living God you are presenting and not some idol that makes them feel good, they are going to turn on you, even people in your own family. There is a great irony here: proclaiming so much love, experiencing so much hate! But don't quit. Don't cave in. It is all well worth it in the end. It is not success you are after in such times but survival. Be survivors! Before you've run out of options, the Son of Man will have arrived.

A student doesn't get a better desk than her teacher. A laborer doesn't make more money than his boss. Be content—pleased, even—when you, my student, my harvest hands, get the same treatment I get. If they call me, the Master, 'Dungface', what can the workers expect?

Don't be intimidated. Eventually everything is going to be out in the open, and everyone will know how things really are. So don't hesitate to go public now.

Don't be bluffed into silence by the threats of bullies. There's nothing they can do to your soul, your core being. Save your fear for God, who holds your entire life—body and soul—in his hands." (Matthew 10:5–28, MSG)

[[Now when he rose early on the first day of the week, he appeared first to Mary Magdalene, from whom he had cast out seven demons. She went and told those who had been with him, as they mourned and wept. But when they heard that he was alive and had been seen by her, they would not believe it.

After these things he appeared in another form to two of them, as they were walking into the country. And they went back and told the rest, but they did not believe them.

Afterward he appeared to the eleven themselves as they were reclining at table, and he rebuked them for their unbelief and hardness of heart, because they had not believed those who saw him after he had risen. And he said to them, "Go into all the world and proclaim the gospel to the whole creation. Whoever believes and is baptized will be saved, but whoever does not believe will be condemned. And these signs will accompany those who believe: in my name they will cast out demons; they will speak in new tongues; they will pick up serpents with their hands; and if they drink any deadly poison, it will not hurt them; they will lay their hands on the sick, and they will recover."

So then the Lord Jesus, after he had spoken to them, was taken up into heaven and sat down at the right hand of God. And they went out and preached everywhere, while the Lord worked with them and confirmed the message by accompanying signs.]] (Mark 16:9–20, ESV)

"Zeal" has no place in your spiritual relationship with your mandate from Christ to *go*!!! The revelation of the "reveal" was necessary to make me a follower of Christ, a Christian.

The "reveal" addresses faith, desire, commitment, and practice. Webster defines "reveal" as an action word (a verb): to make known, disclose, divulge; to reveal a secret; to lay open to view; and to display, exhibit. As a thing (a noun), it is an act or instance of revealing, revelation, or disclosure.

We must learn to become what we believe. The "reveal" is a process that will take your "seed of faith," plant it in the fertile soil of "desire," grow it with your "commitment," and produce "good fruit" with your "practice" of becoming more and more "obedient" to "the will of God for your life."

> *A large crowd was following Jesus. He turned around and said to them, "If you want to be my disciple, you must hate everyone else by comparison— your father and mother, wife and children, brothers and sisters—yes even your own life. Otherwise, you cannot be my disciple. And if you do not carry your own cross and follow me, you cannot be my disciple." (Luke 14:25–27, NLT)*

Being a "disciple of Christ" is not easy. The world is set up to keep your mind off the teachings of Jesus Christ, the Messiah. "Friendly fire" from "undeveloped Christians" impedes God's work more than the natural blockage of the world. Accepting the "reveal" of faith, desire, commitment, and practice will allow us to achieve our mission.

The components that are necessary to be a "disciple of Christ" are "revealed" to us thru:

1) **Faith:** Faith is the confidence that what we hope for will actually happen; it gives us assurance about things we cannot see. Through their faith, the people in days of old earned a good reputation.

> Now faith is the assurance of things hoped for, the conviction of things not see. For by it the people of old received their commendation. By faith we understand that the universe was created by the word of God, so that what is seen was not made out of things that are visible. By faith Abel offered to God a more acceptable sacrifice than Cain, through which he was commended as righteous, God commending him by accepting his gifts. And through his faith, though he died, he still speaks. By faith Enoch was taken up so that he should not see death, and he was not found, because God had taken him. Now before he was taken he was commended as having pleased God. And without faith it is impossible to please him, for whoever would draw near to God must believe that he exists and that he rewards those who seek him. (Hebrews 11:1–6, ESV)
>
> By faith Isaac invoked future blessings on Jacob and Esau. (Hebrews 11:20, ESV)

And all these, though commended through their faith, did not receive what was promised, since God had provided something better for us, that apart from us they should not be made perfect. (Hebrews 11 39 and 40, ESV)

Do you see what this means—all these pioneers who blazed the way, all these veterans cheering us on? It means we'd better get on with it. Strip down, start running—and never quit! No extra spiritual fat, no parasitic sins. Keep your eyes on Jesus, who both began and finished this race we're in. Study how he did it. Because he never lost sight of where he was headed—that exhilarating finish in and with God—he could put up with anything along the way: Cross, shame, whatever. And now he's there, in the place of honor, right alongside God. When you find yourselves flagging in your faith, go over the story again, item by item, that long litany of hostility he plowed through. That will shoot adrenaline into your souls!

In this all-out match against sin, others have suffered far worse than you, to say nothing of what Jesus went through—all that bloodshed! So don't feel sorry for yourselves. Or have you forgotten how good parents treat children, and that God regards you as his children?

My dear child, don't shrug off God's discipline, but don't be crushed by it either. It's the child he loves that he disciplines; the child he embraces, he also corrects.

God is educating you; that's why you must never drop out. He's treating you as dear children. This trouble you're in isn't punishment; it's training, the normal experience of children. Only irresponsible parents leave children to fend for themselves. Would you prefer an irresponsible God? We respect our own parents for training and not spoiling us, so why not embrace God's training so we can truly live? While we were children, our parents did what seemed best to them. But God is doing what is best for us, training us to live God's holy best. At the time, discipline isn't much fun. It always feels like it's going against the grain. Later, of course, it pays off handsomely, for it's the well-trained who find themselves mature in their relationship with God.

So don't sit around on your hands! No more dragging your feet! Clear the path for long-distance runners so no one will trip and fall, so no one will step in a hole and sprain an ankle. Help each other out. And run for it!

Work at getting along with each other and with God. Otherwise you'll never get so much as a glimpse of God. Make sure no one gets left out of God's generosity. Keep a sharp eye out for weeds of bitter discontent. A thistle or two gone to seed can ruin a whole garden in no time. Watch out for the Esau syndrome: trading away God's lifelong gift in order to satisfy a short-term appetite. You well know how Esau later regretted that impulsive act and wanted God's blessing— but by then it was too late, tears or no tears.

Unlike your ancestors, you didn't come to Mount Sinai—all that volcanic blaze and earth-shaking rumble—to hear God speak. The ear-splitting words and soul-shaking message terrified them and they begged him to stop. When they heard the words—"If an animal touches the Mountain, it's as good as dead"—they were afraid to move. Even Moses was terrified.

No, that's not your experience at all. You've come to Mount Zion, the city where the living God resides. The invisible Jerusalem is populated by throngs of festive angels and Christian citizens. It is the city where God is Judge, with judgments that make us just. You've come to Jesus, who presents us with a new covenant, a fresh charter from God. He is the Mediator of this covenant. The murder of Jesus, unlike Abel's—a homicide that cried out for vengeance—became a proclamation of grace.

So don't turn a deaf ear to these gracious words. If those who ignored earthly warnings didn't get away with it, what will happen to us if we turn our backs on heavenly warnings? His voice that time shook the earth to its foundations; this time—he's told us this quite plainly—he'll also rock the heavens: "One last shaking, from top to bottom, stem to stern." The phrase "one last shaking" means a thorough housecleaning, getting rid of all the historical and religious junk so that the unshakable essentials stand clear and uncluttered.

Do you see what we've got? An unshakeable kingdom! And do you see how thankful we must be? Not only thankful, but brimming with worship, deeply reverent before God. For God is not an indifferent bystander. He's actively cleaning house, torching all that needs to burn, and he won't quit until it's all cleansed. God himself is Fire!" (Hebrews 12:1–29, MSG)

2) **Desire:** With our initial involvement, "desire" is high. Our "desire" has not matured to the point that we depend on the Holy Spirit to direct every step. We predetermine things that need to be eliminated, advanced, and put on hold, all

based on a desire based on our "zeal," without the direction of the Holy Spirit. The problem is we are too loud, within ourselves, to hear the whisperings of the Holy Spirit.

"I have said all these things to you to keep you from falling away. They will put you out of the synagogues. Indeed, the hour is coming when whoever kills you will think he is offering service to God. And they will do these things because they have not known the Father, nor me. But I have said these things to you, that when their hour comes you may remember that I told them to you.

I did not say these things to you from the beginning, because I was with you. But now I am going to him who sent me, and none of you asks me, 'Where are you going?' But because I have said these things to you, sorrow has filled your heart. Nevertheless, I tell you the truth: it is to your advantage that I go away, for if I do not go away, the Helper will not come to you. But if I go, I will send him to you. And when he comes, he will convict the world concerning sin and righteousness and judgement: concerning sin, because they do not believe in me; concerning righteousness, because I go to the Father, and you will see no longer; concerning judgment, because the ruler of this world is judged.

I still have many things to say to you, but you cannot bear them now. When the Spirit of truth comes, he will guide you into all the truth, for he will not speak on his own authority, but whatever he hears he will speak, and he will declare to you the things that are to come. He will glorify me, for he will take what is mine and declare it to you. All that the Father has is mine;

therefore I said that he will take what is mine and declare it to you." (John 16:1–15, ESV)

"Desire" is fickle. It could ebb and flow and even wane because of perceptions based on worldly knowledge, of perceived obstacles or actual obstacles that you determine will negatively impact your well-being.

Peter was wildly desirous of defending the Christ (the Messiah) at the time of Christ's arrest.

> When Jesus had spoken these words, he went out with his disciples across the brook Kidron, where there was a garden, which he and his disciples entered. Now Judas, who betrayed him, also knew the place, for Jesus often met there with his disciples. So Judas, having procured a band of soldiers and some officers from the chief priests and the Pharisees, went there with lanterns and torches and weapons. Then Jesus, knowing all that would happen to him, came forward and said to them, "Whom do you seek?" They answered him, "Jesus of Nazareth." Jesus said, "I am he." Judas, who betrayed him, was standing with them. When Jesus said to them, "I am he," they drew back and fell to the ground. So he asked them again, "Whom do you seek?" And they said, "Jesus of Nazareth." Jesus answered, "I told you that I am he. So, if you seek me, let these men go." This was to fulfill the word that he had spoken: "Of those whom you gave me I have lost not one." Then Simon Peter, having a sword, drew it and struck the high priest's servant and cut off his right ear. (The servant's name was Malchus.) So Jesus said to Peter, "Put your sword into its sheath; shall I not drink the cup that the Father has given me?" (John 18:1–11, ESV)

Peter's "desire" was high to protect Christ, his way; but his "faith" was not yet rooted. His "faith" did not have the "desire" to follow Christ's teachings. Peter reacted based on "zeal."

> Simon Peter followed Jesus, and so did another disciple. Since that disciple was known to the high priest, he entered with Jesus into the courtyard of the high priest, but Peter stood outside at the door. So the other disciple, who was known to the high priest, went out and spoke to the servant girl who kept watch at the door, and brought Peter in. The servant girl at the door said to Peter, "You also are not one of this man's disciples, are you?" He said, "I am not." Now the servants and officers had made a charcoal fire, because it was cold, and they were standing and warming themselves. Peter also was with them, standing and warming himself. (John 18:15–18, ESV)
>
> Now Simon Peter was standing and warming himself. So they said to him, "You also are not one of his disciples, are you?" He denied it and said, "I am not." One of the servants of the high priest, a relative of the man whose ear Peter had cut off, asked, "Did I not see you in the garden with him?" Peter again denied it, and at once a rooster crowed. (John 18:25–27, ESV)

"Faith" must be rooted in "desire," and your "faith" has to be unshakeable. Peter, without a personal relationship with the Holy Spirit, had problems with this.

We have to seriously work at not becoming "permanent fans" of Jesus Christ because of lost or dissipating "desire." A loss of "desire" to do the will of the Father keeps our "faith" from being rooted in our "desire." Being rooted requires increasing obedience to God's will.

Our rooted "faith" in our "desire" to be obedient to God requires making our flesh uncomfortable. Rooting requires obedience to God's mandates for our lives, carrying our cross that is given to us, going through the storms of life and suffering. These necessary items cannot be accomplished without stronger nourishment obtained by growing in the word of God.

> In the days of his flesh, Jesus offered up prayers and supplications, with loud cries and tears, to him who was able to save him from death, and he was heard because of his reverence. Although he was a son, he learned obedience through what he suffered. And being made perfect, he became the source of eternal salvation to all who obey him, being designated by God a high priest after the order of Melchizedek. About this we have much to say, and it is hard to explain, since you have become dull of hearing. For though by this time you ought to be teachers, you need someone to teach you again the basic principles of the oracles of God. You need milk, not solid food, for everyone who lives on milk is unskilled in the word of righteousness, since he is a child. But solid food is for the mature, for those who have their powers of discernment trained by constant practice to distinguish good from evil. (Hebrews 5:7–14, ESV)

The lack of rooted "faith" impedes our ability to accept "the strong meat of the reveal." We keep rehashing and choking on "strong teachings" that we need to fulfill our mandate for Christ.

> Therefore let us leave the elementary doctrine of Christ and go on to maturity, not laying again a foundation of repentance from dead works and of faith toward God, and of instruc-

tion about washings, the laying on of hands, the resurrection of the dead, and eternal judgment. And this will do if God permits. For it is impossible, in the case of those who have once been enlightened, who have tasted the heavenly gift, and have shared in the Holy Spirit, and have tasted the goodness of the word of God and the powers of the age to come, and then have fallen away, to restore them again to repentance, since they are crucifying once again the Son of God to their own harm and holding him up to contempt. For land that has drunk the rain that often falls on it, and produces a crop useful to those for whose sake it is cultivated, receives a blessing from God. But if it bears thorns and thistles, it is worthless and near to being cursed, and its end is to be burned.

Though we speak in this way, yet in your case, beloved, we feel sure of better things—things that belong to salvation. For God is not unjust so as to overlook your work and the love that you have shown for his name in serving the saints, as you still do. And we desire each one of you to show the same earnestness to have the full assurance of hope until the end, so that you may not be sluggish, but imitators of those who through faith and patience inherit the promises. (Hebrews 6:1–12, ESV)

The devil will emphasize the importance of our "zeal" to displace our need for the "reveal," making us unacceptable to go forward with Christ. We must always remember our foundation is Jesus Christ.

"But I, brothers, could not address you as spiritual people, but as people of the flesh, as infants in Christ. I fed you with milk, not solid food, for you were not ready for it. And even now you are not yet ready, for you are still of the flesh. For while there is jealousy and strife among you, are you not of the flesh and behaving only in a human way? For when one says, 'I follow Paul,' and another, 'I follow Apollos,' are you not being merely human?

What then is Apollos? What is Paul? Servants through whom you believed, as the Lord assigned to each. I planted, Apollos watered, but God gave the growth. So neither he who plants nor he who waters is anything, but only God who gives the growth. He who plants and he who waters are one, and each will receive his wages according to his labor. For we are God's fellow workers. You are God's field, God's building.

According to the grace of God given to me, like a skilled master builder I laid a foundation, and someone else is building upon it. For no one can lay a foundation other than that which is laid, which is Jesus Christ." (1 Corinthians 3:1–11, ESV)

It's our responsibility to prepare our soil (our lives) for reception of "God's seed" to start our growth in the Lord. God will provide us with whatever we may need to get our soil (our lives) fertile for the "seed of God," but we must do the actual work of preparation.

And when a great crowd was gathering and people from town after town came to him, he said in a parable, "A sower went out to sow his seed. And as he sowed, some fell along the path and was trampled underfoot, and the birds of the air devoured it. And some fell on the rock, and as it grew up, it withered away, because it had no moisture. And some fell among thorns, and the thorns grew up with it and choked it. And some fell into good soil and grew and yielded a hundredfold." As he said these things, he called out, "He who has ears to hear, let him hear."

And when his disciples asked him what this parable meant, he said, "To you it has been given to know the secrets of the kingdom of God, but for others they are in parables, so that seeing they may not see, and hearing they may not understand. Now the parable is this: The seed is the word of God. The ones along the path are those who have heard; then the devil comes and takes away the word from their hearts, so that they may not believe and be saved. And the ones on the rock are those who, when they hear the word, receive it with joy. But these have no root; they believe for a while, and in time of testing fall away. And as for what fell among the thorns, they are those who hear, but as they go on their way they are choked by the cares and riches and pleasures of life, and their fruit does not mature. As for that in the good soil, they are those who, hearing the word, hold it fast in an honest and good heart, and bear fruit with patience." (Luke 8:4–15, ESV)

Faith is that whatever you may be confronted with or must go through, it will advance the Father's kingdom through the teachings of Jesus Christ. A "faith" that creates a "desire" to adhere to the teachings of Christ is paramount, no matter how they have varied from beliefs, doctrines, views, creeds, and/or tenets that have guided you in the past.

One of the criminals who were hanged railed at him saying, "Are you not the Christ?

Save yourself and us!" But the other rebuked him saying, "Do you not fear God, since you are under the same sentence of condemnation? And we indeed justly, for we are receiving the due reward of our deeds; but this man has done nothing wrong." And he said, "Jesus, remember me when you come into your kingdom." And he said to him, "Truly, I say to you, today you will be with me in paradise." (Luke 23:39–43, ESV)

For your "desire" to be rooted and unshakeable, you must be unfailing in your belief about the "authority of Jesus the Christ," the Son of the Father.

Long ago, at many times and in many ways God spoke to our fathers by the prophets, but in these last days he has spoken to us by his Son, whom he appointed the heir of all things, through whom also he created the world. He is the radiance of the glory of god and the exact imprint of his nature, and he upholds the universe by the word of his power. After making purification of sins, he sat down at the right hand of the Majesty on high, having become as much superior to angels as the name he has inherited is more excellent than theirs.

For to which of the angels did God ever say, "You are my Son, today I have begotten you"? Or again, "I will be to him a father, and he shall be to me a son"? And again, when he brings the firstborn into the world, he says, "Let all God's angels worship him." Of the angels he says, "He makes his angels winds, and his ministers a flame of fire." But of the Son he says, "Your throne O God, is forever and ever, the scepter of uprightness is the scepter of your kingdom. You have

loved righteousness and hated wickedness; therefore God, your God, has anointed you with the
oil of gladness beyond your companions." And,
"You, Lord, laid the foundation of the earth in
the beginning, and the heavens are the work of
your hands; they will perish, but you remain;
they will all wear out like a garment, like a robe
you will roll them up, like a garment they will be
changed. But you are the same, and your years
will have no end." And to which of the angels
has he ever said, "Sit at my right hand until I
make your enemies a footstool for your feet"? Are
they not all ministering spirits sent out to serve
for the sake of those who are to inherit salvation?
(Hebrews 1:1–14, ESV)

Peter, who spent three years in training, knew whom Jesus was
and confessed it.

Now when Jesus came into the district of
Caesarea Philippi, he asked his disciples, "Who
do people say that the Son of Man is?" And
they said, "Some say John the Baptist, others say
Elijah, and others Jeremiah or one of the prophets." He said to them, "But who do you say that
I am?" Simon Peter replied, "You are the Christ,
the Son of the living God." And Jesus answered
him, "Blessed are you, Simon Bar-Jonah! For
flesh and blood has not revealed thus to you, but
my Father who is in heaven. And I tell you, you
are Peter, and on this rock I will build my church,
and the gates of hell shall not prevail against it. I
will give you the keys of the kingdom of heaven,
and whatever you bind on earth shall be bound
in heaven, and whatever you loose on earth shall
be loosed in heaven." Then he strictly charged

the disciples to tell no one that he was the Christ. (Matthew 16:13–20, ESV)

The Hebrews coming out of Egypt had "desire problems," and Peter was still trying to root his "faith" in "desire" (determination). Peter struggled with rooting his "faith," but eventually he got it right.

"Take care, brothers, lest there be in any of you an evil, unbelieving heart, leading you to fall away from the living God. But exhort one another every day, as long as it is called 'today,' that none of you may be hardened by the deceitfulness of sin. For we have come to share in Christ, if indeed we hold our original confidence firm to the end. As it is said, 'Today, if you hear his voice, do not harden your hearts as in the rebellion.' For who were those who heard and yet rebelled? Was it not all those who left Egypt led by Moses? And with whom was he provoked for forty years? Was it not with those who sinned, whose bodies fell in the wilderness? And to whom did he swear that they would not enter his rest, but to those who were disobedient? So we see that they were unable to enter because of unbelief." (Hebrews 3:12–19, ESV)

"Therefore, knowing the fear of the Lord, we persuade others. But what we are is known to God, and I hope it is known also to your conscience. We are not commending ourselves to you again but giving you cause to boast about us, so that you may be able to answer those who boast about outward appearance and not about what is in the heart. For if we are beside ourselves, it is for God; if we are in our right mind, it is for you. For the love of Christ controls us, because we have concluded this: that one has died for all, therefore all have died; and he died for all, that those who live might no longer live for themselves but for him who for their sake died and was raised.

From now on, therefore, we regard no one according to the flesh. Even though we once regarded Christ according to the flesh, we regard him thus no longer. Therefore, if anyone is in Christ, he is a new creation. The old has passed away; behold, the new has come. All this is from God, who through Christ reconciled us to himself and gave us the ministry of reconciliation; that is, in Christ God was reconciling the world to himself, not counting their trespasses against them, and entrusting to us the message of reconciliation. Therefore, we are ambassadors for Christ, God making his appeal through us. We implore you on behalf of Christ, be reconciled to God. For our sake he made him to be sin who knew no sin, so that in him we might become the righteousness of God." (2 Corinthians 5:11–21, ESV)

Our "faith" itself needs prepping before it can be rooted in our "desire."

"Therefore, since we are surrounded by so great a cloud of witnesses, let us also lay aside every weight, and sin which clings so closely, and let us run with endurance the race that is set before us, looking to Jesus, the founder and perfecter of our faith, who for the joy that was set before him endured the cross, despising the shame, and is seated at the right hand of the throne of God.

Consider him who endured from sinners such hostility against himself, so that you may not grow weary or fainthearted. In your struggle against sin you have not yet resisted to the point of shedding your blood. And have you forgotten the exhortation that addresses you as sons? 'My son, do not regard lightly the discipline of the Lord, nor be weary when reproved by him. For the Lord disciplines the one he loves, and chastises every son whom he receives.'" (Hebrews 12:1–5, ESV)

The proof of desire is in the pursuit!

3) **Commitment:** "Commitment" is the "in spite of" ingredient necessary to "reveal" and permit growth in obedience to Christ's teachings. "Commitment" allows us to endure and maintain our willingness to be ruled by God's wisdom and understanding, instead of our own. With our "faith" rooted in "desire," "commitment" provides the nourishment (food) for our growth in fulfilling the Father's mandates for our lives on this earth.

Without "commitment," it becomes impossible to stay on the course that God has prepared for your life. As human beings, some of the storms, trials, and tribulations become impossible, if your "faith" is not rooted in "desire" and nourished with "commitment" to God's will for your life.

Some of what you may have to endure is looking ridiculous to the people of the world or not going along with norms that are completely acceptable to the general theme of life on earth, as it is being portrayed.

> "Again, in the ninth year, in the tenth month, on the tenth day of the month, the word of the LORD came to me, saying, 'Son of man, write down the name of the day, this very day— the king of Babylon started his siege against

Jerusalem this very day. And utter a parable to the rebellious house, and say to them, "Thus says the Lord GOD: 'Put on a pot, set it on, and also pour water into it. Gather pieces of meat in it, every good piece, the thigh and the shoulder. Fill it with choice cuts; take the choice of the flock. Also pile fuel bones under it, make it boil well, and let the cuts simmer in it.'

Therefore thus says the Lord GOD: 'Woe to the bloody city, to the pot whose scum is in it, and whose scum is not gone from it! Bring it out piece by piece, on which no lot has fallen. For her blood is in her midst; she set it on top of a rock; she did not pour it on the ground, to cover it with dust. That it may raise up fury and take vengeance, I have set her blood on top of a rock, that it may not be covered.'

Therefore thus says the Lord GOD: 'Woe to the bloody city! I too will make the pyre great. Heap on the wood, kindle the fire; cook the meat well, mix in the spices, and let the cuts be burned up.

Then set the pot empty on the coals, that it may become hot and its bronze may burn, that its filthiness may be melted in it, that its scum may be consumed. She has grown weary with lies, and her great scum has not gone from her. Let her scum be in the fire! In your filthiness is lewdness. Because I have cleansed you, and you were not cleansed, you will not be cleansed of your filthiness anymore, till I have caused My fury to rest upon you. I, the LORD, have spoken it; it shall come to pass, and I will do it; I will not hold back, nor will I spare, nor will I relent; according to your ways and according to your deeds they

will judge you,' Says the Lord GOD."'" (Ezekiel
24:1–14, NKJV)

Yes the *Lord*, God the Father, had the prophet Ezekiel, in
the midst of the Hebrews being under siege and attacked by
Nebuchadnezzar and his Babylonians, pronounce the destruction of
God's city of Jerusalem and the country of Judah. That did not sit
well with his fellow Hebrews. Neither did Jeremiah's work for the
Lord and many other prophets and individuals who were committed
to serving God.

> In the beginning of the reign of Jehoiakim
the son of Josiah, king of Judah, this word came
from the LORD, saying, "Thus says the LORD:
'Stand in the court of the LORD's house, and
speak to all the cities of Judah, which come to
worship in the LORD's house, all the words that
I command you to speak to them. Do not dimin-
ish a word. Perhaps everyone will listen and turn
from his evil way, that I may relent concerning
the calamity which I purpose to bring on them
because of the evil of their doings.' And you shall
say to them, 'Thus says the LORD: "If you will
not listen to Me, to walk in My law which I have
set before you, to heed the words of My servants
the prophets whom I sent to you, both rising
up early and sending them (but you have not
heeded), then I will make this house like Shiloh,
and will make this city a curse to all the nations
of the earth."'"
>
> So the priests and the prophets and all the
people heard Jeremiah speaking these words in
the house of the LORD. Now it happened, when
Jeremiah had made an end of speaking all that
the LORD had commanded him to speak to all
the people, that the priests and the prophets and

all the people seized him, saying, "You will surely die! Why have you prophesied in the name of the LORD, saying, 'This house shall be like Shiloh, and this city shall be desolate, without an inhabitant'?" And all the people were gathered against Jeremiah in the house of the LORD.

When the princes of Judah heard these things, they came up from the king's house to the house of the LORD and sat down in the entry of the New Gate of the LORD's house. And the priests and the prophets spoke to the princes and all the people, saying, "This man deserves to die! For he has prophesied against this city, as you have heard with your ears."

Then Jeremiah spoke to all the princes and all the people, saying: "The LORD sent me to prophesy against this house and against this city with all the words that you have heard. Now therefore, amend your ways and your doings, and obey the voice of the LORD your God; then the LORD will relent concerning the doom that He has pronounced against you. As for me, here I am, in your hand; do with me as seems good and proper to you. But know for certain that if you put me to death, you will surely bring innocent blood on yourselves, on this city, and on its inhabitants; for truly the LORD has sent me to you to speak all these words in your hearing."

So the princes and all the people said to the priests and the prophets, "This man does not deserve to die. For he has spoken to us in the name of the LORD our God."

Then certain of the elders of the land rose up and spoke to all the assembly of the people, saying: "Micah of Moresheth prophesied in the days of Hezekiah king of Judah, and spoke to all the people of Judah, saying, 'Thus says the LORD of hosts: "Zion shall be plowed like a field, Jerusalem shall become heaps of ruins, and the mountain of the temple like the bare hills of the forest."'

Did Hezekiah king of Judah and all Judah ever put him to death? Did he not fear the LORD and seek the LORD's favor? And the LORD relented concerning the doom which He had pronounced against them. But we are doing great evil against ourselves."

Now there was also a man who prophesied in the name of the LORD, Urijah the son of Shemaiah of Kirjath Jearim, who prophesied against this city and against this land according to all the words of Jeremiah. And when Jehoiakim the king, with all his mighty men and all the princes, heard his words, the king sought to put him to death; but when Urijah heard it, he was afraid and fled, and went to Egypt. Then Jehoiakim the king sent men to Egypt: Elnathan the son of Achbor, and other men who went with him to Egypt. And they brought Urijah from Egypt and brought him to Jehoiakim the king, who killed him with the sword and cast his dead body into the graves of the common people.

Nevertheless the hand of Ahikam the son of Shaphan was with Jeremiah, so that they should not give him into the hand of the people to put him to death. (Jeremiah 26:1–24, NKJV)

Total "commitment" is required to grow in the wisdom and understanding that God has for our lives. It is necessary to acquire the wisdom that will permit you to fulfill the will of the Father and accept the understanding that "going along to get along," when it comes to subverting God's mandates, is not acceptable.

Jeremiah presented the word of God and understood that the repercussions of that could mean his death. He understood that God was in control and if the mob was to take his life, so be it. He was "committed" to his service for God. Uriah, son of Shemaiah, had the "wisdom" to do the will of God, but had not yet acquired the "understanding" necessary not to be in fear of the results associated with doing God's will.

Commitment to do the will of God could put you at odds with the world you live in because this world is "the devil's domain."

> Grace to you and peace from God our Father and the Lord Jesus Christ, who gave himself for our sins to deliver us from the present evil age, according to the will of our God and Father to whom be the glory forever and ever. Amen" (Galatians 1:3–5, ESV)

Everyday life occurs every day in the "devil's domain," and its primary function is to attempt to chip at your faith and commitment to God continuously.

> "O foolish Galatians! Who has bewitched you? It was before your eyes that Jesus Christ, was publicly portrayed as crucified. Let me ask you only this: Did you receive the Spirit by works of the law or by hearing with faith? Are you so foolish? Having begun by Spirit, are you now being perfected by the flesh? Did you suffer so many things in vain—if indeed it was in vain? Does he who supplies the Spirit to you and works miracles among you do so by works of the law, or by hearing with faith—just as Abraham 'believed God, and it was counted to him as righteousness'?
>
> Know then that it is those of faith who are the sons of Abraham. And the Scripture, foreseeing that God would justify the Gentiles by faith,

preached the gospel beforehand to Abraham saying, 'In you shall all the nations be blessed.' So then, those who are of faith are blessed along with Abraham, the man of faith." (Galatian 3:1–9, ESV)

And even if our gospel is veiled, it is veiled to those who are perishing. In their case the god of this world has blinded the minds of the unbelievers, to keep them from seeing the light of the gospel of the glory of Christ, who is the image of God. (2 Corinthians 4:3 and 4, ESV)

When Adam sinned, sin entered the world. Adam's sin brought death, so death spread to everyone, for everyone sinned. (Romans 5:12, NLT)

One day the members of the heavenly court came again to present themselves before the LORD, and the Accuser, Satan, came with them. "Where have you come from?" the LORD asked Satan. Satan answered the LORD, "I have been patrolling the earth, watching everything that's going on." (Job 2:1 and 2, NLT)

Our "commitment" to God makes us at odds with Satan and this world day and night (24/7). The "cost of commitment to God" could be extremely high, by earth standards, but the "benefits of commitment to God" far surpass the cost.

Seek the Kingdom of God above all else, and live righteously, and he will give you everything you need. (Matthew 6:33, NLT)

And what do you benefit if you gain the whole world but lose your own soul? Is anything worth more than your soul? (Matthew 16:26, NLT)

If your "faith" is rooted in your "desire" and your "desire" is being feed by your "commitment," then you are prepared to endure building God's kingdom in this devil's domain.

In the beginning of the reign of Jehoiakim the son of Josiah, king of Judah, this word came to Jeremiah from the LORD, saying, "Thus says the LORD to me: 'Make for yourselves bonds and yokes, and put them on your neck, and send them to the king of Edom, the king of Moab, the king of the Ammonites, the king of Tyre, and the king of Sidon, by the hand of the messengers who come to Jerusalem to Zedekiah king of Judah. And command them to say to their masters, "Thus says the LORD of host, the God of Israel—thus you shall say to your masters: 'I have made the earth, the man and the beast that are on the ground, by My great power and by My outstretched arm, and have given it to whom it seemed proper to Me. And now I have given all these lands into the hand of Nebuchadnezzar the king of Babylon, My servant; and the beasts of the field I have also given him to serve him. So all nations shall serve him and his son and his son's son, until the time of his land comes; and then many nations and great kings shall make him serve them. And it shall be, that the nation and kingdom which will not serve Nebuchadnezzar the king of Babylon, and which will not put its neck under the yoke of the king of Babylon, that nation I will punish,' says the LORD, 'with the sword, the famine, and the pestilence, until I have consumed them by his hand. Therefore do not listen to your prophets, your diviners, your dreamers, your soothsayers, or your sorcerers, who speak to you saying, "You shall not serve the king of Babylon." For they prophesy a lie to you, to remove you far from your land; and I will drive you out, and you will perish. But the nations that bring their necks under the yoke of the king of Babylon and serve him, I will let them remain in their own land,' says the LORD, 'and they shall till it and dwell in it.'"'

I also spoke to Zedekiah king of Judah according to all these words, saying, 'Bring your necks under the yoke of the king of Babylon, and serve him and his people, and live! Why will you die, you and your people, by the sword, by the famine, and by the pestilence, as the LORD has spoken against the nation that will not serve the king of Babylon? Therefore do not listen to the words of the prophets who speak to you, saying, "You shall not serve the king of Babylon," for they prophesy a lie to you; for I have not sent them,' says the LORD, 'yet they prophesy a lie in My name, that I may drive you out, and that you may perish, you and the prophets who prophesy to you.'

Also I spoke to the priests and to all the people, saying, 'Thus says the LORD: "Do not listen to the words of your prophets who prophesy to you, saying, 'Behold the vessels of the LORD's house will now shortly be brought back from Babylon'; for they prophesy a lie to you. Do not listen to them; serve the king of Babylon, and live! Why should this city be laid waste? But if they are prophets, and if the word of the LORD is with them, let them now make intercession to the LORD of hosts, that the vessels which are left in the house of the LORD, in the house of the king of Judah, and at Jerusalem, do not go to Babylon."

> For thus says the LORD of hosts concerning the pillars, concerning the Sea, concerning the carts, and concerning the remainder of the vessels that remain in the city, which Nebuchadnezzar king of Babylon did not take, when he carried away captive Jeconiah the son of Jehoiakim, king of Judah, from Jerusalem to Babylon, and all the nobles of Judah and Jerusalem—yes, thus says the LORD of hosts, the God of Israel, concerning the vessels that remain in the house of the king of Judah and of Jerusalem: "They shall be carried to Babylon, and there they shall be until the day that I visit them," says the LORD. "Then I will bring them up and restore them to this place."''"
> (Jeremiah 27:1–22, NKJV)

"Boldness," in God, only comes with growing "commitment." You are no longer functioning on "zeal" that will never help your "faith" become "rooted" in the soil of "determine" which allows you to grow in to the revelation of the "reveal"—God's purpose for your life.

The "obedience" and "boldness" that the Father requires from us in this world, dominated by Lucifer's control, will be contrary to normal earthly events.

> "And it happened in the same year, at the beginning of the reign of Zedekiah king of Judah, in the fourth year and in the fifth month, that Hananiah the son of Azur the prophet, who was from Gibeon, spoke to me in the house of the LORD in the presence of the priests and all the people, saying, 'Thus speaks the LORD of hosts, the God of Israel, saying: "I have broken the yoke of the king of Babylon. Within two full years I will bring back to this place all the vessels of the LORD's house, that Nebuchadnezzar

king of Babylon took away from this place and carried to Babylon. And I will bring back to this place Jeconiah the son of Jehoiakim, king of Judah, with all the captives of Judah who went to Babylon," says the LORD, "for I will break the yoke of the king of Babylon.

Then the prophet Jeremiah spoke to the prophet Hananiah in the presence of the priests and in the presence of all the people who stood in the house of the LORD, and the prophet Jeremiah said, 'Amen! The LORD do so; the LORD perform your words which you have prophesied, to bring back the vessels of the LORD's and all who were carried away captive, from Babylon to this place.

Nevertheless hear now this word that I speak in your hearing and in the hearing of all the people: The prophets who have been before me and before you of old prophesied against many countries and great kingdoms—of war and disaster and pestilence. As for the prophet who prophesies of peace, when the word of the prophet comes to pass, the prophet will be known as one whom the LORD has truly sent.'

Then Hananiah the prophet took the yoke off the prophet Jeremiah's neck and broke it. And Hananiah spoke in the presence of all the people, saying, 'Thus says the LORD: "Even so I will break the yoke of Nebuchadnezzar king of Babylon from the neck of all nations within the space of two full years."'" And the prophet Jeremiah went his way.

Now the word of the LORD came to Jeremiah, after Hananiah the prophet had broken the yoke from the neck of the prophet Jeremiah, saying, "Go and tell Hananiah, saying,

'Thus says the LORD: "You have broken the yokes of wood, but you have made in their place yokes of iron." For thus says the LORD of hosts, the God of Israel: "I have put a yoke of iron on the neck of all these nations, that they may serve Nebuchadnezzar king of Babylon; and they shall serve him. I have given him the beasts of the field also."'"

Then the prophet Jeremiah said to Hananiah the prophet, "Hear now, Hananiah, the LORD has not sent you, but you make this people trust in a lie. Therefore thus says the LORD: 'Behold, I will cast you from the face of the earth. This year you shall die, because you have taught rebellion against the LORD.'"

So Hananiah the prophet died the same year in the seventh month.'" (Jeremiah 28:1–17, NKJV)

In our "zeal" to hold on to what "was" and the "tradition" of what always has been, we become susceptible and inclined to accept offerings from Satan that sound good, feel good, and have plenty of "tradition" to make it seem like the right way to proceed, but is just not in keeping with the teachings given to us by Christ. Hananiah fell into this problem with his desire to maintain Judah and Jerusalem, as they had been for centuries. *This allowed Satan to appear as an "angel of light."*

"But I will continue doing what I have always done. This will undercut those who are looking for an opportunity to boast that their work is just like ours. These people are false apostles. They are deceitful workers who disguise themselves as apostles of Christ. But I am not surprised! Even Satan disguises himself as an angel of light. So it is no wonder that his servants also disguise themselves as servants of righteousness. In the end they will get the punishment their wicked deeds deserve." (2 Corinthians 11:12–15, NLT)

"Commitment" requires total obedience to God's will for your life—a goal that we strive toward our entire life. Just like Abraham, you may have to prepare to make a sacrifice of self or a loved one that you don't understand or wish to avoid.

Just like Christ carrying his cross and dying, so that we may have eternal life with the Father, we must carry our cross also.

> Now King Zedekiah the son of Josiah reigned instead of Coniah the son of Jehoiakim, whom Nebuchadnezzar king of Babylon made king in the land of Judah. But neither he nor his servants nor the people of the land gave heed to the words of the LORD which He spoke by the prophet Jeremiah.
>
> And Zedekiah the king sent Jehucal the son of Shelemiah and Zephaniah the son of Maaseiah, the priest, to the prophet Jeremiah, saying, "Pray now to the LORD our God for us." Now Jeremiah was coming and going among the people for they had not yet put him in prison. Then Pharaoh's army came up from Egypt; and when the Chaldeans who were besieging Jerusalem heard news of them, they departed from Jerusalem.
>
> Then the word of the LORD came to the prophet Jeremiah, saying, "Thus says the LORD, the God of Israel, 'Thus you shall say to the king of Judah, who sent you to Me to inquire of Me: "Behold, Pharaoh's army which has come up to help you will return to Egypt, to their own land. And the Chaldeans shall come back and fight against this city, and take it and burn it with fire."' Thus says the LORD: 'Do not

deceive yourselves, saying "The Chaldeans will surely depart from us," for they will not depart. For though you had defeated the whole army of the Chaldeans who fight against you, and there remained only wounded men among them, they would rise up, every man in his tent, and burn the city with fire.'"

And it happened, when the army of the Chaldeans left the siege of Jerusalem for fear of Pharaoh's army, that Jeremiah went out of Jerusalem to go into the land of Benjamin to claim his property there among the people. And when he was in the Gate of Benjamin, a captain of the guard was there whose name was Irijah the son of Shelemiah, the son of Hananiah; and seized Jeremiah the prophet, saying, "You are defecting to the Chaldeans!"

Then Jeremiah said, "False! I am not defecting to the Chaldeans." But he did not listen to him.

So Irijah seized Jeremiah and brought him to the princes. Therefore the princes were angry with Jeremiah, and they struck him and put him in prison in the house of Jonathan the scribe. For they had made that the prison.

When Jeremiah entered the dungeon and the cells, and Jeremiah had remained there many days, then Zedekiah the king sent and took him out. The king asked him secretly in his house, and said, "Is there any word from the LORD?"

And Jeremiah said, "There is." Then he said, "You shall be delivered into the hands of the king of Babylon!"

Moreover Jeremiah said to King Zedekiah, "What offense have I committed against you, against your servants, or against this people, that you have put me in prison? Where now are your prophets who prophesied to you saying, 'The king of Babylon will not come against you or against this land'? Therefore please hear now, O my lord the king. Please, let my petition be accepted before you, and do not make me return to the house of Jonathan the scribe, lest I die there."

Then Zedekiah the king commanded that they should commit Jeremiah to the court of the prison, and that they should give him daily a piece of bread from the bakers' street, until all the bread in the city was gone. Thus Jeremiah remained in the court of the prison. (Jeremiah 37:1–21, NKJV)

Your "faith," rooted in "desire" and fed by "commitment" to God's word, will transcend the lack of fairness from others, the lack of truth from others, and the acts of Satan to destroy your work for God.

Now Shephatiah the son of Mattan, Gedaliah the son of Pashhur, Jucal the son of Shelemiah, and Pashhur the son of Malchiah heard the words that Jeremiah had spoken to all the people, saying, "Thus says the LORD: 'He who remains in this city shall die by the sword, by famine, and by pestilence; but he who goes over to the Chaldeans shall live; his life shall be as a prize to him, and he shall live.' Thus says the LORD: 'This city shall surely be given into the hand of the king of Babylon's army, which shall take it.'"

Therefore the princes said to the king, "Please, let this man be put to death, for thus he weakens the hands of the men of war who remain in this city, and the hands of all the people, by speaking such words to them. For this man does not seek the welfare of this people, but their harm."

Then Zedekiah the king said, "Look, he is in your hand. For the king can do nothing against you." So they took Jeremiah and cast him into the dungeon of Malchiah the king's son, which was in the court of the prison, and they let Jeremiah down with ropes. And in the dungeon there was no water, but mire. So Jeremiah sank in the mire.

Now Ebed-Melech the Ethiopian, one of the eunuchs, who was in the king's house, heard that they had put Jeremiah in the dungeon. When the king was sitting at the Gate of Benjamin, Ebed-Melech went out of the king's house and spoke to the king, saying: "My lord the king, these men have done evil in all that they have done to Jeremiah the prophet, whom they have cast into the dungeon, and he is likely to die from hunger in the place where he is. For there is no more bread in the city." Then the king commanded Ebed-Melech the Ethiopian, saying, "Take from here thirty men with you, and lift Jeremiah the prophet out of the dungeon before he dies." So Ebed-Melech took the men with him and went into the house of the king under the treasury, and took from there old clothes and old rags, and let them down by ropes into the dungeon to Jeremiah. Then Ebed-Melech the Ethiopian said to Jeremiah, "Please put these clothes and rags under your armpits, under the ropes." And Jeremiah did so. So they pulled Jeremiah up with ropes and lifted him out of the dungeon. And Jeremiah remained in the court of the prison.

Then Zedekiah the king sent and had Jeremiah the prophet brought to him at the third entrance of the house of the LORD. And the king said to Jeremiah, "I will ask you something. Hide nothing from me."

Jeremiah said to Zedekiah, "If I declare it to you, will you not surely put me to death? And if I give you advice, you will not listen to me."

So Zedekiah the king swore secretly to Jeremiah, saying, "As the LORD lives, who made our very souls, I will not put you to death, nor will I give you into the hand of these men who seek your life."

Then Jeremiah said to Zedekiah, "Thus says the LORD, the God of hosts, the God of Israel: 'If you surely surrender to the king of Babylon's princes, then your soul shall live; this city shall not be burned with fire, and you and your house shall live. But if you do not surrender to the king of Babylon's princes, then this city shall be given into the hand of the Chaldeans; they shall burn it with fire, and you shall not escape from their hand.'"

And Zedekiah the king said to Jeremiah, "I am afraid of the Jews who have defected to the Chaldeans, lest they deliver me into their hand, and they abuse me."

But Jeremiah said, "They shall not deliver you. Please, obey the voice of the LORD which I speak to you. So it shall be well with you, and your soul shall live. But if you refuse to surrender, this is the word that the LORD has shown me: 'Now behold, all the women who are left in the king of Judah's house shall be surrendered to the king of Babylon's princes, and those women shall say: "Your close friends have set upon you and prevailed against you; your feet have sunk in the mire, and they have turned away again."

So they shall surrender all your wives and children to the Chaldeans. You shall not escape from their hand, but shall be taken by the hand of the king of Babylon. And you shall cause this city to be burned with fire.'"

Then Zedekiah said to Jeremiah, "Let no one know of these words, and you shall not die. But if the princes hear that I have talked with you, and they come to you and say to you, 'Declare to us now what you have said to the king, and also what the king said to you; do not hide it from us, and we will not put you to death,' then shall you say to them, 'I presented my request before the king, that he would not make me return to Jonathan's house to die there.'"

Then all the princes came to Jeremiah and asked him. And he told them according to all these words that the king had commanded. So they stopped speaking with him, for the conversation had not been heard. Now Jeremiah remained in the court of the prison until the day that Jerusalem was taken. And he was there when Jerusalem was taken. (Jeremiah 38:1–28, NKJV)

In the ninth year of Zedekiah king of Judah, in the tenth month, Nebuchadnezzar king of Babylon and all his army came against Jerusalem, and besieged it. In the eleventh year of Zedekiah, in the fourth month, on the ninth day of the month, the city was penetrated.

Then all the princes of the king of Babylon came in and sat in the Middle Gate: Nergal-Sharezer, Samgar-Nebo, Sarsechim, Rabsaris, Nergal-Sarezer, Rabmag, with the rest of the princes of the king of Babylon.

So it was, when Zedekiah the king of Judah and all the men of war saw them, that they fled and went out of the city by night, by way of the king's garden, by the gate between the two walls. And he went out by way of the plain. But the Chaldean army pursued them and overtook Zedekiah in the plains of Jericho. And when they had captured him, they brought him up to Nebuchadnezzar king of Babylon, to Riblah in the land of Hamath, where he pronounced judgment on him. Then the king of Babylon killed the sons of Zedekiah before his eyes in Riblah; the king of Babylon also killed all the nobles of Judah. Moreover he put out Zedekiah's eyes, and bound him with bronze fetters to carry him off to Babylon. And the Chaldeans burned the king's house and the houses of the people with fire, and broke down the walls of Jerusalem. Then Nebuzaradan the captain of the guard carried away captive to Babylon the remnant of the people who remained in the city and those who defected to him, with the rest of the people who remained. But Nebuzaradan the captain of the guard left in the land of Judah the poor people, who had nothing and gave them vineyards and fields at the same time.

Now Nebuchadnezzar king of Babylon gave charge concerning Jeremiah to Nebuzaradan the captain of the guard, saying, "Take him and look after him, and do him no harm; but do to him just as he says to you." So Nebuzaradan the captain of the guard sent Nebushasban, Rabsaris, Nergal-Sharezer, Rabmag, and all the king of Babylon's chief officers; then they sent someone to take Jeremiah from the court of the prison, and committed him to Gedaliah the son of Ahikam, the son of Shaphan, that he should take him home. So he dwelt among the people.

Meanwhile the word of the LORD had come to Jeremiah while he was shut up in the court of the prison, saying, "Go and speak to Ebed-Melech the Ethiopian, saying, 'Thus says the LORD of hosts, the God of Israel: "Behold, I will bring My words upon this city for adversity and not for good, and they shall be performed in that day before you. But I will deliver you in that day," says the LORD, "and you shall not be given into the hand of the men of whom you are afraid. For I will surely deliver you and you shall not fall by the sword; but your life shall be as a prize to you, because you have put your trust in Me," says the LORD.'" (Jeremiah 39:1–18, NKJV)

The word that came to Jeremiah from the LORD after Nebuzaradan the captain of the guard had let him go from Ramah, when he had taken him bound in chains among all who were carried away captive from Jerusalem and Judah, who were carried away captive to Babylon.

And the captain of the guard took Jeremiah and said to him: "The LORD your God has pronounced this doom on this place. Now the LORD has brought it, and has done just as He said. Because you people have sinned against the LORD, and not obeyed His voice, therefore this thing has come upon you. And now look, I free you this day from the chains that were on your hand. If it seems good to you to come with me to Babylon, come, and I will look after you. But if it seems wrong for you to come with me to Babylon, remain here. See, all the land is before you; wherever it seems good and convenient for you to go, go there."

Now while Jeremiah had not yet gone back, Nebuzaradan said, "Go back to Gedaliah the son of Ahikam, the son of Shaphan, whom the king of Babylon has made governor over the cities of Judah, and dwell with him among the people. Or go wherever it seems convenient for you to go." So the captain of the guard gave him rations and a gift and let him go. Then Jeremiah went to Gedaliah the son of Ahikam, to Mizpah, and dwelt with him among the people who were left in the land. (Jeremiah 40:1–6, NKJV)

Your "commitment" has to be based on what you are seeking.

On the following day, when the people who were standing on the other side of the sea saw that there was no other boat there, except that one which His disciples had entered, and that Jesus had not entered the boat with His disciples, but His disciples had gone away alone—however, other boats came from Tiberias, near the place where they ate bread after the Lord had given thanks—when the people therefore saw that Jesus was not there, nor His disciples, they also got into boats and came to Capernaum, seeking Jesus. And when they found Him on the other side of the sea, they said to Him, "Rabbi, when did You come here?"

Jesus answered them and said, "Most assuredly, I say to you, you seek Me, not because you saw the signs, but because you ate of the loaves and were filled. Do not labor for the food which perishes, but for the food which endures to everlasting life, which the Son of Man will give you, because God the Father has set His seal on Him."

Then they said to Him, "What shall we do, that we may work the works of God?"

Jesus answered and said to them, "This is the work of God, that you believe in Him whom He sent."

Therefore they said to Him, "What sign will You perform then, that we may see it and believe You? What work will You do? Our fathers ate the manna in the desert; as it is written, 'He gave them bread from heaven to eat.'"

Then Jesus said to them, "Most assuredly, I say to you, Moses did not give you the bread from heaven, but My Father gives you the true bread from heaven. For the bread of God is He who comes down from heaven and gives life to the world."

Then they said to Him, "Lord, give us this bread always."

And Jesus said to them, "I am the bread of life. He who comes to Me shall never hunger, and he who believes in Me shall never thirst. But I said to you that you have seen Me and yet do not believe. All that the Father gives Me will come to Me, and the one who comes to Me I will by no means cast out. For I have come down from heaven, not to do My own will, but the will of Him who sent Me. This is the will of the Father who sent Me, that of all He has given Me I should lose nothing, but should raise it up at the last day. And this is the will of Him who sent Me, that everyone who sees the Son and believes in Him may have everlasting life; and I will raise him up at the last day."

The Jews then complained about Him, because He said, "I am the bread which came down from heaven." And they said. "Is not this Jesus, the son of Joseph, whose father and mother we know? How is it then that He says, 'I have come down from heaven'?"

Jesus therefore answered and said to them, "Do not murmur among yourselves. No one can come to Me unless the Father who sent Me draws him; and I will raise him up at the last day. It is written in the prophets, 'And they shall all be taught by God.' Therefore everyone who has heard and learned from the Father comes to Me. Not that anyone has seen the Father, except He who is from God; He has seen the Father. Most assuredly, I say to you, he who believes in Me has everlasting life. I am the bread of life. Your fathers ate the manna in the wilderness, and are dead. This is the bread which comes down from heaven, that one may eat of it and not die. I am the living bread which came down from heaven. If anyone eats of this bread, he will live forever; and the bread that I shall give is My flesh, which I shall give for the life of the world."

The Jews therefore quarreled among themselves, saying, "How can this Man give us His flesh to eat?"

Then Jesus said to them, "Most assuredly, I say to you, unless you eat the flesh of the Son of Man and drink His blood, you have no life in you. Whoever eats My flesh and drinks My blood has eternal life, and I will raise him up at the day last day. For My flesh is food indeed, and My blood is drink indeed. He who eats My flesh and drinks My blood abides in Me, and I in him. As the living Father sent Me, and I live because of the Father, so he who feeds on Me will live because of Me. This is the bread which came down from heaven—not as your fathers ate the manna, and are dead. He who eats this bread will live forever."

These things He said in the synagogue as He taught in Capernaum.

Therefore many of His disciples, when they heard this, said, "This is a hard saying; who can understand it?"

When Jesus knew in Himself that His disciples complained about this, He said to them, "Does this offend you? What then if you should see the Son of Man ascend where He was before? It is the Spirit who gives life; the flesh profits nothing. The words that I speak to you are spirit, and they are life. But there are some of you who do not believe." For Jesus knew from the beginning who they were who did not believe, and who would betray Him. And He said, "Therefore I have said to you that no one can come to Me unless it has been granted to him by My Father."

From that time many of His disciples went back and walked with Him no more. Then Jesus said to the twelve, "Do you also want to go away?"

But Simon Peter answered Him, "Lord, to whom shall we go? You have the words of eternal life. Also we have come to believe and know that You are the Christ, the Son of the living God."

Jesus answered them, "Did I not choose you, the twelve, and one of you is a devil?" He spoke of Judas Iscariot, the son of Simon, for it was he who would betray Him, being one of the twelve. (John 6:22–71, NKJV)

"Commitment" requires your righteousness to be better than....

"Do not think that I have come to abolish the Law or the Prophets; I have not come to abolish them but to fulfill them. For truly, I say to you, until heaven and earth pass away, not an iota, not a dot, will pass away the Law until all is accomplished. Therefore whoever relaxes one of the least of these commandments and teaches others to do the same will be called least in the kingdom of heaven, but whoever does them and teaches them will be called great in the kingdom of heaven. For I tell you, unless your righteousness exceeds that of the scribes and Pharisees, you will never enter the kingdom of heaven." (Matthew 5:17–20, ESV)

"Commitment," which produces "obedience," leads to "peace of mind."

"These things I have spoken to you while I am still with you. But the Helper, the Holy Spirit, whom the Father will send in my name, he will teach you all things and bring to your remembrance all that I have said to you. Peace I leave with you; my peace I give to you. Not as the world gives do I give to you. Let not your hearts be troubled, neither let them be afraid. You heard me say to you, 'I am going away, and I will come to you.' If you loved me, you would have rejoiced, because I am going to the Father, for the Father is greater than I. And now I have told you before it takes place, so that when it does take place you may believe. I will no longer talk much with you, for the ruler of this world is coming. He has no claim on me, but I do as the Father has commanded me, so that the world may know that I love the Father. Rise, let us go from here." (John 14:25–31, ESV)

The purpose of the necessary "reveal" of "commitment" is to solidify our willingness to do the "Will of God" by carrying out our mandate to "GO"!

"You did not choose me, but I chose you and appointed you that you should go and bear fruit and that your fruit should abide, so that whatever you ask the Father in my name, he may give it to you. These things I command you, so that you will love one another." (John 15:16 and 17, ESV)

"But when the Helper comes, whom I will send to you from the Father, the Spirit of truth, who proceeds from the Father, he will bear witness about me. And you also will bear witness, because you have been with me from the beginning." (John 15:26 and 27, ESV)

"I have said all these things to you to keep you from falling away. They will put you out of the synagogues. Indeed, the hour is coming when whoever kills you will think he is offering service to God. And they will do these things because they have not known the Father, nor me. But I have said these things to you, that when their hour comes you may remember that I told them to you."

"I did not say these things to you from the beginning, because I was with you." (John 16:1–4, ESV)

Then he said to them, "These are my words that I spoke to you while I was still with you, that everything written about me in the Law of Moses and the Prophets and the Psalms must be fulfilled." Then he opened their minds to understand the Scriptures, and said to them, "Thus it is written, that the Christ should suffer and on the third day rise from the dead, and that repentance for the forgiveness of sins should be proclaimed in his name to all nations, beginning from Jerusalem. You are witnesses of these things. And behold, I am sending the promise of my Father upon you. But stay in the city until you are clothed with power from on high." (Luke 24:44–49, ESV)

So when the apostles were with Jesus, they kept asking him, "Lord, has the time come for you to free Israel and restore our kingdom?"

He replied, "The Father alone has the authority to set those dates and times, and they are not for you to know. But you will receive power when the Holy Spirit comes upon you. And you will be my witnesses, telling people about me everywhere—in Jerusalem, throughout Judea, in Samaria, and to the ends of the earth." (Acts 1:6–8, NLT)

Abandoning their "zeal" and accepting the revelations of Christ's "reveal" for them, the apostles were finally able to "understand the scriptures" (Luke 24:45).

In like manner, when we move from a shallow *zeal* for Christ to the acceptance of the *reveal* necessary to complete our mandate to *go*, our *faith* gets rooted in the soil of our *desire* and is fed by our *commitment*, which produces *good fruit* from our *practice*.

4) **Practice:** "Practice" is learning to "be obedient to the will of God for your life." "Practice" produces fruit. The sweetness and maturity of your fruit is based on your obedience to the will of God for your life. *The work you must do in order to produce the "good fruit" is determined by the Father, instructed by Christ, and guided by the Holy Spirit. "Practice" grows "fruit for the kingdom of God!!!*

There were some present at that very time who told him about the Galileans whose blood Pilate had mingled with their sacrifices. And he answered them, "Do you think that these Galileans were worse sinners than all the other Galileans, because they suffered in this way? No, I tell you; but unless you repent, you will all likewise perish. Or those eighteen on whom the tower of Siloam fell and killed them: do you think that they were worse offenders than all the others who lived in Jerusalem? No, I tell you; but unless you repent, you will all likewise perish."

And he told this parable: "A man had a fig tree planted in his vineyard, and he came seeking fruit on it and found none. And he said to the vinedresser, 'Look, for three years now I have come seeking fruit on this fig tree, and I find none. Cut it down. Why should it use up the ground?' And he answered him, 'Sir, let it alone this year also, until I dig around it and put on manure. Then if it should bear fruit next year, well and good; but if not, you can cut it down.'"
(Luke 13:1–9, ESV)

The great "I *AM* that I *AM*" (God) has endowed every human being with "giftings" necessary to fulfill the reason for their birth. As mentioned earlier, the two most important days in a person's life are the day they were born and the day they discover the purpose of their birth (Mark Twain). To fulfill this purpose, we practice at becoming more and more obedient to God's will for our lives and the use of our talents and skills that God gave us. In order to work at these giftings, God, the Father, directs it through the Holy Spirit in order to achieve his goals. If we do not take the time to learn from the Father and "practice" being "obedient," the outcome could be fatal to our eternal existence.

For the kingdom of heaven is like a man traveling to a far country, who called his own servants and delivered his goods to them. And to one he gave five talents, to another two, and to another one, to each according to his own ability; and immediately he went on a journey. Then he who had received the five talents went and traded with them, and made another five talents. And likewise he who had received two gained two more also. But he who had received one went and dug in the ground, and hid his lord's money. After a long time the lord of those servants came and settled accounts with them.

So he who had received five talents came and brought five other talents, saying, "Lord, you delivered to me five talents; look, I have gained five more talents besides them." His lord said to him, "Well done, good and faithful servant; you were Faithful over a few things, I will make you ruler over many things. Enter into the joy of your lord." He also who had received two talents came and said, "Lord, you delivered to me two talents; look, I have gained two more talents besides them." His lord said to him, "Well done, good and faithful servant; you have been faithful over a few a few things, I will make you ruler over many things. Enter into the joy of your lord."

Then he who had received the one talent came and said, "Lord, I knew you to be a hard man, reaping where you have not sown, and gathering where you have not scattered seed. And I was afraid, and went and hid your talent in the ground. Look, there you have what is yours."

But his lord answered and said to him, "You wicked and lazy servant, you knew that I reap where I have not sown, and gather where

I have not scattered seed. So you ought to have deposited my money with the bankers, and at my coming I would have received back my own with interest. So take the talent from him, and give it to him who has ten talents.

For to everyone who has, more will be given, and he will have abundance; but from him who does not have, even what he has will be taken away. And cast the unprofitable servant into the outer darkness. There will be weeping and gnashing of teeth." (Matthew 25:14–30, NKJV)

It is never what "we think" must be done or "how it should be done." It's imperative that we address everything "God's way." This has to become a lifetime goal by moving step by step closer to the model of perfection the Father gave us in the Messiah, Jesus the Christ. The alternative is to become counterproductive to God's purpose for our lives.

And he entered Jerusalem and went into the temple. And when he had looked around at everything, as it was already late, he went out to Bethany with the twelve.

On the following day, when they came from Bethany, he was hungry. And seeing in the distance a fig tree in leaf, he went to see if he could find anything on it. When he came to it, he found nothing but leaves, for it was not the season for figs. And he said to it, "May no one ever eat fruit from you again." And his disciples heard it. (Mark 11:11–14, ESV)

As they passed by in the morning, they saw the fig tree withered away to its roots. And Peter remembered and said to him, "Rabbi, look! The fig tree that you cursed has withered." And Jesus answered them, "Have faith in God. Truly, I say to you, whoever says to this mountain, 'Be taken up and thrown into the sea,' and does not doubt in his heart, but believes that what he says will come to pass, it will be done for him. Therefore I tell you, whatever you ask in prayer, believe that you have received it, and it will be yours. And whenever you stand praying, forgive, if you have anything against anyone, so that your Father also who is in heaven may forgive you your trespasses." (Mark 11:20–26, ESV)

In your working toward producing good fruit for God by "practicing" growing in "obedience to God," you must be careful not to take on the characteristics of this fig tree. The tree giving the appearance of being in full development, with the display of its leaves, is barren and useless by not being obedient to its purpose as defined by God.

When the leaves appear on a fig tree, there is at least supposed to be a small edible knob known as a "taqsh." If the leaves are in full bloom and there are no taqsh or figs, then that tree will not be producing any fruit. It is existing for itself. It looks good, like it's fulfilling its purpose as defined by the Father, but that is only a pretense.

As a follower of Christ, you must be very careful not to fall into the same predicament.

Christ talked about the goats on the left (Matthew 25:31–46), where so-called followers of Christ, "undeveloped followers of Christ," were sentenced to eternal damnation of hell because they chose not to bear fruit, according to their purpose.

The key to producing "good fruit" for God is your heart.

Our hearts are filthy. When the Bible tells us to "guard our hearts," it's not telling us to guard it, like it's in Fort Knox, but to guard it because it is in Leavenworth Federal Prison. Our goal is to get our hearts as close to the heart of Christ as we can get them, when it's time to depart this world.

"The human heart is the most deceitful of all things, and desperately wicked. Who really knows how bad it is?

> But I, the LORD, search all hearts and examine secret motives. I give all people their due rewards, according to what their actions deserve." (Jeremiah 17:9 and 10, NLT)
>
> But Peter said to him, "Explain the parable to us." And he said, "Are you also still without understanding? Do you not see that whatever goes into the mouth passes into the stomach and is expelled? But what comes out of the mouth proceeds from the heart, and this defiles a person. For out of the heart come evil thoughts, murder, adultery, sexual immorality, theft, false witness, slander. These are what defile a person. But to eat with unwashed hands does not defile anyone." (Matthew 15:15–20, ESV)

Our hearts could never be like Christ's heart, but it is something that we can work toward step by step until the day we die. The only way conditions can rehabilitate our hearts to be more Christ-like is by:

- Accepting the directives of the Father
- Following the instructions given to us by Jesus the Christ in order to comply correctly with the Father's directives
- Availing ourselves of and utilizing the moment-by-moment guidance of the Holy Spirit

Thus says the LORD: "Cursed is the man who trust in man and makes flesh his strength, whose heart turns away from the LORD. He is like a shrub in the desert, and shall not see any good come. He shall dwell in the parched places of the wilderness, in an uninhabited salt land.

> Blessed is the man who trust in the LORD, whose trust is the LORD. He is like a tree planted by water, that sends out its roots by the stream,

and does not fear when heat comes, for its leaves remain green, and is not anxious in the year of drought, for it does not cease to bear fruit." (Jeremiah 17:5–8, ESV)

"The human heart is the most deceitful of all things, and desperately wicked. Who really knows how bad it is? But I, the LORD, search all hearts and examine secret motives. I give all people their due rewards, according to what their actions deserve." (Jeremiah 17:9 and 10, NLT)

Guard your heart above all else, for it determines the course of your life. (Proverbs 4:23, NLT)

There is a way which seemeth right unto a man, but the end thereof are the ways of death. (Proverbs 14:12, KJV)

Everyone that is proud in heart is an abomination to the LORD: though hand join in hand, he shall not be unpunished. (Proverbs 16:5, KJV)

Fire tests the purity of silver and gold, but the LORD tests the heart. (Proverbs 17:3, NLT)

There are many devices in a man's heart; nevertheless the counsel of the LORD, that shall stand. (Proverbs 19:21, KJV)

Though good advice lies deep within the heart, a person with understanding will draw it out. (Proverbs 20:5, NLT)

The LORD's light penetrates the human spirit, exposing every hidden motive. (Proverbs 20:27, NLT)

People may be right in their own eyes, but the LORD examines their heart. (Proverbs 21:2, NLT)

Haughty eyes, a proud heart, and evil actions are all sin. (Proverbs 21:4, NLT)

Apply thine heart unto instruction, and thine ears to the words of knowledge. (Proverbs 23:12, KJV)

"My child, if your heart is wise, my own heart will rejoice!" (Proverbs 23:15, NLT)

"My child, listen and be wise: Keep your heart on the right course." (Proverbs 23:19, NLT)

"O my son, give me your heart. May your eyes take delight in following my ways." (Proverb 23:26, NLT)

Rejoice not when thine enemy falleth, and let not thine heart be glad when he stumbleth: Lest the LORD see it, and it displease him, and he turns away his wrath from him. (Proverbs 24:17 and 18, KJV)

He that is of a proud heart stirreth up strife: but he that putteth his trust in the LORD shall be made fat. He that trusteth in his own heart is a fool: but whoso walketh wisely, he shall be delivered." (Proverbs 28:25 and 26, KJV)

The heart promotes the flesh and attempts to keep you from doing God's will for your life. It needs constant admonishment, prepping, and supervision to stay on course.

At that time Joshua summoned the Reubenites and the Gadites and the half-tribe of Manasseh, and said to them, "You have kept all that Moses the servant of the LORD commanded you and have obeyed my voice in all that I have commanded you. You have not forsaken your brothers these many days, down to this day, but have been careful to keep the charge of the LORD your God. And now the LORD your God has given rest to your brothers, as he promised them. Therefore turn and go to your tents in the land where your possession lies, which Moses the servant of the LORD gave you on the other side of the Jordan. Only be very careful to observe the commandment and the law that Moses the servant of the LORD commanded you, to love the LORD your God, and to walk in all his ways and to keep his commandments and to cling to him and to serve him with all your heart and with all your soul." So Joshua blessed them and sent them away, and they went to their tents. (Joshua 22:1–6, ESV)

Even after your heart has been on course to follow Christ's instructions, insurrection in your heart occurs. "Wants," "thoughts," "opinions," "position in the world," etc. create chaos. You've been listening intently to the Holy Spirit and having more and more of the Father's manual on how to operate your life revealed to you, but you still have to stay on guard.

Then Samuel took a flask of oil and poured it on his head, and kissed him and said: "Is it not because the LORD has anointed you commander over His inheritance? When you have departed from me today, you will find two men by Rachel's tomb in the territory of Benjamin at Zelzah; and they will say to you, 'The donkeys which you went to look for have been found. And now your father has ceased caring about the donkeys and is worrying about you, saying, "What shall I do about my son?"' Then you shall go on forward from there and come to the terebinth tree of Tabor. There three men going up to God at Bethel will meet you, one carrying three young goats, another carrying three loaves of bread, and another carrying a skin of wine. And they shall greet you and give you two loaves of bread, which you shall receive from their hands. After that you shall come to the hill of God where the Philistine garrison is. And it will happen, when you have come there to the city, that you will meet a group of prophets coming down from the high place with a stringed instrument, a tambourine, a flute, and a harp before them; and they will be prophesying. Then the Spirit of the LORD will come upon you, and you will prophesy with them and be turned into another man. And let it be, when these signs come to you, that you do as the occasion demands; for God is with you. You shall go down before me to Gilgal; and surely I will come down to you to offer burnt offerings and make sacrifices of peace offerings. Seven days you shall wait, till I come to you and show you what you should do."

So it was, when he had turned his back to go from Samuel, that God gave him another heart; and all those signs came to pass that day. When they came there to the hill, there was a group of prophets to meet him; then the Spirit of God came upon him, and he prophesied among them. And it happened, when all who knew him formerly saw that he indeed prophesied among the prophets, that the people said to one another, "What is this that has come upon the son of Kish? Is Saul also among the prophets?" Then a man from there answered and said, "But who is their father?" Therefore it became a proverb: "Is Saul also among the prophets?" And when he had finished prophesying, he went to the high place.

Then Saul's uncle said to him and his servant, "Where did you go?"

So he said, "To look for the donkeys. When we saw that they were nowhere to be found, we went to Samuel."

And Saul's uncle said, "Tell me please, what Samuel said to you."

So Saul said to his uncle, "He told us plainly that the donkeys had been found." But about the matter of the kingdom, he did not tell him what Samuel had said.

Then Samuel called the people together to the LORD at Mizpah, and said to the children of Israel, "Thus says the LORD God of Israel: 'I brought up Israel out of Egypt, and delivered you from the hand of the Egyptians and from the hand of all kingdoms and from those who oppressed you.' But you have today rejected your God, who Himself saved you from all your adversities and your tribulations; and have said to Him, 'No, set a king over us!' Now therefore, present yourselves before the LORD by your tribes and by your clans."

And when Samuel had caused all the tribes of Israel to come near, the tribe of Benjamin was chosen. When he had caused the tribe of Benjamin to come near by their families, the family of Matri was chosen. And Saul the son of Kish was chosen. But when they sought him, he could not be found. Therefore they inquired of the LORD further, "Has the man come here yet?"

And the LORD answered, "There he is, hidden among the equipment."

So they ran and brought him from there; and when he stood among the people, he was taller than any of the people from his shoulders upward. And Samuel said to all the people, "Do you see him whom the LORD has chosen, that there is no one like him among all the people?"

So all the people shouted and said, "Long live the king!"

Then Samuel explained to the people the behavior of royalty, and wrote it in a book and

laid it up before the LORD. And Samuel sent
all the people away, every man to his house. And
Saul also went home to Gibeah; and valiant men
went with him, whose hearts God had touched.
But some rebels said, "How can this man save
us?" So they despised him, and brought him no
presents. But he held his peace." (1 Samuel 10:1–
27, NKJV)

According to the "Dead Sea Scroll, 4QSam," King Nahash of
the Ammonites had been attacking the tribes of Reuben and Gad,
which had settled outside of the "promise land" (the wrong side of
the Jordan). His favorite practice was gouging out the right eye of the
Israelites. There were a few thousand men who had fled and lived in
Jabesh-Gilead.

Then Nahash the Ammonite came up and
encamped against Jabesh Gilead; and all the men
of Jabesh said to Nahash, "Make a covenant with
us, and we will serve you."
And Nahash the Ammonite answered them,
"On this condition I will make a covenant with
you, that I may put out all your right eyes, and
bring reproach on all Israel."
Then the elders of Jabesh said to him, "Hold
off for seven days, that we may send messengers
to all the territory of Israel. And then, if there is
no one to save us, we will come out to you."
So the messengers came to Gibeah of Saul
and told the news in the hearing of the people.
And all the people lifted up their voices and
wept. Now there was Saul, coming behind a herd
from the field; and Saul said, "What troubles the
people, that they weep?" And they told him the
words of the men of Jabesh. Then the Spirit of
God came upon Saul when he heard this news,

and his anger was greatly aroused. So he took a yoke of oxen and cut them in pieces, and sent them throughout all the territory of Israel by the hands of the messengers, saying, "Whoever does not go out with Saul and Samuel to battle, so it shall be done to his oxen."

And the fear of the LORD fell on the people, and they came out with one consent. When he numbered them in Bezek, the children of Israel were three hundred thousand, and the men of Judah thirty thousand. And they said to the messengers who came, "Thus you shall say to the men of Jabesh Gilead: 'Tomorrow, by the time the sun is hot, you shall have help.'" Then the messengers came and reported it to the men of Jabesh, and they were glad. Therefore the men of Jabesh said, "Tomorrow we will come out to you, and you may do with us whatever seems good to you."

So it was, on the next day, that Saul put the people in three companies; and they came into the midst of the camp in the morning watch, and killed Ammonites until the heat of the day. And it happened that those who survived were scattered, so that no two of them were left together.

Then the people said to Samuel, "Who is he who said, 'Shall Saul reign over us?' Bring the men, that we may put them to death."

But Saul said, "Not a man shall be put to death this day, for today the LORD has accomplished salvation in Israel."

Then Samuel said to the people, "Come, let us go to Gilgal and renew the kingdom there." So all the people went to Gilgal, and there they made Saul king before the LORD in Gilgal. There they made sacrifices of peace offerings before the

LORD, and there Saul and all the men of Israel rejoiced greatly. (1 Samuel 11:1–15, NKJV)

Saul reigned one year; and when he had reigned two years over Israel, Saul chose for himself three thousand men of Israel. Two thousand were with Saul in Michmash and in the mountains of Bethel, and a thousand were with Jonathan in Gibeah of Benjamin. The rest of the people he sent away, every man to his tent.

And Jonathan attacked the garrison of the Philistines that was in Geba, and the Philistines heard of it. Then Saul blew the trumpet throughout all the land, saying, "Let the Hebrews hear!" Now all Israel heard it said that Saul had attacked a garrison of the Philistines, and that Israel had also become an abomination to the Philistines. And the people were called together to Saul at Gilgal.

Then the Philistines gathered together to fight with Israel, thirty thousand chariots and six thousand horsemen, and people as the sand which is on the seashore in multitude. And they came up and encamped in Michmash, to the east of Beth Aven. When the men of Israel saw that they were in danger (for the people were distressed), then the people hid in caves, in thickets, in rocks, in holes, and in pits. And some of the Hebrews crossed over the Jordan to the land of Gad and Gilead.

As for Saul, he was still in Gilgal, and all the people followed him trembling. Then he waited seven days, according to the time set by Samuel. But Samuel did not come to Gilgal; and the people were scattered from him. So Saul said, "Bring a burnt offering and peace offerings here to me." And he offered the burnt offering. Now it happened, as soon as he had finished presenting the burnt offering, that Samuel came; and Saul went out to meet him, that he might greet him.

And Samuel said, "What have you done?"

Saul said, "When I saw that the people were scattered from me, and that you did not come within the days appointed, and that the Philistines gathered together at Michmash, then I said, 'The Philistines will now come down on me at Gilgal, and I have not made supplication to the LORD.' Therefore I felt compelled, and offered a burnt offering."

And Samuel said to Saul, "You have done foolishly. You have not kept the commandment of the LORD your God, which He commanded you. For now the LORD would have established your kingdom over Israel forever. But now your kingdom shall not continue. The LORD has sought for Himself a man after His own heart, and the LORD has commanded him to be commander over His people, because you have not kept what the LORD commanded you." (1 Samuel 13:1–14, NKJV)

"Practice," being "obedient to God," requires your complete attention at all times. During your efforts to produce "good fruit," help others to get a step closer to God. If you stay resolute in listening to the Holy Spirit, God will:

- Guide you into an understanding of the giftings that he has placed within you and "reveal" more of the "personal operational manual" he has written for your life.
- Help you "prune" your "free will" that constantly wells up from the depths of your heart and wants to compete with God, concerning the direction of your life.

- Show you how to "clean up and remove" earthly impediments like unforgiveness, self-worth issues, "friendly fire" from family and friends, zeal-laden followers of religion, and the world in general.
- Enhance your "efforts" in everything you do to advance the kingdom of God, according to what the Father wants and how he wants it.

Where do wars and fights come from among you? Do they not come from your desires for pleasure that war in your members? You lust and do not have. You murder and covet and cannot obtain. You fight and war. Yet you do not have because you do not ask. You ask and do not receive, because you ask amiss, that you may spend it on your pleasures. Adulterers and adulteresses! Do you not know that friendship with the world is enmity with God? Whoever therefore wants to be a friend of the world makes himself an enemy of God. Or do you think that the Scripture says in vain, "The Spirit who dwells in us yearns jealously"?

But He gives more grace. Therefore He says: "God resists the proud, But gives grace to the humble."

Therefore submit to God. Resist the devil and he will flee from you. Draw near to God and He will draw near to you. Cleanse your hands, you sinners; and purify your hearts, you double minded. Lament and mourn and weep! Let your laughter be turned to mourning and your joy to gloom. Humble yourselves in the sight of the LORD, and He will lift you up.

Do not speak evil of one another, brethren. He who speaks evil of a brother and judges his brother, speaks evil of the law and judges the law.

But if you judge the law, you are not a doer of the law but a judge. There is one Lawgiver, who is able to save and to destroy. Who are you to judge another?

Come now, you who say, "Today or tomorrow we will go to such and such a city, spend a year there, buy and sell, and make a profit"; whereas you do not know what will happen tomorrow. For what is your life? It is even a vapor that appears for a little time and then vanishes away. Instead you ought to say, "If the Lord wills, we shall live and do this or that." But now you boast in your arrogance. All such boasting is evil.

Therefore, to him who knows to do good and does not do it, to him it is sin. (James 4:1–17, NKJV)

What causes quarrels and what causes fights among you? Is it not this, that your passions are at war within you? You desire and do not have, so you murder. You covet and cannot obtain, so you fight and quarrel. You do not have, because you do not ask. You ask and do not receive, because you ask wrongly, to spend it on your passions. You adulterous people! Do you not know that friendship with the world is enmity with God? Therefore whoever wishes to be a friend of the world makes himself an enemy of God. Or do you suppose it is to no purpose that the Scriptures says, "He yearns jealously over the spirit that he has made to dwell in us"? But he gives more grace. Therefore it says, "God opposes the proud but gives grace to the humble." Submit yourselves therefore to God. Resist the devil, and he will flee from you. Draw near to God, and he will draw near to you. Cleanse your hands, you sinners, and purify your hearts, you double-minded. Be wretched and mourn and weep. Let your laughter be turned to mourning and your joy to gloom. Humble yourselves before the Lord, and he will exalt you.

Do not speak evil against one another, brothers. The one who speaks against a brother or judges his brother, speaks evil against the law and judges the law. But if you judge the law, you are not a doer of the law but a judge. There is only one lawgiver and judge, he who is able to save and to destroy. But who are you to judge your neighbor?

Come now, you who say, "Today or tomorrow we will go into such and such a town and spend a year there and trade and make a profit"—yet you do not know what tomorrow will bring. What is your life? For you are a mist that appears for a little time and then vanishes. Instead you ought to say, "If the Lord wills, we will live and do this or that." As it is, you boast in your arrogance. All such boasting is evil. So whoever knows the right thing to do and fails to do it, for him it is sin. (James 4:1–17, ESV)

When your "faith" is rooted in "desire" and nourished with "commitment" and pruned with the "practice" of being "obedient to the will of God" for your life, your life will produce the "good fruit" of bringing others closer to God. That is what our heavenly Father requires of you, and that is what will fulfill "the desires of your heart."

Fret not yourself because of evildoers; be not envious of wrongdoers! For they will soon fade like the grass and wither like the green herb. Trust in the LORD, and do good; dwell in the land and befriend faithfulness. Delight yourself in the LORD, and he will give you the desires of your heart. Commit your way to the LORD; trust in him, and he will act. He will bring forth your righteousness as the light, and your justice as the noonday. Be still before the LORD and wait patiently for him; fret not yourself over the one who prospers in his way, over the man who carries out evil devices! Refrain from anger, and forsake wrath! Fret not yourself; it tends only to evil. For the evildoers shall be cut off, but those who wait for the LORD shall inherit the land." (Psalm 37:1–9, ESV)

Section 3

"Prayer Makes the Difference!"

Chapter 7

UNDERSTANDING PRAYER AND MEDITATION IN YOUR HEARING LIFE

You may be asking, "What is it that I need to know about prayer?" Great question. The Lord taught us the basics of prayer (the "Our Father," Matthew 6:9–13), but tradition and human folkways and mores have altered and mitigated the power of prayer. Have you ever been in a prayer session where you don't feel the prayers are ascending to the throne of God but bouncing off the walls and hitting you in the head? That is usually not based on intent, unless the person aims to put on a show, but on the infusion of tradition and repetition (rote).

The goal here is to increase the effectiveness of your communication with the Father. In order to do this, it will be necessary to reaffirm the "directives" of the Father, the "instructions" of Jesus the Christ as to how to do it, and the "guidance" of the Holy Spirit as to how to carry out and accomplish our goal of producing "good fruit" for the Father.

- The "directives" of the Father as to what to do

  Don't become partners with those who do not believe. For what partnership is there between righteousness and lawlessness? Or what fellowship does light have with darkness? What agreement does Christ have with Belial? Or what does a believer have in common with an unbeliever? And what agreement does the temple of God have with idols? For we are the temple of the living God, as God said: "I will dwell and walk among them, and I will be their God, and they will be my people. Therefore, come out from among them and be separate, says the Lord; do not touch any unclean thing, and I will welcome you. And I will be a Father to you, and you will be sons and daughters to me, says the Lord Almighty. (2 Corinthians 6:14–18, CSB)

- The "instructions" of Jesus the Christ as to how to do it

So Jesus said to them, "When you have lifted up the Son of Man, then you will know that I am he, and that I do nothing on my own authority, but speak just as the Father taught me. And he who sent me is with me. He has not left me alone, for I always do the things that are pleasing to him." As he was saying these things, many believed in him." (John 8:28–30, ESV)

His disciples said, "Ah, now you are speaking plainly and not using figurative speech! Now we know that you know all things and do not need anyone to question you; this is why we believe that you came from God." Jesus answered them, "Do you know believe? Behold, the hour is coming, indeed it has come, when you will be scattered, each to his own home, and will leave me alone. Yet I am not alone, for the Father is with me. I have said these things to you, that in me you may have peace. In the world you will have tribulation. But take heart; I have overcome the world." (John 16:29–33, ESV)

Jesus spoke these things, looked up to heaven, and said, "Father, the hour has come. Glorify your Son so that the Son may glorify you, since you gave him authority over all flesh, so that he may give eternal life to everyone you have given him. This is eternal life: that they may know you, the only true God, and the one you have sent—Jesus Christ. I have glorified you on the earth by completing the work you gave me to do. Now, Father, glorify me in your presence with that glory I had with you before the world existed.

I have revealed your name to the people you gave me from the world. They were yours, you gave them to me, and they have kept your word. Now they know that everything you have given is from you, because I have given them the words you gave me. They have received them and have known for certain that I came from you. They have believed that you sent me.

I pray for them. I am not praying for the world but for those you have given me, because they are yours. Everything I have is yours, and everything you have is mine, and I am glorified in them. I am no longer in the world, but they are in the world, and I am coming to you. Holy Father, protect them by your name that you have given me, so that they may be one as we are one. While I was with them, I was protecting them by your name that you have given me. I guarded them and not one of them is lost, except the son of destruction, so that the Scripture may be fulfilled. Now I am coming to you, and I speak these things in the world so that they may have my joy completed in them. I have given them your word. The world hated them because they are not of the world, just as I am not of this world. I am not praying that you take them out of the world but that you protect them from the evil one. They are not of the world, just as I am not of the world. Sanctify them by the truth; your word is truth. As you sent me into the world, I also have sent them into the world. I sanctify myself for them, so that they also may be sanctified by the truth.

I pray not only for these, but also for those who believe in me through their word. May they all be one, as you, Father, are in me and I am in you. May they also be in us, so that the world may believe you sent me. I have given them the glory you have given me, so that they may be one as we are one. I am in them and you are in me, so that they may be made completely one, that the world may know you have sent me and have loved them as you have loved me.

Father, I want those you have given me to be with me where I am, so that they will see my glory, which you have given me because you loved me before the world's foundation. Righteous Father, the world has not known you. However, I have known you, and they have known that you sent me. I made your name known to them and will continue to make it known, so that the love you have loved me with may be in them and I may be in them." (John 17:1–26, CSB)

- The "guidance" of the Holy Spirit as to how to carry out and accomplish our goal for the Father

But you have been anointed by the Holy One, and you all have knowledge. I write to you, not because you do not know the truth, but because you know it, and because no lie is of the truth. Who is the liar but he who denies that Jesus is the Christ? This is the antichrist, he who denies the Father and the Son. No one who denies the Son has the Father. Whoever confesses the Son has the Father also. Let what you heard from the beginning abide in you. If what you heard from the beginning abides in you, then you too will abide in the Son and in the Father. And this is the promise that he made to us—eternal life.

I write these things to you about those who are trying to deceive you. But the anointing that you received from him abides in you, and you have no need that anyone should teach you. But as his anointing teaches you about everything, and is true, and is no lie—just as it has taught you abide in him. (1 John 2:20–27, ESV)

We often do not ask the Holy Spirit for guidance. We let our own understanding and wisdom guide us. Our goal in life, which we should strive toward until our journey on this planet is over, should be to submit everything in life to the Holy Spirit.

This should also be the governing approach to our prayer life. Before we utter or think of what to say in prayer, we must ask the Holy Spirit what to pray about.

"So then, brothers, we are debtors, not to the flesh, to live according to the flesh. For if you live according to the flesh you will die, but if by the Spirit you put to death the deeds of the body, you will live. For all who are led by the Spirit of God are sons of God. For you did not receive the spirit of slavery to fall back into fear, but you have received the Spirit of adoption as sons, by whom we cry, 'Abba! Father!' The Spirit himself bears witness with our spirit that we are children of God, and if children, then heirs—heirs of God and fellow heirs with Christ, provided we suffer with him in order that we may also be glorified with him.

For I consider that sufferings of this present time are not worth comparing with the glory that is to be revealed to us. For the creation waits with eager longing for the revealing of the sons to God. For the creation was subjected to futility, not willingly, but because of him who subjected it, in hope that the creation itself will be set free from its bondage to corruption and obtain the freedom of the glory of the children of God. For we know that the whole creation has been groaning together in the pains of childbirth until now. And not only the creation, but we ourselves, who have the firstfruits of the Spirit, groan inwardly as we wait eagerly for adoption as sons, the redemption of our bodies. For in this hope we were saved. Now hope that is seen is not hope. For who hopes for what he sees? But if we hope for what we do not see, we wait for it with patience.

Likewise the Spirit helps us in our weakness. For we do not know what to pray for as we ought, but the Spirit himself intercedes for us with groanings too deep for words. And he who searches hearts knows what is the mind of the Spirit, because the Spirit interceded for the saints according to the will of God. And we know that for those who love God all things work together for good, for those who are called according to his purpose. For those whom he foreknew he also predestined to be conformed to the image of his Son, in order that he might be the firstborn among many brothers. And those whom he predestined he also called, and those whom he called he also justified, and those whom he justified he also glorified." (Romans 8:12–30, ESV)

And the gospel must first be published among all nations.

But when they shall lead you, and deliver you up, take no thought beforehand what ye shall speak, neither do ye premeditate: but whatsoever shall be given you in that hour, that speak ye: for it is not ye that speak, but the Holy Ghost. (Mark 13:10 and 11, KJV)

And Jesus being full of the Holy Ghost returned from Jordan, and was led by the Spirit into the wilderness. (Luke 4:1, KJV)

Now there was a man in Jerusalem, whose name was Simeon, and this man was righteous and devout, waiting for the consolation of Israel, and the Holy Spirit was upon him. And it had been revealed to him by the Holy Spirit that he would not see death before he had seen the Lord's Christ. And he came in the Spirit into the temple, and when the parents brought in the child Jesus, to do for him according to the custom of the Law, he took him up in his arms and blessed God and said, "Lord, now you are letting your servant depart in peace, according to your word; for my eyes have seen your salvation that you have prepared in the presence of all peoples, a light for revelation to the Gentiles, and for glory to your people Israel."

And his father and his mother marveled at what was said about him. And Simeon blessed them and said to Mary his mother, "Behold, this child is appointed for the fall and rising of many in Israel, and for a sign that is opposed (and a sword will pierce through your own soul also), so

that thoughts from many hearts may be revealed."
(Luke 2:25–35, ESV)

Likewise the Spirit also helpeth our infirmities: for we know not what we should pray for as we ought: but the Spirit itself maketh intercession for us with groanings which cannot be uttered. (Romans 8:26, KJV)

And the Father who knows all hearts knows what the Spirit is saying, for the Spirit pleads for us believers in harmony with God's own will. And we know that God causes everything to work together for the good of those who love God and are called according to his purpose for them. (Romans 8:27 and 28, NLT)

"Therefore, dear brothers and sisters, dear brothers and sisters, you have no obligation to do what your sinful nature urges you to do. For if you live by its dictates, you will die. But if through the power of the Spirit you put to death the deeds of your sinful nature, you will live. For all who are led by the Spirit of God are children of God." (Romans 8:12–14, NLT)

At this point there is a need to clarify the utilization of "speaking in tongues." "Speaking in tongues" is a communication process shared between God the Father and that piece of the Father that he places in every human being known as "spirit" (remember we are made up of three parts: flesh, spirit, and soul). So "speaking in tongues" is a conversation between God the Father and his tracking device, his spirit in us. God only uses his tracking device "speaking in tongues" one of two ways:

- Privately – In the privacy of yourself, your spirit is speaking to God the Father, in "tongues."
- Publicly – God gives an individual the ability to translate your spirit speaking in "tongues" for the benefit of all who

may hear. If there is no one assigned by God to interrupt, then the "tongues" do not benefit the people hearing it.

Go after a life of love as if your life depended on it—because it does. Give yourselves to the gifts God gives you. Most of all, try to proclaim his truth. If you praise him in the private language of tongues, God understands you but no one else does, for you are sharing intimacies just between you and him. But when you proclaim his truth in everyday speech, you're letting others in on the truth so that they can grow and be strong and experience his presence with you.

The one who prays using a private "prayer language" certainly gets a lot out of it, but proclaiming God's truth to the church in its common language brings the whole church into growth and strength. I want all of you to develop intimacies with God in prayer, but please don't stop with that. Go on and proclaim his clear truth to others. It's more important that everyone have access to the knowledge and love of God in language everyone understands than that you go off and cultivate God's presence in a mysterious prayer language—unless, of course, there is someone who can interpret what you are saying for the benefit of all.

Think, friends: If I come to you and all I do is pray privately to God in a way only he can understand, what are you going to get out of that? If I don't address you plainly with some insight or truth or proclamation or teaching, what help am I to you? If musical instruments—flutes, say, or harps—aren't played so that each note is distinct and in tune, how will anyone be able to catch the melody and enjoy the music? If the trumpet call can't be distinguished, will anyone show up for the battle?

So if you speak in a way no one can understand, what's the point of opening your mouth? There are many languages in the world and they all mean something to someone. But if I don't understand the language, it's not going to do me much good. It's no different with you. Since you're so eager to participate in what God is doing, why don't you concentrate on doing what helps everyone in the church?

So, when you pray in your private prayer language, don't hoard the experience for yourself. Pray for the insight and ability to bring others into that intimacy. If I pray in tongues, my spirit prays but my mind lies fallow, and all that intelligence is wasted. So what's the solution? The answer is simple enough. Do both. I should be spiritually free and expressive as I pray, but I should be thoughtful and mindful as I pray. I should sing with my spirit, and sing with my mind. If you give a blessing using your private prayer language, which no one else understands, how can some outsider who has just shown up and has no idea what's going on know when to say "Amen"? Your blessing might be beautiful, but you have very effectively cut that person out of it.

I'm grateful to God for the gift of praying in tongues that he gives us for praising him, which leads to wonderful intimacies we enjoy with him. I enter into this as much or more than any of you. But when I'm in church assembled for worship, I'd rather say five words that everyone can understand and learn from than say ten thousand that sound to others like gibberish.

To be perfectly frank, I'm getting exasperated with your infantile thinking. How long before you grow up and use your head—your adult head? It's all right to have childlike unfamiliarity with evil; a simple no is all that's needed there. But there's far more to saying yes to something. Only mature and well-exercised intelligence can save you from falling into gullibility. It's written in Scripture that God said,

In strange tongues and from the mouths of strangers I will preach to this people, but they'll neither listen nor believe.

So where does it get you, all this speaking in tongues no one understands? It doesn't help believers, and it only gives unbelievers something to gawk at. Plain truth-speaking, on the other hand, goes straight to the heart of believers and doesn't get in the way of unbelievers. If you come together as a congregation and some unbelieving outsiders walk in on you as you're all praying in tongues, unintelligible to each other and to them, won't they assume you've taken leave of your senses and get out of there as fast as they can? But if some unbelieving outsiders walk in on a service where people are speaking out God's truth, the plain words will bring them up against the truth and probe their hearts. Before you know it, they're going to be on their faces before God, recognizing that God is among you. (1 Corinthians 14:1–25, MSG)

The first thing that you must remind yourself is that prayer and meditation are tantamount for having a "hearing life." The incorporation of both is necessary to producing the "good fruit" that God requires. Some preparatory work must be done to better prepare us to improve our ability to pray and meditate.

This is what the LORD says to the people of Judah and Jerusalem: "Plow up the hard ground of your hearts! Do not waste your good seed among thorns. O people of Judah and Jerusalem, surrender your pride and power. Change your hearts before the LORD, or my anger will burn like an unquenchable fire because of all your sins." (Jeremiah 4:3 and 4, NLT)

Don't let anyone capture you with empty philosophies and high-sounding nonsense that come from human thinking and from the spiritual powers of this world, rather than from Christ. For in Christ lives all the fullness of God in a human body. So you also are complete through your union with Christ, who is the head over every ruler and authority. (Colossians 2:8–10, NLT)

If then you have been raised with Christ, seek the things that are above, where Christ is, seated at the right hand of God. Set your minds on things that are above, not on things that are on earth. For you have died, and your life is hidden with Christ in God. When Christ who is your life appears, then you also will appear with him in glory.

Put to death therefore what is earthly in you: sexual immorality, impurity, passion, evil desire, and covetousness, which is idolatry. On account of these the wrath of God is coming. In these you too once walked, when you were living in them. But now you must put them all away: anger, wrath, malice, slander, and obscene talk from your mouth. Do not lie to one another, seeing that you have put off the old self with its practices and have put on the new self, which is being renewed in knowledge after the image of its

creator. Here there is not Greek and Jew, circumcised and uncircumcised, barbarian, Scythian,
slave, free; but Christ is all, and in all.

Put on then, as God chosen ones, holy
and beloved, compassionate hearts, kindness,
humility, meekness, and patience, bearing with
one another and, if one has a complaint against
another, forgiving each other; as the Lord has forgiven you, so you also must forgive. And above
all these put on love, which binds everything
together in perfect harmony. And let the peace of
Christ rule in your hearts, to which indeed you
were called in one body. And be thankful. Let the
word of Christ dwell in you richly, teaching and
admonishing one another in all wisdom, singing psalms and hymns and spiritual songs, with
thankfulness in your hearts to God. And whatever you do, in word or deed, do everything in the
name of the Lord Jesus, giving thanks to God the
Father through him. (Colossians 3:1–17, ESV)

The world may offer you trinkets and components to focus on,
but God is the only entity that we need to learn to "pray" to and
"meditate" on. Both require us to improve our "hearing life" in order
to make our prayer life effective and our meditation time decisive.
You need both to make your "hearing life" complete.
Effective prayer, that is, prayer that garners an audience with
our Father, requires spiritual preparation. We can pray anytime, anywhere, and in any situation. Our goal is to make sure we are not
holding pride, unforgiveness, hatred, dislike, confrontation, and/or
ulterior motives, as we approach the throne.

"Dear children, keep away from anything
that might take God's place in your hearts." (1
John 5:21, NLT)

"Paul, an apostle of Christ Jesus by command of God our Savior and of Christ Jesus our hope, to Timothy, my true child in the faith: Grace, mercy, and peace from God the Father and Christ Jesus our Lord.

As I urged you when I was going to Macedonia, remain at Ephesus so that you may charge certain persons not to teach any different doctrine, nor to devote themselves to myths and endless genealogies, which promote speculations rather than the stewardship from God that is by faith. The aim of our charge is love that issues from a pure heart and a good conscience and a sincere faith. Certain persons, by swerving from these, have wandered away into vain discussion, desiring to be teachers of the Law, without understanding either what they are saying or the things about which they make confident assertions." (1 Timothy 1:1–7, ESV)

Followers of Christ mitigate the power of their prayers by being entangled in these circumstances and conditions presented by the world and its spiritual thinking.

Therefore, since God in his mercy has given us this new way, we never give up. We reject all shameful deeds and underhanded methods. We don't try to trick anyone or distort the word of God. We tell the truth before God, and all who are honest know this. (2 Corinthians 4:1 and 2, NLT)

Chapter 8

THE AWAKENING: HEARING AIDS FOR YOUR HEARING LIFE

There is some prep work (hearing aids) that must be done to make your "hearing life" (prayer and meditation) more impactful in your mission to "go" and produce "good fruit" for the Father. Your spiritual and/or religious leader(s) will be your sous-chef (supporter in the process) in this venture, but you must take the lead for yourself.

Webster defines "awakening" as an adjective, rousing, quickening, and as a noun, the act of awaking from sleep; a revival of interest or attention; a recognition, realization, or coming into awareness of something; a renewal of interest.

It's not for me to determine where you are on the continuum of "awakening"; that is between you and the Holy Spirit.

> "I suspect you would never intend this, but this is what happens. When you attempt to live by your own religious plans and projects, you are cut off from Christ, you fall out of grace. Meanwhile we expectantly wait for a satisfying relationship with the Spirit. For in Christ, neither our most conscientious religion nor disregard of religion

amounts to anything. What matters is something far more interior: faith expressed in love.

You were running superbly! Who cut in on you, deflecting you from the true course of obedience? This detour doesn't come from the One who called you into the race in the first place. And please don't toss this off as insignificant. It only takes a minute amount of yeast, you know, to permeate an entire loaf of bread. Deep down, the Master has given me confidence that you will not defect. But the one who is upsetting you, whoever he is, will bear the divine judgment." (Galatians 5:4–10, MSG)

Well the one who is upsetting you is Satan and his imps. They are constantly working at destroying your "peace of mind" and destroying your mission of producing "good fruit" by bringing human beings closer to God.

It makes no sense to "live in Hell, on your way to Heaven!!!

This is because our "hearing life" needs "hearing aids" in order to hear and utilize the Holy Spirit's global positioning system (holy GPS). The moment you wake up to the moment you fall asleep, your holy GPS must be on. The "hearing aids" will allow you to keep your holy GPS switch on and activate a more consistent use of "meditation." Thus with "prayer and "meditation," you have a "guided path."

The LORD says, "I will guide you along the best pathway for your life. I will advise you and watch over you. Do not be like a senseless horse or mule that needs a bit and bridle to keep it under control." (Psalm 32:8 and 9, NLT)

Let's explore some "hearing aids" that are foundational to our task:

- **That all "people" (men and women) know God**

"I will climb up to my watchtower and stand at my guardpost. There I will wait to see what the LORD says and how he will answer my complaint.

Then the LORD said to me, 'Write my answer plainly on tablets, so that a runner can carry the correct message to others. This vision is for a future time. It describes the end, and it will be fulfilled. If it seems slow in coming, wait patiently, for it will surely take place. It will not be delayed.

Look at the proud! They trust in themselves, and their lives are crooked. But the righteous will live by their faithfulness to God. Wealth is treacherous, and the arrogant are never at rest. They open their mouths as wide as the grave, and like death, they are never satisfied. In their greed they have gathered up many nations and swallowed many peoples.'" (Habakkuk 2:1–5, NLT)

"For I am not ashamed of the gospel, for it is the power of God for salvation to everyone who believes, to the Jew first and also to the Greek. For in it the righteousness of God is revealed from faith for faith, as it is written, 'The righteous shall live by faith.'

For the wrath of God is revealed from heaven against all ungodliness and unrighteousness of men, who by their unrighteousness suppress the truth. For what can be known about God is plan to them, because God has shown it to them. For his invisible attributes, namely, his eternal power and divine nature, have been clearly perceived, ever since the creation of the world, in the things that have been made. So they are without excuse. For although they knew God, they did not honor him as God or give thanks to him, but they became futile in their thinking, and their foolish hearts were darkened. Claiming to be wise, they became fools, and exchanged the glory of the immortal God for images resembling mortal man and birds and animals and creeping things.

Therefore God gave them up in the lusts of their hearts to impurity, to the dishonoring of their bodies among themselves, because they exchanged the truth about God for a lie and worshiped and served the creature rather than the Creator, who is blessed forever! Amen." (Romans 1:16–25, ESV)

- **What makes the Holy Spirit's global positioning system so necessary for our "peace of mind" and our mission to produce "good fruit" for the Father?**

Our "holy GPS" is based on God being **omnipotent**, "all powerful"; **omniscient**, "all knowing"; and **omnipresent**, "everywhere."

Omnipotent

God is "all powerful," "all mighty." Nothing can compare with God. God is above "human logic."

> "And I heard as it were the voice of a great multitude, and as the voice of many waters, and as the voice of mighty thunderings, saying, Alleluia: for the Lord God omnipotent reigneth." (Revelation 19:6, KJV)
>
> First this: God created the Heavens and Earth—all you see, all you don't see. Earth was a soup of nothingness, a bottomless emptiness, an inky blackness. God's Spirit brooded like a

bird above the watery abyss. (Genesis 1:1 and 2, MSG)

Jesus looked at them intently and said, "Humanly speaking, it is impossible. But with God everything is possible." (Matthew 19:26, NLT)

"I know the greatness of the LORD—that our Lord is greater than any other god. The LORD does whatever pleases him throughout all heaven and earth, and on the seas and in their depths. He causes the clouds to rise over the whole earth. He sends the lightning with the rain and releases the wind from his storehouses." (Psalms 135:5–7, NLT)

Then came the word of the LORD unto Jeremiah, saying, "Behold, I am the LORD, the God of all flesh: is there anything too hard for me?" (Jeremiah 32:26 and 27, KJV)

For nothing is impossible with God. (Luke 1:37, NLT)

"For I can do everything through Christ, who gives me strength." (Philippians 4:13, NLT)

Omniscient

God is "all knowing." God is above "human logic." Nothing can be hidden from "I Am That I Am" [Exodus 3:14 is where this reference can be found; this is from the KJV].

"Your word is a lamp to guide my feet and a light for my path." (Psalm 119: 105, NLT)

For the word of God is alive and powerful. It is sharper than the sharpest two-edged sword, cutting between soul and spirit, between joint and marrow. It exposes our innermost thoughts and desires. Nothing in all creation is hidden from God. Everything is naked and exposed before his eyes, and he is the one to whom we are accountable. (Hebrews 4:12 and 13, NLT)

"The human heart is the most deceitful of all things, and desperately wicked. Who really knows how bad it is? But I, the LORD, search all hearts and examine secret motives. I give all people their due rewards, according to what their actions deserve." (Jeremiah 17:9 and 10, NLT)

"If we had forgotten the name of our God or spread our hands in prayer to foreign gods, God would surely have known it, for he knows the secrets of every heart." (Psalm 44:20 and 21, NLT)

But it was to us that God revealed these things by his Spirit. For his Spirit searches out everything and shows us God's deep secrets. (1 Corinthians 2:10, NLT)

Omnipresence

God is "everywhere" at the same time period.

"LORD, you have searched me and know me. You know when I sit down and when I stand up; you understand my thoughts from far away. You observe my travels and my rest; you are aware of all my ways. Before a word is on my tongue, you know all about it, LORD. You have encircled me; you have placed your hand on me. This wondrous knowledge is beyond me. It is lofty; I am unable to reach it. Where can I go to escape your Spirit? Where can I flee from your presence? If I go to heaven, you are there; If I make my bed in Sheol, you are there. If I live at the eastern horizon or settle at the western limits, even there your hand will lead me; your right hand will hold on to me. If I say, 'Surely the darkness will hide me, and the light around me will be night'—even the darkness is not dark to you. The night shines like the day; darkness and light are alike to you." (Psalms 139:1–12, CSB)

But the LORD is in his holy Temple; the LORD still rules from heaven. He watches everyone closely, examining every person on earth.

The LORD examines both the righteous and the wicked. He hates those who love violence. (Psalm 11:4 and 5, NLT)

"Can anyone hide from me in a secret place? Am I not everywhere in all the heavens and earth?" says the LORD." (Jeremiah 23:24, NLT)

"Don't you realize that all of you together are the temple of God and that the Spirit of God lives in you?" (1 Corinthians 3:16, NLT)

On that day the announcement to Jerusalem will be, "Cheer up, Zion! Don't be afraid!

For the LORD your God is living among you. He is a mighty savior. He will take delight in you with gladness. With his love, he will calm all your fears. He will rejoice over you with joyful song." (Zephaniah 3:16 and 17, NLT)

"Teach these new disciples to obey all the commands I have given you. And be sure of this: I am with you always, even to the end of the age." (Matthew 28:20, NLT)

Christ is the visible image of the invisible God. He existed before anything was created and is supreme over all creation, for through him God created everything in the heavenly realms and on earth. He made the things we can see and the things we can't see—such as thrones, kingdoms, rulers, and authorities in the unseen world. Everything was created through him and for him.

He existed before anything else, and he holds all creation together. Christ is also the head of the church, which is his body. He is the beginning, supreme over all who rise from the dead. So he is first in everything.

For God in all his fullness was pleased to live in Christ, and through him God reconciled everything to himself. He made peace with everything in heaven and on earth by means of Christ's blood on the cross. (Colossians 1:15–20, NLT)

To develop the "hearing life," we need to go forward. There are some "hearing aids" we must incorporate and "do" and some things we must "surrender":

- [Do] – You must forgive everyone that has ever harmed, hurt, or caused damage to you while they were sinning against you and God. This is not for their sake but yours. God cannot forgive you of your sins until you forgive others.

If you forgive those who sin against you, your heavenly Father will forgive you. But if you refuse to forgive others, your Father will not forgive your sins. (Matthew 6:14 and 15, NLT)

The Holy Spirit who was sent by the Father operates in our lives with the same attributes of the Father. Remember all humans have three parts, flesh, soul, and the "spirit of God."

The battle is over our souls. With the introduction of "pride" (the original sin) combined with our ability to use "free will," you and I have hurt people, created harm, and sinned daily. We shut down our holy GPS in order to do what we thought was wise to do with our earthly understanding.

- [Do] – Accept your forgiveness from God.

Jesus knew that the Father had given him authority over everything and that he had come from God and would return to God. So he got up from the table, took off his robe, wrapped a towel around his waist, and poured water into a basin. Then he began to wash the disciples' feet, drying them with the towel he had around him." (John 13:3–5, NLT)

When Jesus came to Simon Peter, Peter said to him, "Lord, are you going to wash my feet?"

Jesus replied, "You don't understand now what I am doing, but someday you will."

"No," Peter protested, "you will never ever wash my feet!"

Jesus replied, "Unless I wash you, you won't belong to me."

Simon Peter exclaimed, "Then wash my hands and head as well, Lord, not just my feet!"

Jesus replied, "A person who has bathed all over does not need to wash, except for the feet, to be entirely clean. And you disciples are clean, but not all of you." For Jesus knew who would betray him. That is what he meant when he said, "Not all of you are clean." (John 13:6–11, NLT)

You and I sin daily, but that does not mean you have lost or jeopardized your salvation.

Only you and God know if you have accepted the free gift of salvation that Jesus the Christ, the Son of the Father, gave us. God knows your heart; don't end up being one of the "goats on the left-hand side"—Matthew 25:31–46.

The gravity of our sins against God and other human beings can sometime create a devil-inspired thought that makes us feel that just asking and receiving forgiveness from God is not enough.

Some individuals have a difficult time approaching a relationship with God because of the hurt, pain, betrayal, and suffering imposed on them by you and me or past experiences afflicted and/or inflicted on them by the "free will" of other human beings dead or alive or life in general.

It's important to note that God did not abandon you.

It was others' selfish "free will" that unleashed the same thing that caused Adam and Eve to create the "original sin" of "pride."

- [Surrender] the need or desire to forgive yourself.

"O my soul, bless God. From head to toe, I'll bless his holy name! O my soul, bless God, don't forget a single blessing!

He forgives your sins—every one.

He heals your diseases—every one.

He redeems you from hell—saves your life!

He crowns you with love and mercy—a paradise crown.

He wraps you in goodness—beauty eternal.

He renews your youth—you're always young in his presence.

God makes everything come out right; he puts victims back on their feet. He showed Moses how he went about his work, opened up his plans to all Israel. God is sheer mercy and grace; not easily angered, he's rich in love. He doesn't endlessly nag and scold, nor hold grudges forever. He doesn't treat us as our sins deserve, nor pay us back in full for our wrongs. As high as heaven is over the earth, so strong is his love to those who fear him. And as far as sunrise is from sunset, he has separated us from our sins. As parents feel for their children, God feels for those who fear him. He knows us inside out, keeps in mind that we're made of mud. Men and women don't live very long; like wildflowers they spring up and blossom, but a storm snuffs them out just as quickly, leaving nothing to show they were here. God's love, though, is ever and always, eternally present to all who fear him, making everything right for them and their children as they follow his Covenant ways and remember to do whatever he said. God has set his throne in heaven; he rules over us all. He's the King! So bless God, you angels, ready and able to fly at his bidding, quick to hear and do what he says. Bless God, all you armies of angels, alert to respond to whatever he wills. Bless God, all creatures, wherever you are—everything and everyone made by God.

And you, O my soul, bless God." (Psalm 103:1–22, MSG)

When God has forgiven you of your sins, you are forgiven. There are no additional steps necessary for your forgiveness. Yes, it would be wonderful to receive the forgiveness of people you have sinned against and seeking that promotes great healing for you, but it is not a criteria for gaining your salvation.

The criteria for being the "administrator" of "forgiveness" is that you are the great "I AM" and have control over the placement of "souls" in heaven or hell, in other words, only God.

In our early church history, there was the introduction of a practice known as "flagellation." These "flagellants" believed that their forgiveness was not complete until they punished their flesh by whipping.

There is nothing else that needs to be added to the "forgiveness of God." Stop impeding your "growth in service" to God and your "peace of mind" by thinking that you have to forgive yourself.

It is a lie from the pits of hell.

"Come now, let's settle this," says the LORD. "Though your sins are like scarlet, I will make them as white as snow. Though they are red like crimson, I will make them as white as wool.

If you will only obey me, you will have plenty to eat. But if you turn away and refuse to listen, you will be devoured by the sword of your enemies. I the LORD, have spoken!" (Isaiah 1:18–20, NLT)

"Where is another God like you, who pardons the guilt of the remnant, overlooking the sins of his special people? You will not stay angry with your people forever, because you delight in showing unfailing love.

Once again you will have compassion on us. You will trample our sins under your feet and throw them into the depths of the ocean!" (Micah 7:18 and 19, NLT)

"It seems it was good for me to go through all those troubles. Throughout them all you held tight to my lifeline. You never let me tumble over the edge into nothing. But my sins you let go of, threw them over your shoulder—good riddance!" (Isaiah 38:17, MSG)

"I—yes, I alone—will blot out your sins for my own sake and will never think of them again." (Isaiah 43: 25, NLT)

- [Surrender] doubts and inhibitions: Related to what you are created for and/or what you are able to do, in order to carry out what God wants done.

"Now the word of the LORD came to me, saying, 'Before I formed you in the womb I knew you, and before you were born I consecrated you; I appointed you a prophet to the nations.' Then I said, 'Ah, Lord God! Behold, I do not know how to speak, for I am only a youth.' But the LORD said to me, 'Do not say, "I am only a youth"; for to all to whom I send you, you shall go, and whatever I command you, you shall speak. Do not be afraid of them, for I am with you to deliver you, declares the LORD.' Then the LORD put out his hand and touched my mouth. And the LORD said to me,

'Behold, I have put my words in your mouth. See, I have set you this day over nations and over kingdoms, to pluck up and to break down, to destroy and to overthrow, to build and to plant.'" (Jeremiah 1:4-10, ESV)

> One day the angel of God came and sat down under the oak in Ophrah that belonged to Joash the Abiezrite, whose son Gideon was threshing wheat in the winepress, out of sight of the Midianites. The angel of God appeared to him and said, "God is with you, O mighty warrior!"
>
> Gideon replied, "With me, my master? If God is with us, why has all this happened to us? Where are all the miracle-wonders our parents and grandparents told us about, telling us, 'Didn't God deliver us from Egypt?' The fact is, God has nothing to do with us—he has turned us over to Midian."
>
> But God faced him directly: "Go in this strength that is yours. Save Israel from Midian. Haven't I just sent you?"
>
> Gideon said to him, "Me, my master? How and with what could I ever save Israel? Look at me. My clan's the weakest in Manasseh and I'm the runt of the litter."
>
> God said to him, "I'll be with you. Believe me, you'll defeat Midian as one man."
>
> Gideon said, "If your serious about this, do me a favor: Give me a sign to back up what you're telling me. Don't leave until I come back and bring you my gift."
>
> He said, "I'll wait till you get back."
>
> Gideon went and prepared a young goat and a huge amount of unraised bread (he used over a half a bushel of flour!). He put the meat

in a basket and the broth in a pot and took them back under the shade of the oak tree for a sacred meal.

The angel of God said to him, "Take the meat and unraised bread, place them on that rock, and pour the broth on them." Gideon did it.

The angel of God stretched out the tip of the stick he was holding and touched the meat and the bread. Fire broke out of the rock and burned up the meat and bread while the angel of God slipped away out of sight. And Gideon knew it was the angel of God!

Gideon said, "Oh no! Master, God! I have seen the angel of God face-to-face!"

But God reassured him, "Easy now. Don't panic. You won't die."

Then Gideon built an altar there to God and named it "God's Peace." It's still called that at Ophrah of Abiezer.

That night this happened. God said to him, "Take your father's best seven-year old bull, the prime one. Tear down your father's Baal altar and chop down the Asherah fertility pole beside it. Then build an altar to God, your God, on the top of this hill. Take the prime bull and present it as a Whole-Burnt-Offering, using firewood from the Asherah pole that you cut down."

Gideon selected ten men from his servants and did exactly what GOD had told him. But because of his family and the people in the neighborhood, he was afraid to do it openly, so he did it that night.

Early in the morning, the people in town were shocked to find's Baal's altar torn down, the Asherah pole beside it chopped down, and the prime bull burning away on the altar that had been built.

They kept asking, "Who did this?"

Questions and more questions, and then the answer: "Gideon son of Joash did it."

The men of the town demanded of Joash: "Bring out your son! He must die! Why, he tore down the Baal altar and chopped down the Asherah tree!"

But Joash stood up to the crowd pressing on him, "Are you going to fight Baal's battles for him? Are you going to save him? Anyone who takes Baal's side will be dead by morning. If Baal is a god in fact, let him fight his own battles and defend his own altar."

They nicknamed Gideon that day Jerub-Baal because after he had torn down the Baal altar, he had said, "Let Baal fight his own battles." (Judges 6:11–32, MSG)

• [Surrender] "I Know Me": The belief that you have the "instruction manual" for your life. God reveals your "instruction manual for service" one page at a time, based on your growing "obedience."

Now Jephthah the Gileadite was a mighty warrior, but he was the son of a prostitute. Gilead was the father of Jephthah. And Gilead's wife also bore him sons. And when his wife's sons grew up, they drove Jephthah out and said to him, "You shall not have an inheritance in our father's house, for you are the son of another woman." Then Jephthah fled from his brothers and lived in the land of Tob, and worthless fellows collected around Jephthah and went out with him.

After a time the Ammonites made war against Israel. And when the Ammonites made war against Israel, the elders of Gilead went to bring Jephthah from the land of Tob. And they said to Jephthah, "Come and be our leader, that we may fight against the Ammonites." But Jephthah said to the elders of Gilead, "Did you not hate me and drive me out of my father's house? Why have you come to me now when you are in distress?" And the elders of Gilead said to Jephthah, "That is why we have turned to you now, that you may go with us and fight against the Ammonites and be our head over all the inhabitants of Gilead." Jephthah said to the elders of Gilead, "If you bring me home again to fight against the Ammonites, and the LORD gives them over to me, I will be your head." And the elders of Gilead said to Jephthah, "The LORD will be witness between us, if we do not do as you say." So Jephthah went with the elders of Gilead, and the people made him head and leader over them. And Jephthah spoke all his words before the LORD at Mizpah. (Judges 11:1–11, ESV)

- [Do] – Keep on the "whole armor of God": Once you have acquired the "whole armor of God" and learned to put it on correctly, never take it off!!! It doesn't require to be washed or repair, so it does not have to come off. The "key of free will" [lack of "obedience" to "God's will" for your life] dismantles the "whole armor of God." The only piece of the "whole armor of God," once it is accepted, that cannot come off is the "helmet of salvation."

"While I was with them in the world, I kept them in thy name: those that thou gavest me I have kept, and none of them is lost, but the son of perdition; that the scripture might be fulfilled." (John 17:12, KJV)

Any time a piece of the "whole armor of God" is missing, we become susceptible to "spiritual illness" [attacks from the spiritual world opposed to God], "mental illness" [the translation of "spiritual illness" into an "earthly format" based on mood-changing and mind-altering medication], and/or "physical maladies."

"Finally, be strong in the Lord and in the strength of his might. Put on the whole armor of God, that you may be able to stand against the schemes of the devil. For we do not wrestle against flesh and blood, but against the rulers, against the authorities, against the cosmic powers over this present darkness, against spiritual forces of evil in the heavenly places. Therefore take up the whole armor of God, that you may be able to withstand in the evil day, and having done all, to stand firm. Stand therefore, having fastened on the belt of truth, and having put on the breastplate of righteousness, and, as shoes for your feet, having put on the readiness given by the gospel of peace. In all circumstances take up the shield of faith, with which you can extinguish all the flaming darts of the evil one; and take the helmet of salvation, and the sword of the Spirit, which is the word of God, praying at all times in the Spirit, with all prayer and supplication. To that end, keep alert with all perseverance, making supplication for all the saints, and also for me, that words may be given to me in opening my mouth boldly to proclaim the mystery of the gospel, for which I am an ambassador in chains, that I may declare it boldly, as I ought to speak." (Ephesians 6:10–20, ESV)

Chapter 9

AWAKE

Your "hearing life" completes your "prayer life."

Your "prayer life" is your "life"!!! Your "prayer life" consists of "prayer" [petitioning God] and meditation [listening to God]. Meditation, the key component to "listening to God," is the "prayer booster." Meditation [listening to God] reduces the amount of "know not what to pray for" in our lives. Meditation [listening to God] increases our receptiveness to accepting more of the Holy Spirit's "step-by-step" guidance for our lives. Meditation [listening to God] increases our ability to "know what to pray for" in our lives. Meditation [listening to God] brings "peace of mind" no matter what earthly thing you may be going through. Meditation [listening to God] is your "hearing life." "Hearing life" and "meditation" are synonymous. Meditation [listening to God] makes your "prayer life" complete!

While we know that having a "prayer life" is something we must wholeheartedly embrace, it becomes something that the majority of us do not define nor develop.

Our "prayer life" is the "process" by which God communicates to us and we communicate with God. It consists of three components:

A. The foundational level – prayer and meditation
B. The intercessory level – prayer for others

C. The favor level – "a prayer fest" (personal guidance meditation, Psalm 1, Enoch)

God provides directions for our lives and a response to our needs and requests through the use of the three components of a "prayer life," by our willingness to utilize one or all of these components. Our "hearing life" is perfected by fine-tuning our willingness to meditate [listening to God], instead of spending the majority of our time "talking to God."

With our mouth, mind, and heart, we pray and meditate.

"Let the words of my mouth, and the meditation of my heart, be acceptable in thy sight, O LORD, my strength and my redeemer." (Psalm 19:14, KJV)

You will find out that the more you listen, the more you will want to listen. The clarity and "peace of mind" it brings will strengthen the desires of your heart.

"As the deer pants for the water brooks,
So pants my soul for You, O God.
My soul thirsts for God, for the living God.
When shall I come and appear before God?"
(Psalms 42:1 and 2, NKJV)

Somebody right now is saying to themselves, "I need to talk to God. I need help. I've got problems and issues. *I need his help!!!*"

In my ministry I have encountered this concern more than any other. The Holy Spirit has instructed me every time to share this, "I have given you everything that you need to clean the situation up, according to my will, but I gave you free will. You must do the work."

It's like standing there in a filthy room complaining about how disgusting it is. You're standing there with bleach, disinfect, mops, rags, hot water, and anything else you would need to get the place cleaned, but you're just standing there complaining. What you need is more listening and doing. Get to work!!!

We need more listening and less talking in our relationship with God.

Complete and total utilization of our "prayer life" is a growth process.

A. It starts with the "foundational level," personal prayer and meditation.

B. It advances to the "intercessory level," praying for others, which can be done privately (by yourself) or in a group.

C. It culminates with the "favor level," a "prayer fest" where you are constantly working toward unbroken communication with your God day and night. You know and utilize the Holy Spirit. You have accepted the Holy Spirit over your "free will." You have allowed the Holy Spirit to be your "guidance system," step by step, through this world and your life.

At level "C," you receive the "favor of the *Lord*." Enoch was a perfect example of this, only the seventh generation from Adam (Adam was still alive).

> When Jared had lived 162 years, he fathered Enoch. Jared lived after he fathered Enoch 800 years and had other sons and daughters. Thus all the days of Jared were 962 years, and he died.
>
> When Enoch had lived 65 years, he fathered Methuselah. Enoch walked with God after he fathered Methuselah 300 years and had other sons and daughters. Thus all the days of Enoch were 365 years. Enoch walked with God, and he was not, for God took him. (Genesis 5:18–24, ESV)

Not only did God decide to walk with Enoch, the Father showed us his original plan for us joining him in heaven. His plan was to translate (convert) us, soul, spirit, and flesh. Adam and Eve altered that plan by sinning in the garden. Now only the soul and spirit of a person can be translated, at death, but the sinful flesh must stay here on earth until Christ returns. Enoch is our example from God of how it was supposed to be.

Because of Enoch's desire to hear from God (next to Jesus the Christ, the greatest example of a "hearing life"), the *Lord* told him all about Christ and what he will do.

> Enoch, who lived in the seventh generation after Adam, prophesied about these people. He said, "Listen! The Lord is coming with countless thousands of his holy ones to execute judgement on the people of the world. He will convict every person of all the ungodly things they have done and for all the insults that ungodly sinners have spoken against him." (Jude 1:14 and 15, NLT)

Our goal in our relationship with God is to reach the attributes enunciated in Psalm 1:

> Blessed is the man who walks not in the counsel of the wicked, nor stands in the way of sinners, nor sits in the seat of scoffers; but his delight is in the law of the LORD, and on his law he meditates day and night.
>
> He is like a tree planted by streams of water that yields its fruit in its season, and its leaf does not wither. In all that he does, he prospers. The wicked are not so, but are like chaff that the wind drives away.
>
> Therefore the wicked will not stand in the judgment, nor sinners in the congregation of the righteous; for the LORD knows the way of the

righteous, but the way of the wicked will perish.
(Psalm 1:1–6, ESV)

Utilizing the three components of our "prayer life" will get us there. The components are progressive for completeness.

The "foundational level" (A level) is the building block. It always must be the first thing done. Petitioning God through prayer is extremely important, but we must learn to meditate [listening to God] more than we talk.

> And he told them a parable to the effect that they ought always to pray and not lose heart. He said, "In a certain city there was a judge who neither feared God nor respected man. And there was a widow in that city who kept coming to him and saying, 'Give me justice against my adversary.' For a while he refused, but afterward he said to himself, 'Though I neither fear God nor respect man, yet because this widow keeps bothering me, I will give her justice, so that she will not beat me down by her continual coming.'" And the Lord said, "Hear what the unrighteous judge says. And will not God give justice to his elect, who cry to him day and night? Will he delay long over them? I tell you, he will give justice to them speedily. Nevertheless, when the Son of Man comes, will he find faith on earth?" (Luke 18:1–8, ESV)

A. The foundational level: Prayer and meditation – building a prayer life

We start by learning to pray. As a child my parents taught me to pray over my food and to pray before I went to bed. "Now I lay me down to sleep. I pray the LORD my soul to keep. If I die before I wake, I pray the LORD my soul to take. Amen." As soon as I could talk, I would mumble along with my mother or father until I could recite it myself, without their assistance. I had found prayer. Prayer is the first step in learning to communicate with God.

> "I will answer them before they even call to me. While they are still talking about their needs. I will go ahead and answer their prayers!" (Isaiah 65:24, NLT)

Everything you will ever need to know about prayer is contained in the gospel of Matthew 6:5–15.

> "And when you pray, you must not be like the hypocrites. For they love to stand and pray in the synagogues and at the street corners, that they may be seen by others. Truly I say to you, they have received their reward. But when you pray, go into your room and shut the door and pray to your Father who is in secret. And your Father who sees in secret will reward you.
> And when you pray, do not heap up empty phrases as the Gentiles do, for they think that they will be heard for their many words. Do not be like them, for your Father knows what you need before you ask him. Pray then like this:
> 'Our Father in heaven, hallowed be your name. Your kingdom come, your will be done, on earth as it is in heaven. Give us this day our daily bread, and forgive us our debts, as we also have forgiven our debtors. And lead us not into temptation, but deliver us from evil. For if you forgive others their trespasses, your heavenly Father will also forgive you, but if you do not forgive others their trespasses, neither will your Father forgive your trespasses.'" (Matthew 6:5–15, ESV)

[It's important to note for your own orientation that "For thine is the kingdom, and the power, and the glory forever" was added during the time of the Protestant Reformation.]

The purpose of a "prayer life" is to obtain the ultimate results that God has for our lives and the lives of others. We obtain these results from "obedience" to God's will for all mankind on this earth. The ultimate results are the salvation of people, meeting the needs of people, peace of mind, clarity, blessings, miracles, and favor.

> Don't let anyone capture you with empty philosophies and high-sounding nonsense that come from human thinking and from the spiritual powers of this world, rather than from Christ. For in Christ lives all the fullness of God in a human body. So you also are complete through your union with Christ, who is the head over every ruler and authority. (Colossians 2:8–10, NLT)

When "petitioning God" through "prayer," make yourself small and shut yourself off so it's just you and God. Even in a group, put yourself in a bubble with the Holy Spirit and then proceed to intercede for the concerns being addressed.

We have allowed tradition and custom to impede our "prayer life." In early church history those individuals who had accepted the teachings of Jesus the Christ were being extremely persecuted by the Roman Empire and others. Early followers of Christ when confronted by persecutors would "stand up" to be identified as Christians. The custom initiated from there. People would "stand up" to show their commitment to Christ in their services. That evolved into "stand up" to show your commitment to Christ and "let us pray" to the Father.

> "And when thou prayest, thou shall not be as the hypocrites are: for thy love to pray standing in the synagogues and in the corners of the streets, that they may be seen by men. Verily I

say unto you, They have their reward." (Matthew 6:5, KJV)

"But when ye pray, use not vain repetitions, as the heathen do: for they think that they shall be heard for their much speaking." (Matthew 6:7, KJV)

Make yourself small (bend low if other options are not available, sit, kneel, lay prostrate). Never go before the throne of the "great *I AM*," our God, standing upright.

If this adjustment to "tradition and custom" causes any unsettlement in your spirit, this would be a perfect time to exercise the process of "meditation—listening to God."

Getting used to meditation [listening to God] requires preparation. If you are internally engaged in worldly and personal thoughts about problems, concerns, desires, and/or life, you will not be able to hear God's still small voice.

- First: "Dismiss your pride." To what you've been doing all your life, what the patriarchs and matriarchs of your family had accepted pertaining to this matter and beliefs, practice, and notions of your spiritual leaders that follow or practice a "stand up to pray" approach.
- Second: "Quiet yourself." To external and internal "noises of the world" (problems, concerns, situations, etc.). Shhhhhhhhhhhhhhhhh.
- Third: "Ask the Father."
- Fourth: "Accept his answer." It will be something Jesus Christ would say or do. Christ's instruction for us may be different from the custom we have been practicing, like this one of standing to pray.
- Fifth: "Do it." Knowing what to do and not doing it could create serious consequences for you at "judgment time." Read Matthew 25:31–46. Don't let the "church crowd" or the "worldly crowd" dictate your growth in Christ. Don't

let your mission for Jesus become impeded, like it did in Laodicea.

> "I know all the things you do, that you are neither hot nor cold. I wish that you were one or the other! But since you are like lukewarm water, neither hot nor cold, I will spit you out of my mouth! You say, 'I am rich. I have everything I want. I don't need a thing!' And you don't realize that you are wretched and miserable and poor and blind and naked. So I advise you to buy gold from me—gold that has been purified by fire. Then you will be rich. Also buy white garments from me so you will not be shamed by your nakedness, and ointment for your eyes so you will be able to see. I correct and discipline everyone I love. So be diligent and turn from your indifference.
>
> Look! I stand at the door and knock. If you hear my voice and open the door, I will come in, and we will share a meal together as friends. Those who are victorious will sit with me on my throne, just as I was victorious and sat with my Father on his throne.
>
> Anyone with ears to hear must listen to the Spirit and understand what he is saying to the churches." (Revelation 3:15–22, NLT)

At home shut yourself off. Create a separate space reserved for your private "pray life" with God.

Remember this level of prayer is only between you and God. You must hear God 90 percent of the time and talk 10 percent. Anyone that may think this is a radical change in how they view prayer needs to ask God. [Make sure you follow the steps provided.]

> "Understand this, my dear brothers and sisters: You must all be quick to listen, slow to

speak, and slow to get angry. Human anger does not produce the righteousness God desires. So get rid of all the filth and evil in your lives, and humbly accept the word God has planted in your hearts, for it has the power to save your souls.

But don't just listen to God's word. You must do what it says. Otherwise, you are only fooling yourselves. For if you listen to the word and don't obey, it is like glancing at your face in a mirror. You see yourself, walk away, and forget what you look like.

But if you look carefully into the perfect law that that sets you free, and if you do what it says and don't forget what you heard, then God will bless you for doing it." (James 1:19–27, NLT)

The prayer formula as taught by Paul will also make your "prayer life" more impactful.

See that no one pays back evil for evil, but always try to do good to each other and to all people.

Always be joyful. Never stop praying. Be thankful in all circumstances, for this is God's will for you who belong to Christ Jesus. (1 Thessalonians 5:15–18, NLT)

Study this Book of Instruction continually. Meditate on it day and night so you will be sure to obey everything written in it. Only then will you prosper and succeed in all you do. (Joshua 1:8, NLT)

"For my thoughts are not your thoughts, neither are your ways my ways," saith the LORD.

"For as the heavens are higher than the earth, so are my ways higher than your ways, and my thoughts than your thoughts." (Isaiah 55:8 and 9, KJV)

B. The intercessory level: Individually and group – building an intercessory prayer life, "God-defined involvement"

An "intercessory prayer life" [your God-defined involvement] is your willingness to spend time in the presence of God for others. It has everything to do with what others need collectively or individually.

If you're wondering why it's called "intercessory prayer life" [your God-defined involvement] instead of just "intercessory prayer," it is because now you are learning to become an active participant in interceding. Interceding for others is an extremely powerful weapon.

We will look at "expanding the impact" of an "intercessory prayer life" [your God-defined involvement] on others by your intervention. It is important for you to understand that "expanding the impact" of your "intercessory prayer life" is a process. A progression from learning:

> ➤ To build your personal "prayer life" made up of:
> o Prayer [petitioning God] with
> o Meditation [listening to God]
> ➤ To an "intercessory prayer life that is made up of:
> o Prayer [petitioning God] with
> o Meditation [listening to God] combined with
> o Intervention [your God-defined involvement]) that is more impactful
> o Monastic involvement [denial of self before God] – an optional approach some individuals are comfortable in entering, because of the "calling of God"

While you improve your personal "prayer life" [prayer and meditation], your intervention through your "intercessory prayer life" [your God-defined involvement] will become more in keeping with what God wants from you, making interceding more effective.

Don't worry about anything; instead, pray about everything. Tell God what you need, and thank him for all he has done. Then you will experience God's peace, which exceeds anything we can understand. His peace will guard your hearts and minds as you live in Christ Jesus." (Philippians 4:6 and 7, NLT)

Who hath believed our report? And to whom is the arm of the LORD revealed? (Isaiah 53:1, KJV)

"I urge you, first of all, to pray for all people. Ask God to help them; intercede on their behalf, and give thanks for them. Pray this way for kings and all who are in authority so that we can live peaceful and quiet lives marked by godliness and dignity. This is good and pleases God our Savior, who wants everyone to be saved and to understand the truth. For there is only one God and one Mediator who can reconcile God and humanity—the man Christ Jesus. He gave his life to purchase freedom for everyone. This is the message God gave to the world at just the right time. And I have been chosen as a preacher and apostle to teach the Gentiles this message about faith and truth. I'm not exaggerating—just telling the truth." (1 Timothy 2:1–7, NLT)

Intercessory Prayer Life: Your God-Defined Involvement (Group or Individual)

Our traditional approach to intercessory prayer has us gathering as a group or doing it by ourselves. Either approach is acceptable to accomplish the intercessory goal of "impacting outcomes."

"Impacting outcomes" in the most spiritual way translates effectively in our earthly realm. Learning what the Father wants and then applying it to our intercessory prayer life will produce some amazing outcomes.

To enhance your intercessory efforts in behalf of others:

1) Make sure you bring your improving personal "prayer life" to the "intercessory prayer event" (individual or group format). This will allow you to hear from the Father before you petition him. If you enter into intercessory prayer without the intent to "listen to God" first, you minimize the impact of your intercessory prayer.

2) Ask the Father what you need to add or delete from the introductory request or need for intercessory prayer. While you're praying for "safe travel" for your parents, the spirit might tell you to pray that they stay mindful of promoting Christ's work for them on the way. A perfect example is when the benediction is given at the end of service:

> May God be merciful and bless us. May his face smile with favor on us. *Interlude*
>
> May your ways be known throughout the earth, your saving power among people everywhere. May the nations praise you, O God. Yes, may all the nations praise you. Let the whole world sing for joy, because you govern the nations with justice and guide the people of the whole world. *Interlude*
>
> May the nations praise you, O God. Yes, may all the nations praise you. Then the earth will yield its harvests, and God, our God will richly bless us. Yes, God will bless us, and people all over the world will fear him. (Psalm 67, NLT)
>
> After church you, get into your vehicle covered in God and Jesus bumper stickers and customized front license plates; and then two blocks from church, you become a "road demon." You're looking like a person on the border of "road

rage." If we asked the Holy Spirit what needs to be included in that benediction, the spirit will tell us: "Let our drive home reflect the love Christ wants us to show to our neighbors (fellow human beings)."

3) Ask the Father, "What must I do to impact the outcome?" You must ask the Father to maximize the impact of your intercessory prayer in group or by yourself. This permits God through the Holy Spirit to tell you what you must do. We must have a sense of total involvement in our intercessory prayer. You could be praying for children or people thousands of miles away, and the spirit might tell you that I want you to spend more time in the word. So now you're praying for your children and spending more time with God in the word. Watch how the impact of your intercessory prayer increases.

> Don't copy the behavior and customs of this world, but let God transform you into a new person by changing the way you think. Then you will learn to know God's will for you, which is good and pleasing and perfect. (Romans 12:2, NLT)

Monastic Intercessory Prayer Life: Denial of Self before God (Individual or Group)

Do nothing from selfishness or empty conceit, but with humility of mind regard one another as more important than yourselves; do not merely look out for your own personal interest, but also for the interest of others. (Philippians 2:3 and 4, NASB)

A "monastic intercessory prayer life" is led by a "calling by God" and a personal commitment to that "calling by God."

The early church knew that the cares of the world could impede our focus on God and others, so they cloistered individuals who had a "monastic calling" on their lives. This allowed them to only focus on God and others.

Get rid of all bitterness, rage, anger, harsh words, and slander, as well as all types of evil behavior. Instead, be kind to each other, tenderhearted, forgiving one another, just as God through Christ has forgiven you. (Ephesians 4:31 and 32, NLT)

While this activity continues today, we have the opportunity to participate in a "monastic intercessory prayer life," individually and collectively.

The nineteenth-century evangelist Charles Grandison Finney was the leader of the Second Great Awakening in the United States. Pastor Finney conducted revivals in upstate New York in the 1820s and 1830s. Finney is known as the father of modern-day revivalism. A key component of his ministry was an intercessory prayer warrior named Daniel Nash better known as Father Nash.

These are taken from the HopeFaithPrayer.com, website:

> Daniel Nash served as Charles Finney's personal intercessor. He was key to the revival that followed Finney's ministry. We can all look at the life of Daniel Nash and see an example of how important prayer is to see the kingdom of God revealed.

From *Daniel Nash: Prevailing Prince of Prayer* by J. Paul Reno:

> When God would direct where a meeting was to be held, Father Nash would slip quietly into town and seek to get two or three people to enter into a covenant of prayer with him. Sometimes he had with him a man of similar prayer ministry, Abel Clary. Together they would begin to pray fervently for God to move in the community.
>
> One record of such is told by Leonard Ravenhill: "I met an old lady who told me a story

about Charles Finney that has challenged me over the years. Finney went to Bolton to minister, but before he began, two men knocked on the door of her humble cottage, wanting lodging. The poor woman looked amazed, for she had no extra accommodations. Finally, for about twenty-five cents a week, the two men, none other than Father Nash and Clary, rented a dark and damp cellar for the period of the Finney meetings (at least two weeks), and there in that self-chosen cell, those prayer partners battled the forces of darkness."

Another record tells: "On one occasion when I got to town to start a revival a lady contacted me who ran a boarding house. She said, 'Brother Finney, do you know a Father Nash? He and two other men have been at my boarding house for the last three days, but they haven't eaten a bite of food. I opened the door and peeped in at them because I could hear them groaning, and I saw them down on their faces. They have been this way for three days, lying prostrate on the floor and groaning. I thought something awful must have happened to them. I was afraid to go in and didn't know what to do.

Would you please come see about them?' 'No, it isn't necessary,' Finney replied. 'They just have a spirit of travail in prayer.'"

Another states: "Charles Finney so realized the need of God's working in all his service that he was wont to send godly Father Nash on in advance to pray down the power of God into the meetings which he was about to hold."

Not only did Nash prepare the communities for preaching, but he also continued in prayer during the meetings.

Often Nash would not attend meetings, and while Finney was preaching Nash was praying for the Spirit's outpouring upon him. Finney stated, "I did the preaching altogether, and Brother Nash gave himself up almost continually to prayer."

Often while the evangelist preached to the multitudes, Nash in some adjoining house would be upon his face in agony of prayer, and God answered in the marvels of His grace. With all due credit to Mr. Finney for what was done, it was the praying men who held the ropes. The tears they shed, the groans they uttered are written in the book of the chronicles of the things of God. (*Prevailing Prince of Prayer* by J. Paul Reno)

You do not have to be cloistered to engage in "monastic intercessory prayer." You only have to "deny yourself" as "God directs," before entering into "monastic intercessory prayer".

The premise to a "monastic intercessory prayer life" is that God has called you to "deny yourself" for the sake of others. Such sacrifice, as directed by God, enhances the impact of your intercession.

Make sure your "listening to God" [meditating] in order to make sure your "self-denial" is "God driven" not "self-inspired."

C.   The favor level: The favor of the Lord – a prayer life fest

Our goal while we walk this planet is to be more like Christ in our earthly endeavors. While we will never be able to achieve the "Christ level" during our lives, constant pursuit of that goal is essential.

It culminates with the "favor level," a "prayer fest" where you are constantly working toward unbroken communication with your God day and night. You know and utilize the Holy Spirit. You have accepted the Holy Spirit over your "free will." You have allowed the

Holy Spirit to be your "guidance system," step by step, through this world and your life.

People often identify individuals like David and Noah and Moses and Abraham and Isaac and Jacob (and more) as heroes of the "faith" and rightfully so. But there are some Bible individuals that exuded the "favor of the *Lord* (the Father)" that should be mentioned more. Examples of how to surrender your will and become "obedient" to the "will of God," no matter how your life started or what you have done during it:

Enoch

Enoch exhibited such a willingness to be "obedient" to the "will of God" for his life that God could walk the earth with him. Even after God could no longer walk the earth because of man's sinful nature, God could walk with Enoch. During Seth's time, God forced man to get "his attention" through "worship" (Genesis 4:26).

> When Jared was 162 years old, he became the father of Enoch. After the birth of Enoch, Jared lived another 800 years, and he had other sons and daughters. Jared lived 962 years, and then he died.
>
> When Enoch was 65 years old, he became the father of Methuselah. After the birth of Methuselah, Enoch lived in close fellowship with God for another 300 years, and he had other sons and daughters. Enoch lived 365 years, walking in close fellowship with God. Then one day he disappeared, because God took him. (Genesis 5:18–24, NLT)

Not only did God decide to walk with Enoch, God showed him his original plan for us joining the Father in heaven. His plan was to translate (convert) us, soul, spirit, and flesh. Adam and Eve altered that plan by sinning in the garden. Now only the soul and spirit of a person can be translated, at death, but the sinful flesh must stay here on earth until Christ returns. Enoch is our example from God of how it was supposed to be.

Because of Enoch's desire to hear from God (next to Jesus the Christ, the greatest example of a "hearing life"), we have an example of a man entering the "favor level."

The *Lord* (the Father) told him all about Christ and what he will do.

> Enoch, who lived in the seventh generation after Adam, prophesied about these people. He said, "Listen! The Lord is coming with countless thousands of his holy ones to execute judgement on the people of the world. He will convict every person of all the ungodly things they have done and for all the insults that ungodly sinners have spoken against him." (Jude 1:14 and 15, NLT)

Enoch in the "favor of the *Lord*" was a perfect example of "the favor level (prayer life fest), only the seventh generation from Adam (Adam was still alive).

Ruth

> Once upon a time—it was back in the days when judges led Israel—there was a famine in the land. A man from Bethlehem in Judah left home to live in the country of Moab, he and his wife and his two sons. The man's name was Elimelech; his wife's name was Naomi; his sons were named Mahlon and Kilion—all Ephrathites from Bethlehem in Judah. They all went to the country of Moab and settled there.
>
> Elimelech died and Naomi was left, she and her two sons. The sons took Moabite wives; the name of the first was Orpah, the second Ruth.

They lived there in Moab for the next ten years. But then the two brothers, Mahlon and Kilion, died. Now the woman was left without either her young men or her husband. (Ruth 1:1–5, MSG)

Ruth was a Moabite. She was a child of incest. Moabites were frowned upon and had fought against the Hebrews. They were the children of Lot, Abraham's nephew, and Lot's oldest daughter. In spite of what life has led us into, God is always there for us.

Lot left Zoar and went into the mountains to live with his two daughters; he was afraid to stay in Zoar. He lived in a cave with his daughters.

One day the older daughter said to the younger, "Our father is getting old and there's not a man left in the country by whom we can get pregnant. Let's get our father drunk with wine and lie with him. We'll get children through our father—it's our only chance to keep our family alive."

They got their father drunk with wine that very night. The older daughter went and lay with him. He was oblivious, knowing nothing of what she did. The next morning the older said to the younger, "Last night I slept with my father. Tonight, it's your turn. We'll get him drunk again and then you sleep with him. We'll both get a child through our father and keep our family alive." So that night they got their father drunk again and the younger went in and slept with him. Again he was oblivious, knowing nothing of what she did.

Both daughters became pregnant by their father, Lot. The older daughter had a son and named him Moab, the ancestor of the present-day Moabites. The younger daughter had a son and

named him Ben-Ammi, the ancestor of the present-day Ammonites. (Genesis 19:30–38, MSG)

Lot had always been a problem since he left Haran with Uncle
Abraham (Abram, until God changed his name, Genesis 17:3–6).
Lot was a very self-centered person, who couldn't work with his
Uncle Abraham. The land that Sodom and Gomorrah sat on was
near his land. Lot's daughters were as self-centered as their father.

Finally Abram said to Lot, "Let's not allow
this conflict to come between us or our herds-
men. After all, we are close relatives! The whole
countryside is open to you. Take your choice of
any section of the land you want, and we will
separate. If you want the land to the left, then I'll
take the land to the right. If you prefer the land
on the right, then I'll go to the left."
Lot took a long look at the fertile plains of
the Jordan Valley in the direction of Zoar. The
whole area was well watered everywhere, like
the garden of the LORD or the beautiful land
of Egypt. (This was before the LORD destroyed
Sodom and Gomorrah.) Lot chose for himself
the whole Jordan Valley to the east of them. He
went there with his flocks and servants and parted
company with his uncle Abram. So Abram settled
in the land of Canaan, and Lot moved his tents
to a place near Sodom and settled among the cities of the plain. But the people of this area were
extremely wicked and constantly sinned against
the LORD. (Genesis 13:8–13, NLT)

This is what happens when we embellish a directive from God.
Abram was told by God to leave his relatives and leave with his family
(his wife Sarai). Abraham took Lot with him, which created problems for him and his children for centuries to come.

Now God was going to show Ruth the Moabite, the child of incest, great "favor" by changing her earthly status based on her devotion to Naomi and her willingness to accept the God of Israel as her God. Ruth would be the foremother of King David of Israel, Mary the mother of Christ, and Joseph the earthly father of Christ.

> One day she got herself together, she and her two daughters-in-law, to leave the country of Moab and set out for home; she had heard that GOD had been pleased to visit his people and give them food. And so she started out from the place she had been living, she and her two daughters-in-law with her, on the road back to the land of Judah.
>
> After a short while on the road, Naomi told her two daughters-in-law, "Go back. Go home and live with your mothers. And may GOD treat you as graciously as you treated your deceased husbands and me. May GOD give each of you a new home and a new husband!" She kissed them and they cried openly.
>
> They said, "No, we're going on with you to your people."
>
> But Naomi was firm: "Go back, my dear daughters. Why would you come with me? Do you suppose I still have sons in my womb who can become your future husbands? Go back, dear daughters—on your way, please! I'm too old to get a husband. Why, even if I said, 'There's still hope!' and this very night got a man and had sons, can you imagine being satisfied to wait until they were grown? Would you wait that long to get married again? No, dear daughters; this is a bitter pill for me to swallow—more bitter for me than for you. GOD has dealt me a hard blow."

Again they cried openly. Oprah kissed her
mother-in-law good-bye; but Ruth embraced her
and held on.

Naomi said, "Look, your sister-in-law is
going back home to live with her own people and
gods; go with her."

But Ruth said, "Don't force me to leave you;
don't make me go home. Where you go, I go;
and where you live, I'll live. Your people are my
people, your GOD is my god; where you die, I'll
die, and that's where I'll be buried, so help me
GOD—not even death itself is going to come
between us!"

When Naomi saw that Ruth had her heart
set on going with her, she gave in. And so the two
of them traveled on together to Bethlehem.

When they arrived in Bethlehem the whole
town was soon buzzing: "Is this really our Naomi?
And after all this time!"

But she said, "Don't call me Naomi; call me
Bitter. The Strong One has dealt me a bitter blow.
I left here full of life, and GOD has brought me
back with nothing but the clothes on my back.
Why should you call me Naomi? God certainly
doesn't. The Strong One ruined me."

And so Naomi was back, and Ruth the foreigner with her, back from the country of Moab.
They arrived in Bethlehem at the beginning of
the barley harvest. (Ruth 1:6–22, MSG)

It so happened that Naomi had a relative by
marriage, a man prominent and rich, connected
with Elimelech's family. His name was Boaz.

One day Ruth, the Moabite foreigner, said
to Naomi, "I'm going to work; I'm going out to
glean among the sheaves, following after some
harvester who will treat me kindly."

Naomi said, "Go ahead, dear daughter."

And so she set out. She went and started gleaning in a field, following in the wake of the harvesters. Eventually she ended up in the part of the field owned by Boaz, her father-in-law Elimelech's relative. A little later Boaz came out from Bethlehem, greeting his harvesters, "God be with you!" They replied, "And God bless you!"

Boaz asked his young servant who was foreman over the farm hands, "Who is this young woman? Where did she come from?"

The foreman said, "Why, that's the Moabite girl, the one who came with Naomi from the country of Moab. She asked permission. 'Let me glean,' she said, 'and gather among the sheaves following after your harvesters.' She's been at it steady ever since, from early morning until now, without so much as a break."

Then Boaz spoke to Ruth: "Listen, my daughter. From now on don't go to any other field to glean—stay right here in this one. And stay close to my young women. Watch where they are harvesting and follow them. And don't worry about a thing; I've given orders to my servants not to harass you. When you get thirsty, feel free to go and drink from the water buckets that the servants have filled."

She dropped to her knees, then bowed her face to the ground. "How does this happen that you should pick me out and treat me so kindly— me, a foreigner?"

Boaz answered her, "I've heard all about you—heard about the way you treated your mother-in-law after the death of her husband, and how you left your father and mother and the land of your birth and have come to live among a bunch of total strangers. GOD reward you well for what you've done—and with a generous bonus besides from GOD, to whom you've come seeking protection under his wings."

She said, "Oh sir, such grace, such kindness—I don't deserve it. You've touched my heart, treated me like one of your own. And I don't even belong here!"

At the lunch break, Boaz said to her, "Come over here; eat some bread. Dip it in the wine."

So she joined the harvesters. Boaz passed the roasted grain to her. She ate her fill and even had some left over.

When she got up to go back to work, Boaz ordered his servants: "Let her glean where there's still plenty of grain on the ground—make it easy for her. Better yet, pull some of the good stuff out and leave it for her to glean. Give her special treatment."

Ruth gleaned in the fields until evening. When she threshed out what she had gathered, she ended up with nearly a full sack of barley! She gathered up her gleanings, went back to town, and showed her mother-in-law the results of her day's work; she also gave her the leftovers from her lunch.

Naomi asked her, "So where did you glean today? Whose field? GOD bless whoever it was who took such good care of you!"

Ruth told her mother-in-law, "The man with whom I worked today? His name is Boaz."

Naomi said to her daughter-in-law, "Why, GOD bless that man! GOD hasn't quite walked out on us after all! He still loves us, in bad times as well as good!"

Naomi went on, "That man, Ruth, is one of our circle of covenant redeemers, a close relative of ours!"

Ruth the Moabitess said, "Well, listen to this: He also told me, 'Stick with my workers until my harvesting is finished.'"

Naomi said to Ruth, "That's wonderful, dear daughter! Do that! You'll be safe in the company of his young women; no danger now of being raped in some stranger's field."

So Ruth did it—she stuck close to Boaz's young women, gleaning in the fields daily until both the barley and wheat harvesting were finished. And she continued living with her mother-in-law. (Ruth 2:1–23, MSG)

One day her mother-in law Naomi said to Ruth, "My dear daughter, isn't it about time I arranged a good home for you so you can have a happy life? And isn't Boaz our close relative, the one with whose young women you've been working? Maybe it's time to make our move. Tonight is the night of Boaz's barley harvest at the threshing floor.

Take a bath. Put on some perfume. Get all dressed up and go to the threshing floor. But don't let him know you're there until the party is well under way and he's had plenty of food and drink. When you see him slipping off to sleep, watch where he lies down and then go there. Lie at his feet to let him know that you are available to him for marriage. Then wait and see what he says. He'll tell you what to do."

Ruth said, "If you say so, I'll do it, just as you've told me."

She went down to the threshing floor and put her mother-in-law's plan into action.

Boaz had a good time, eating and drinking his fill—he felt great. Then he went off to get some sleep, lying down at the end of a stack of barley. Ruth quietly followed; she lay down to signal her availability for marriage.

In the middle of the night the man suddenly startled and sat up. Surprised! This woman asleep at his feet!

He said, "And who are you?"

She said, "I am Ruth, your maiden; take me under your protecting wing. You're my close relative, you know, in the circle of covenant redeemers—you do have the right to marry me."

He said, "GOD bless you, my dear daughter! What a splendid expression of love! And when you could have had your pick of any of the young men around. And now, my dear daughter, don't worry about a thing; I'll do all you could want or ask. Everybody in town knows what a courageous woman you are—a real prize! You're right, I am a close relative to you, but there is one even closer than I am. So stay the rest of the night. In the morning, if he wants to exercise his customary rights and responsibilities as the closest covenant redeemer, he'll have his chance; but if he isn't interested, as GOD lives, I'll do it. Now go back to sleep until morning."

Ruth slept at his feet until dawn, but she got up while it was still dark and wouldn't be recognized. Then Boaz said to himself, "No one must know that Ruth came to the threshing floor."

So Boaz said, "Bring the shawl you're wearing and spread it out."

She spread it out and he poured it full of barley, six measures, and put it on her shoulders. Then she went back to town.

When she came to her mother-in-law, Naomi asked, "And how did things go, my dear daughter?"

Ruth told her everything that the man had done for her, adding, "And he gave me all this barley besides—six quarts! He told me, 'You can't go back empty-handed to your mother-in-law!'"

Naomi said, "Sit back and relax, my dear daughter, until we find out how things turn out; that man isn't going to fool around. Mark my words, he's going to get everything wrapped up today." (Ruth 3:1–18, MSG)

Boaz went straight to the public square and took his place there. Before long the "closer relative," the one mentioned earlier by Boaz, strolled by. "Step aside, old friend," said Boaz. "Take a seat." The man sat down.

Boaz then gathered ten of the town elders together and said, "Sit down here with us; we've got some business to take care of." And they sat down.

Boaz then said to his relative, "The piece of property that belonged to our relative Elimelech is being sold by his widow Naomi, who has just returned from the country of Moab. I thought you ought to know about it. Buy it back if you want it—you can make it official in the presence of those sitting here and before the town elders. You have first redeemer rights. If you don't want it, tell me so I'll know where I stand. You're first in line to do this and I'm next after you."

He said, "I'll buy it."

Then Boaz added, "You realize, don't you, that when you buy the field from Naomi, you also get Ruth the Moabite, the widow of our dead relative, along with the redeemer responsibility to have children with her to carry on the family inheritance."

Then the relative said, "Oh, I can't do that—I'd jeopardize my own family's inheritance. You go ahead and buy it—you can have my rights—I can't do it."

In the olden times in Israel, this is how they handled official business regarding matters of property and inheritance: a man would take off his shoe and give it to the other person. This was the same as an official seal or personal signature in Israel.

So when Boaz's "redeemer" relative said, "Go ahead and buy it," he signed the deal by pulling off his shoe.

Boaz then addressed the elders and all the people in the town square that day: "You are witnesses today that I have bought from Naomi everything that belonged to Elimelech and Kilion and Mahlon, including responsibility for Ruth the foreigner, the widow of Mahlon—I'll take her as my wife and keep the name of the deceased alive along with his inheritance. The memory and reputation of the deceased is not going to disappear out of this family or from his hometown. To all this you are witnesses this very day."

All the people in the town square that day, backing up the elders, said, "Yes, we are witnesses. May GOD make this woman who is coming into your household like Rachel and Leah, the two women who built the family of Israel. May GOD make you a pillar in Ephrathah and famous in Bethlehem! With the children GOD gives you from this young woman, may your family rival the family of Perez, the son Tamar bore to Judah."

Boaz married Ruth. She became his wife. Boaz slept with her. By GOD's gracious gift she conceived and had a son.

The town women said to Naomi, "Blessed be GOD! He didn't leave you without family to carry on your life. May this baby grow up to be famous in Israel! He'll make you young again! He'll take care of you in old age. And this daughter-in-law who has brought him into the world and loves you so much, why, she's worth more to you than seven sons!"

Naomi took the baby and held him in her arms, cuddling him, cooing over him, waiting on him hand and foot.

The neighborhood women started calling him "Naomi's baby boy!" But his real name was Obed. Obed was the father of Jesse, and Jesse the father of David.

This is the family tree of Perez:

- Perez had Hezron,
- Hezron had Ram,
- Ram had Amminadab,
- Amminadab had Nahshon,
- Nahshon had Salmon,
- Salmon had Boaz,
- Boaz had Obed,
- Obed had Jesse,
- And Jesse had David." (Ruth 4:1–22, MSG)

Esther

God had showed Persian kings great "favor." Kings Cyrus, Darius, Ardashir (Artaxerxes), and Khashayarshah (Xerxes or Ahasuerus) were servants of the Lord.

God mentioned Cyrus as the shepherd and being anointed. Isaiah spoke of King Cyrus 150 years before he was born and what he would do for the *Lord*. King Cyrus would conquer Babylon and would allow the Jewish exiles to return to Jerusalem.

> "When I say of Cyrus, 'He is my shepherd,' he will certainly do as I say. He will command, 'Rebuild Jerusalem'; he will say, 'Restore the Temple.'" (Isaiah 44:28, NLT)

> This is what the LORD says to Cyrus, his anointed one, whose right hand he will empower. Before him mighty kings will be paralyzed with fear. Their fortress gates will be opened, never to shut again.

> This is what the LORD says: "I will go before you Cyrus, and level the mountains, I will smash down gates of bronze and cut through bars of iron. And I will give you treasures hidden in the darkness—secret riches. I will do this so you may know that I am the LORD, the God of Israel, the one who calls you by name." (Isaiah 45:1–3, NLT)

> In the first year of King Cyrus of Persia, the LORD fulfilled the prophecy he had given through Jeremiah. He stirred the heart of Cyrus to put this proclamation in writing and to send it throughout his kingdom:

> This is what King Cyrus of Persia says: "The LORD, the God of heaven, has given me all the kingdoms of the earth. He has appointed me to build him a Temple at Jerusalem, which is in Judah. Any of you who are the LORD'S people may go there for this task. And may the LORD your God be with you!" (2 Chronicles 36:22 and 23, NLT)

Rebuilding the temple in Jerusalem was resumed under King Darius.

So the work on the Temple of God in Jerusalem had stopped, and it remained at a standstill until the second year of the reign of King Darius of Persia. (Ezra 4:24, NLT)

King Artaxerxes (Ardashir) sent Nehemiah back to repair Jerusalem's walls.

> "These are the memoirs of Nehemiah son of Hacaliah. In late autumn, in the month of Kislev, in the twentieth year of King Artaxerxes' reign, I was at the fortress of Susa. Hanani, one of my brothers, came to visit me with some other men who had just arrived from Judah. I asked them about the Jews who had returned there from captivity and about how things were going in Jerusalem.
>
> They said to me, "Things are not going well for those who returned to the province of Judah. They are in great trouble and disgrace. The wall of Jerusalem has been torn down, and the gates have been destroyed by fire."
>
> When I heard this, I sat down and wept. In fact, for days I mourned, fasted, and prayed to the God of heaven." (Nehemiah 1:1–4, NLT)

The result of "prayer" and "meditation" brings tangible outcomes from God. When you're not on the same page with God according to "God's personal manual for your life," then "fasting" is a must.

> "The king asked, 'Well, how can I help you?' With a prayer to the God of heaven, I replied, 'If it please the king, and if you are pleased with me, your servant, send me to Judah to rebuild the city where my ancestors are buried.'

The king, with the queen sitting beside him, asked, 'How long will you be gone? When will you return?' After I told him how long I would be gone, the king agreed to my request." (Nehemiah 2:4–6, NLT)

King Xerxes (Khashayarshah) [his Hebrew translation would be Ahasuerus] would marry Esther and save the Jewish population from a diabolical plot of Haman.

Now there was a Jew who lived in the palace complex in Susa. His name was Mordecai the son of Jair, the son of Shimei, the son of Kish—a Benjaminite. His ancestors had been taken from Jerusalem with the exiles and carried off with King Jehoiachin of Judah by King Nebuchadnezzar of Babylon into exile. Mordecai had reared his cousin Hadassah, otherwise known as Esther, since she had no father or mother. The girl had a good figure and a beautiful face. After her parents died, Mordecai had adopted her. (Esther 2:5–7, MSG)

When the king's order had been publicly posted, many young girls were brought to the palace complex of Susa and given over to Hegai who was overseer of the women. Esther was among them.

Hegai liked Esther and took a special interest in her. Right off he started her beauty treatments, ordered special food, assigned her seven personal maids from the palace, and put her and her maids in the best rooms in the harem. Esther didn't say anything about her family and racial background because Mordecai had told her not to.

Every day Mordecai strolled beside the court of the harem to find out how Esther was and get news of what she was doing. (Esther 2:8–11, MSG)

Each girl's turn came to go in to King Xerxes after she had completed the twelve months of prescribed beauty treatments—six months' treatment with oil of myrrh followed by six months with perfumes and various cosmetics. When it was time for the girl to go to the king, she was given whatever she wanted to take with her when she left the harem for the king's quarters. She would go there in the evening; in the morning she would return to a second harem overseen by Shaashgaz, the king's eunuch in charge of the concubines. She never again went back to the king unless the king took a special liking to her and asked for her by name.

When it was Esther's turn to go to the king (Esther the daughter of Abihail the uncle of Mordecai, who adopted her as his daughter), she asked for nothing other than what Hegai, the king's eunuch in charge of the harem, had recommended. Esther, just as she was, won the admiration of everyone who saw her.

She was taken to King Xerxes in the royal palace in the tenth month, the month of Tebeth, in the seventh year of the king's reign.

The king fell in love with Esther far more than with any of his other women or any of the other virgins—he was totally smitten by her. He placed a royal crown on her head and made her queen in place of Vashti. Then the king gave a great banquet for all his nobles and officials—"Esther's Banquet." He proclaimed a holiday for all the provinces and handed out gifts with royal generosity.

On one of the occasions, when the virgins were being gathered together, Mordecai was sitting at the King's Gate. All this time, Esther had kept her family background and race a secret as Mordecai had ordered; Esther still did what Mordecai told her, just as when she was being raised by him. (Esther 2:12–20, MSG)

On this day, with Mordecai sitting at the King's Gate, Bigthana and Teresh, two of the king's eunuchs who guarded the entrance, had it in for the king and were making plans to kill King Xerxes. But Mordecai learned of the plot and told Queen Esther, who told King Xerxes, giving credit to Mordecai. When the thing was investigated and confirmed as true, the two men were hanged on a gallows. This was all written down in a logbook kept for the king's use. (Esther 2:21–23, MSG)

Some time later, King Xerxes promoted Haman son of Hammedatha the Agagite, making him the highest-ranking official in the government. All the king's servants at the King's Gate used to honor him by bowing down and kneeling before Haman—that's what the king had commanded.

Except Mordecai. Mordecai wouldn't do it, wouldn't bow down and kneel. The king's servants at the King Gate asked Mordecai about it: "Why do you cross the king's command?" Day after day they spoke to him about this but he wouldn't listen, so they went to Haman to see whether something shouldn't be done about it. Mordecai had told them that he was a Jew.

When Haman saw for himself that Mordecai didn't bow down and kneel before him, he was outraged. Meanwhile, having learned that

Mordecai was a Jew, Haman hated to waste his fury on just one Jew; he looked for a way to eliminate not just Mordecai but all Jews throughout the whole kingdom of Xerxes.

In the first month, the month of Nisan, of the twelfth year of Xerxes, the pur—that is, the lot—was cast under Haman's charge to determine the propitious day and month. The lot turned up the thirteenth day of the twelfth month, which is the month of Adar.

Haman then spoke with King Xerxes: "There is an odd set of people scattered through the provinces of your kingdom who don't fit in. Their customs and ways are different from those of everybody else. Worse, they disregard the king's laws. They're an affront; the king shouldn't put up with them. If it please the king, let orders be given that they be destroyed. I'll pay for it myself. I'll deposit 375 tons of silver in the royal bank to finance the operation."

The king slipped his signet ring from his hand and gave it to Haman son of Hammedatha the Agagite, archenemy of the Jews.

"Go ahead," the king said to Haman. "It's your money—do whatever you want with those people."

The king's secretaries were brought in on the thirteenth day of the first month. The orders were written out word for word as Haman had addressed them to the king's satraps, the governors of every province, and the officials of every people. They were written in the script of each province and the language of each people in the name of King Xerxes and sealed with the royal signet ring.

Bulletins were sent out by couriers to all the king's provinces with orders to massacre, kill, and eliminate all the Jews—youngsters and old men, women and babies—on a single day, the thirteenth day of the twelfth month, the month of Adar, and to plunder their goods. Copies of the bulletin were to be posted in each province, publicly available to all the peoples, to get them ready for that day.

At the king's command, the couriers took off; the order was also posted in the palace complex of Susa. The king and Haman sat back and had a drink while the city of Susa reeled from the news. (Esther 3:115, MSG)

When Mordecai learned what had been done, he ripped his clothes to shreds and put on sackcloth and ashes. Then he went out in the streets of the city crying out loud and bitter cries. He came only as far as the King's Gate, for no one dressed in sackcloth was allowed to enter the King's Gate. As the king's order was posted in every province, there was loud lament among Jews—fasting, weeping, wailing. And most of them stretched out on sackcloth and ashes.

Esther's maids and eunuchs came and told her. The queen was stunned. She sent fresh clothes to Mordecai so he could take off his sackcloth but he would not accept them. Esther called for Hathach, one of the royal eunuchs whom the king had assigned to wait on her, and told him to go to Mordecai and get the full story of what was happening. So Hathach went to Mordecai in the town square in front of the King's Gate. Mordecai told him everything that had happened to him. He also told him the exact amount of money that Haman had promised to deposit in the royal bank to finance the massacre of the Jews. Mordecai also gave him a copy of the bulletin that had been posted in Susa ordering the massacre so he could show it to Esther when he reported back with instructions to go to the king and intercede and plead with him for her people.

Hathach came back and told Esther everything Mordecai had said. Esther talked it over with Hathach and then sent him back to Mordecai with this message: "Everyone who works for the king here, and even the people out in the provinces, knows that there is a single fate for every man or woman who approaches the king without being invited: death. The one exception is if the king extends his gold scepter; then he or she may live. And it's been thirty days now since I've been invited to come to the king."

When Hathach told Mordecai what Esther had said, Mordecai sent her this message: "Don't think that just because you live in the king's house you're the one Jew who will get out of this alive. If you persist in staying silent at a time like this, help and deliverance will arrive for the Jews from someplace else; but you and your family will be wiped out. Who knows? Maybe you were made queen for such a time as this."

Esther sent back her answer to Mordecai, "Go and get all the Jews living in Susa together. Fast for me. Don't eat or drink for three days, either day or night. I and my maids will fast with you. If you will do this, I'll go to the king, even though it's forbidden. If I die, I die."

Mordecai left and carried out Esther's instructions. (Esther 4:1–17, MSG)

Three days later Esther dressed in her royal robes and took up a position in the inner court of the palace in front of the king's throne room. The king was on his throne facing the entrance. When he noticed Queen Esther standing in the court, he was pleased to see her; the king extended the gold scepter in his hand. Esther approached and touched the tip of the scepter. The king asked, "And what's your desire, Queen Esther? What do you want? Ask and it's yours—even if it's half my kingdom!"

"If it please the king," Esther said, "let the king come with Haman to a dinner I've prepared for him."

"Get Haman at once," said the king, "so we can go to dinner with Esther."

So the king and Haman joined Esther at the dinner she had arranged. As they were drinking wine, the king said, "Now, what is it you want? Half of my kingdom isn't too much to ask! Just ask."

Esther answered, "Here's what I want. If the king favors me and is pleased to do what I desire and ask, let the king and Haman come again tomorrow to dinner that I will fix for them. Then I'll give a straight answer to the king's question." (Esther 5:1–8, MSG)

Haman left the palace that day happy, beaming. And then he saw Mordecai sitting at the King's Gate ignoring him, oblivious to him. Haman was furious with Mordecai. But he held himself in and went on home. He got his friends together with his wife Zeresh and started bragging about how much money he had, his many sons, all the times the king had honored him, and his promotion to the highest position of government. "On top of all that," Haman continued, "Queen Esther invited me to a private dinner she gave for the king, just the three of us. And she's invited me to another one tomorrow. But I can't enjoy any of it when I see Mordecai the Jew sitting at the King's Gate."

His wife Zeresh and all his friends said, "Build a gallows seventy-five feet high. First thing in the morning speak with the king; get him to order Mordecai hanged on it. Then happily go with the king to dinner."

Haman liked that. He had the gallows built. (Esther 5:9–14, MSG)

That night the king couldn't sleep. He ordered the record book, the day-by-day journal of events, to be brought and read to him. They came across the story there about the time that Mordecai had exposed the plot of Bigthana and Teresh—the two royal eunuchs who guarded the entrance and who had conspired to assassinate King Xerxes.

The king asked, "What great honor was given to Mordecai for this?"

"Nothing," replied the king's servants who were in attendance. "Nothing has been done for him."

The king said, "Is there anybody out in the court?"

Now Haman had just come into the outer court of the king's palace to talk to the king about hanging Mordecai on the gallows he had built for him.

The king's servants said, "Haman is out there, waiting in the court."

"Bring him in," said the king.

When Haman entered, the king said, "What would be appropriate for the man the king especially wants to honor?"

Haman thought to himself, "He must be talking about honoring me—who else?" So he answered the king, "For the man the king delights to honor, do this: Bring a royal robe that the king has worn and a horse the king has ridden, one with a royal crown on its head. Then give the robe and the horse to one of the king's most noble princes. Have him robe the man whom the king especially wants to honor; have the prince lead him on horseback through the city square, proclaiming before him. 'This is what is done for the man whom the king especially wants to honor!'"

"Go and do it," the king said to Haman. "Don't waste another minute. Take the robe and horse and do what you have proposed to Mordecai the Jew who sits at the King's Gate. Don't leave out a single detail of your plan."

So Haman took the robe and horse; he robed Mordecai and led him through the city square, proclaiming before him, "This is what is done for the man whom the king especially wants to honor!"

Then Mordecai returned to the King's Gate, but Haman fled to his house, thoroughly mortified, hiding his face. When Haman had finished telling his wife Zeresh and all his friends everything that had happened to him, his knowledgeable friends who were there and his wife Zeresh said, "If this Mordecai is in fact a Jew, your bad luck has only begun. You don't stand a chance against him—you're as good as ruined."

While they were still talking, the king's eunuchs arrived and hurried Haman off to the dinner that Esther had prepared. (Esther 6:1–14, MSG)

So, the king and Haman went to dinner with Queen Esther. At this second dinner, while they were drinking wine the king again asked, "Queen Esther, what would you like? Half of my kingdom! Just ask and it's yours."

Queen Esther answered, "If I have found favor in your eyes, O King, and if it please the king, give me my life, and give my people their lives.

We've been sold, I and my people, to be destroyed—sold to be massacred, eliminated. If we had just been sold off into slavery. I wouldn't even have brought it up; our troubles wouldn't have been worth bothering the king over."

King Xerxes exploded, "Who? Where is he? This is monstrous!"

"An enemy. An adversary. This evil Haman," said Esther.

Haman was terror-stricken before the king and queen.

The king, raging, left his wine and stalked out into the palace garden.

Haman stood pleading with Queen Esther for his life—he could see that the king was finished with him and that he was doomed. As the king came back from the palace garden into the banquet hall, Haman was groveling at the couch on which Esther reclined. The king roared out, "Will he even molest the queen while I'm just around the corner?"

When that word left the king's mouth, all the blood drained from Haman's face.

Harbona, one of the eunuchs attending the king, spoke up: "Look over there! There's the gallows that Haman had built for Mordecai, who saved the king's life. It's right next to Haman's house—seventy-five feet high!"

The king said, "Hang him on it!"

So Haman was hanged on the very gallows that he had built for Mordecai. And the king's hot anger cooled. (Esther 7:1–10, MSG)

That same day King Xerxes gave Queen Esther the estate of Haman, archenemy of the Jews. And Mordecai came before the king because Esther had explained their relationship. The king took off his signet ring, which he had taken back from Haman, and gave it to Mordecai. Esther appointed Mordecai over Haman's estate. (Esther 8:1 and 2, MSG)

The Book of Esther continues to explain how Haman's plot was rectified and Mordecai's role with King Xerxes. It also explains the creation of "the festival of Purim."

Haman had a true hatred of the Jews, and Mordecai appeared not to be too fond of Agagites. Joseph Ben Matthias better known as Josephus (Flavius Josephus), a first-century (AD) historian, wrote in his *The Antiquities of the Jews* (book 11, chapter 6, section 5, verse 209): "Now there was one Haman, the son of Amedatha, by birth an Amalekite…."

The Amalekites were the archenemy of the Jews. Amalek was the grandson of Esau (Genesis 36:11).

Amalek came and fought Israel at Rephidim. Moses ordered Joshua: "Select some men for us and go out and fight Amalek. Tomorrow I will take my stand on top of the hill holding God's staff."

Joshua did what Moses ordered in order to fight Amalek. And Moses, Aaron, and Hur went to the top of the hill. It turned out that whenever Moses raised his hands, Israel was winning, but whenever he lowered his hands, Amalek was winning. But Moses' hands got tired. So they got a stone and set it under him. He sat on it and Aaron and Hur held up his hands, one on each side. So his hands remained steady until the sun went down. Joshua defeated Amalek and its army in battle.

GOD said to Moses, "Write this up as a reminder to Joshua, to keep it before him, because I will most certainly wipe the very memory of Amalek off the face of the Earth."

Moses built an altar and named it "GOD My Banner." He said,

"Salute GOD's rule!
GOD at war with Amalek
Always and forever!" (Exodus 17:8–16, MSG)

Manasseh

King Manasseh is a perfect example of an individual who surrendered completely to the desires and urgings of his "free will" combined with his view of what was right. King Manasseh learned the value of being a man "seeking God's heart."

Manasseh was twelve years old when he became king. He ruled for fifty-five years in Jerusalem. His mother's name was Hephzibah. In GOD's judgment he was a bad king—an evil king. He reintroduced all the moral rot and spiritual corruption that had been scoured from the country when GOD dispossessed the pagan nations in favor of the children of Israel. He rebuilt all the sex-and-religion shrines that his father Hezekiah had torn down, and he built altars and phallic images for the sex god Baal and the sex goddess Asherah, exactly what Ahaz king of Israel had done. He worshiped the cosmic powers, taking orders from the constellations. He even built these pagan altars in The Temple of GOD, the very Jerusalem Temple dedicated exclusively by GOD's decree ("in Jerusalem I place my Name") to GOD's Name. And he built shrines to cosmic powers and placed them in both courtyards of The Temple of GOD. He burned his own son in a sacrificial offering. He practiced black magic and fortunetelling. He held séances and consulted spirits from the underworld. Much evil— in GOD's judgment, a career in evil. And GOD was angry.

As a last straw he placed the craved image of the sex goddess Asherah in The Temple of GOD, a flagrant and provocative violation of GOD's well-known statement to both David and Solomon, "In this Temple and in this city Jerusalem, my choice out of all the tribes of Israel, I place my Name—exclusively and forever. Never again will I let my people Israel wander off from this land I gave their ancestors. But here's the condition: They must keep everything I've commanded in the instructions my servant Moses passed on to them."

But the people didn't listen. Manasseh led them off the beaten path into practices of evil even exceeding the evil of the pagan nations that GOD had earlier destroyed.

GOD, thoroughly fed up, sent word through his servants the prophets: "Because Manasseh king of Judah has committed these outrageous sins, eclipsing the sin-performance of the Amorites before him, setting new records of evil, using foul idols to debase Judah into a nation of sinners, this is my judgment, GOD's

verdict: I, the GOD of Israel, will visit catastro-
phe on Jerusalem and Judah, a doom so terrible
that when people hear of it they'll shake their
heads in disbelief, saying, 'I can't believe it!'

I'll visit the fate of Samaria on Jerusalem,
a rerun of Ahab's doom. I'll wipe out Jerusalem
as you would wipe out a dish, wiping it out and
turning it over to dry. I'll get rid of what's left of
my inheritance, dumping them on their enemies.
If their enemies can salvage anything from them,
they're welcome to it. They've been nothing but
trouble to me from the day their ancestors left
Egypt until now. They pushed me to my limit; I
won't put up with their evil any longer."

The final word of Manasseh was that he
was an indiscriminate murderer. He drenched
Jerusalem with the innocent blood of his victims.
That's on top of all the sins in which he involved
his people. As far as GOD was concerned, he'd
turned them into a nation of sinners." (1 King
21:1–16, MSG)

Even when it looks like your life story has
been written and society and the world have concluded your total worth, seeking forgiveness and
the "favor of God" can greatly alter your future.

But Manasseh led Judah and the citizens of
Jerusalem off the beaten path into practices of
evil exceeding even the evil of the pagan nations
that GOD had earlier destroyed. When GOD
spoke to Manasseh and his people about this,
they ignored him.

Then GOD directed the leaders of the
troops of the king of Assyria to come after
Manasseh. They put a hook in his nose, shackles
on his feet, and took him off to Babylon. Now
that he was in trouble, he went to his knees in

prayer asking for help—total repentance before the God of his ancestors. As he prayed, GOD was touched; GOD listened and brought him back to Jerusalem as king. That convinced Manasseh that GOD was in control.

After that Manasseh rebuilt the outside defensive wall of the City of David to the west of the Gihon spring in the valley. It went from the Fish Gate and around the hill of Ophel. He also increased its height. He tightened up the defense system by posting army captains in all the fortress cities in Judah. He also did a good spring cleaning on The Temple, carting out the pagan idols and the goddess statue. He took all the altars he had set up on the Temple hill and throughout Jerusalem and dumped them outside the city. He put the Altar of GOD back in working order and restored worship, sacrificing Peace-Offerings and Thank-Offerings. He issued orders to the people: "You shall serve and worship GOD, the GOD of Israel." But the people didn't take him seriously—they used the name "GOD" but kept on going to the old pagan neighborhood shrines and doing the same old things.

The rest of the history of Manasseh—his prayer to his God, and the sermons the prophets personally delivered by authority of GOD, the God of Israel—this is all written in The Chronicles of the Kings of Israel. His prayer and how God was touched by his prayer, a list of all his sins and the things he did wrong, the actual places where he built the pagan shrines, the installation of the sex-goddess Asherah sites, and the idolatrous images that he worshiped previous to his conversion—this is all described in the records of the prophets.

When Manasseh died, they buried him in the palace garden. His son Amon was the next king. (2 Chronicles 33:10–20, MSG)

Josiah

When people talk about the greatest king, during the period of "kingship" in the "promised land" (Israel in totality), people's attention often turns to King David or his son King Solomon. The first king of the "promised land" (Israel) was King Saul. The people of the "promised land" (Israel) wanted to be like the countries around them with a king. They wanted this because Samuel had done the same thing Eli did (1 Samuel 2:12–26). When Samuel got old, he appointed his sons to take over his responsibilities (1 Samuel 8:1–9).

Saul was everything Israel (the promised land) thought they wanted. He was from a wealthy prominent family, he was the most handsome man in Israel, and he stood a head and shoulder taller than anyone else in the "promise land" (1 Samuel 9:1 and 2). King Saul's problem was that he leaned on his own understanding, instead of seeking God's. He sought man's forgiveness instead of God's forgiveness (1 Samuel 15:10–35).

King David understood the importance of seeking God. David had major qualities and flaws that we see in ourselves. David was ruthless, treacherous, and selfish. David's saving quality was that he knew how to turn to God for forgiveness. He was a man after God's heart (2 Samuel 12:13–25).

King Solomon received special Giftings from God (1 Kings chapter 3). Solomon built God's temple in Jerusalem and received a promise from God based on Solomon's faithfulness (1 Kings 9:1–9). Solomon clouded his giftings from the *Lord*, the God of Israel, with his wants and desires (1 Kings 11:1–13). King Solomon recognized his foolishness and attempted to alert his son about the vainness of vanity and seeking earthly items over God's desires for your life (the books of Proverbs and Ecclesiastes).

King Josiah is referred to, in the Bible, as the greatest king of Israel (the promised land) whole or divided.

Never before had there been a king like
Josiah, who turned to the LORD with all his
heart and soul and strength, obeying all the laws
of Moses. And there has never been a king like
him since. (2 Kings 23:25, NLT)

As we will see the Israelites, God's chosen people, were functioning without the book of the law that God gave Moses for years.
It will be Josiah's efforts that would create a right relationship with
the God of Israel.

Josiah was eight years old when he became
king. He ruled for thirty-one years in Jerusalem.
He behaved well before GOD. He kept straight
on the path blazed by his ancestor David, not one
step to the left or right.
When he had been king for eight years—he
was still only a teenager—he began to seek the
God of David his ancestor. Four years later, the
twelfth year of his reign, he set out to cleanse the
neighborhood of sex-and-religion shrines, and
get rid of sacred Asherah groves and the god and
goddess figurines, whether carved or cast, from
Judah. He wrecked the Baal shrines, tore down
the altars connected with them, and scattered the
debris and ashes over the graves of those who had
worshiped at them. He burned the bones of the
priests on the same altars they had used when
alive. He scrubbed the place clean, Judah and
Jerusalem, clean inside and out. The cleanup campaign ranged outward to the cities of Manasseh,
Ephraim, Simeon, and the surrounding neigh-
borhoods—as far north as Naphtali. Throughout
Israel he demolished the altars and Asherah groves,
pulverized the god and goddess figures, chopped
up the neighborhood shrines into firewood. With

Israel once more intact, he returned to Jerusalem. (2 Chronicles 34:1–7, MSG)

King Josiah developed an "obedient relationship with God." Josiah's desire to be obedient to God led the Father to allow Josiah to be the first king to have influence over all of Israel, since Solomon's son Rehoboam lost it (1 Kings 12:1–20). God showed Josiah great favor because of his intimate relationship with God.

Josiah tore down and burned everything that was not of God in all of Israel, and he did it not knowing God's law. It reiterates the special kind of relationship that the Father makes available to Enoch, Josiah, and you, through a "prayer life" of prayer and meditation.

One day in the eighteenth year of his kingship, with the cleanup of country and Temple complete, King Josiah sent Shaphan son of Azaliah, Maaseiah the mayor of the city, and Joah son of Joahaz the historian to renovate The Temple of GOD. First they turned over to Hilkiah the high priest all the money collected by the Levitical security guards from Manasseh and Ephraim and the rest of Israel, and from Judah and Benjamin and the citizens of Jerusalem. It was then put into the hands of the foremen managing the work on The Temple of GOD who then passed it on to the workers repairing GOD's Temple—the carpenters, construction workers, and masons—so they could buy the lumber and dressed stone for rebuilding the foundations the kings of Judah had allowed to fall to pieces. (2 Chronicles 34:8–11, MSG)

While the money that had been given for The Temple of GOD was being received and dispersed, Hilkiah the high priest found a copy

TED FREEMAN

of The Revelation of Moses. He reported to
Shaphan the royal secretary, "I've just found the
Book of GOD's Revelation, instructing us in
GOD's way—found it in the Temple!" He gave
it to Shaphan, who then gave it to the king. And
along with the book, he gave this report: "The
job is complete—everything you ordered done is
done. They took all the money that was collected
in The Temple of GOD and handed it over to the
managers and workers."

And then Shaphan told the king, "Hilkiah
the priest gave me a book." Shaphan proceeded
to read it out to the king.

When the king heard what was written
in the book, GOD's Revelation, he ripped his
robes in dismay. And then he called for Hilkiah,
Ahikam son of Shaphan, Abdon son of Micah,
Shaphan the royal secretary, and Asaiah the king's
personal aide. He ordered them all: "Go and
pray to GOD for me and what's left of Israel and
Judah. Find out what we must do in response to
what is written in this book that has just been
found! GOD's anger must be burning furiously
against us—our ancestors haven't obeyed a thing
written in this book of GOD, followed none of
the instructions directed to us."

Hilkiah and those picked by the king went
straight to Huldah the prophetess. She was the
wife of Shallum son of Tokhath, the son of Hasrah,
who was in charge of the palace wardrobe. She
lived in Jerusalem in the Second Quarter. The
men consulted with her. In response to them she
said, "GOD's word, the God of Israel: Tell the
man who sent you here, 'GOD has spoken, I'm
on my way to bring the doom of judgment on
this place and this people. Every word written in

286

the book read by the king of Judah will happen.
And why? Because they've deserted me and taken
up with other gods; they've made me thoroughly
angry by setting up their god-making businesses.
My anger is raging white-hot against this place
and nobody is going to put it out.'

And also tell the king of Judah, since he sent
you to ask GOD for direction, GOD's comment
on what he read in the book: 'Because you took
seriously the doom of judgment I spoke against
this place and people, and because you responded
in humble repentance, tearing your robe in dismay and weeping before me, I'm taking you seriously. GOD's word. I'll take care of you; you'll
have a quiet death and be buried in peace. You
won't be around to see the doom that I'm going
to bring upon this place and people.'"

The men took her message back to the king.

The king acted immediately, assembling all
the elders of Judah and Jerusalem, and then pro-
ceeding to The Temple of GOD bringing everyone in his train—priests and prophets and people
ranging from the least to the greatest. Then he
read out publicly everything written in the Book
of the Covenant that was found in The Temple
of GOD. The king stood by his pillar and before
GOD solemnly committed himself to the covenant: to follow GOD believingly and obediently;
to follow his instructions, heart and soul, on what
to believe and do; to confirm with his life the
entire covenant, all that was written in the book.

Then he made everyone in Jerusalem and
Benjamin commit themselves. And they did it.
They committed themselves to the covenant of
God, the God of their ancestors.

Josiah did a thorough job of cleaning up the pollution that had spread throughout Israelite territory and got everyone started fresh again, serving and worshiping their GOD. All through Josiah's life the people kept to the straight and narrow, obediently following GOD, the God of their ancestors. (2 Chronicles 34:14–33, MSG)

Chapter 10

TURNING AWAY:
ACCEPTING THE REVEAL

So we must listen very carefully to the truth we have heard, or we may drift away from it. For the message God delivered through angels has always stood firm, and every violation of the law and every act of disobedience was punished. So what makes us think we can escape if we ignore this great salvation that was first announced by the Lord Jesus himself and then delivered to us by those who heard him speak? And God confirmed the message by giving signs and wonders and various miracles and gifts of the Holy Spirit whenever he chose.

—Hebrews 2:1–4, NLT

You have just been reacquainted with, enlightened by, stimulated by, energized by, convicted by, motivated by, and conflicted by learning that "resolved by the love the Father has for you, the sacrifice the Messiah made for your salvation, and the efforts of the Holy Spirit to enlighten and guide you" to do better.

"To do better" in keeping God first even in traffic. "To do better" in learning to love the unfamiliar in our neighbors (everybody). "To do better" in sharing what God has given us as a nation, not until it allows us to wash our hands like Pontius Pilate but until it "pleases" the Father, through the "teachings" of the Son (that we have learned) and the "obedience" to the guidance of the Holy Spirit.

You have studied to "approve yourself."

Study to shew thyself approved unto God, a workman that needeth not to be ashamed, rightly dividing the word of truth. (2 Timothy 2:15, KJV)

Now that you have "approved yourself" (committing to God's will for your life), studying becomes a liability.

> The words of the wise are like cattle prods— painful but helpful. Their collected sayings are like a nail studded stick with which a shepherd drives the sheep.
>
> But my child, let me give you some further advice: Be careful for writing books is endless, and much study wears you out.
>
> That's the whole story. Here now is my final conclusion: Fear God and obey his commands, for this is everyone's duty. God will judge us for everything we do, including every secret thing, whether good or bad. (Ecclesiastes 12:11–14, NLT)

Now you move from studying and "making yourself approved" by accepting the "will of God" for your life to learning and being "obedient" to the guidance of the Holy Spirit.

Overstudying allows your opinions and thoughts to become coagulated with "God's word." This promotes inconsequential etiology and etymology and other items that will just make your head hurt and could lead to a life of mitigating your giftings from God.

> For the word of the cross is folly to those who are perishing, but to us who are saved it is the power of God. For it is written, "I will destroy the wisdom of the wise, and the discernment of the

discerning I will thwart." Where is the one who is wise? Where is the scribe? Where is the debater of this age? Has not God made foolish the wisdom of the world? For since, in the wisdom of God, the world did not know God through wisdom, it pleased God through the folly of what we preach to save those who believe. For Jews demand signs and Greeks seek wisdom, but we preach Christ crucified, a stumbling block to Jews and folly to Gentiles, but to those who are called, both Jews and Greeks, Christ the power of God and the wisdom of God. For the foolishness of God is wiser than men, and the weakness of God is stronger than men.

For consider your calling, brothers: not many of you were wise according to worldly standards, not many were powerful, not many were of noble birth. But God chose what is foolish in the word to shame the wise; God chose what is weak in the world to shame the strong; God chose what is low and despised in the world, even things that are not, to bring to nothing things that are, so that no human being might boast in the presence of God. And because of him you are in Christ Jesus, who became to us wisdom from God, righteousness and sanctification and redemption, so that, as it is written, "Let the one who boasts, boast in the Lord." (1 Corinthians 1:18–31, ESV)

Now that you have "studied to approve yourself" (you have accepted the "will of God" for your life), it's time to focus on "learning." "Learning" is becoming more "obedient" to the guidance of the Holy Spirit in spite of what is being presented by the world. "Learning" from the Holy Spirit does not require your opinion, interpretation, education, and "ed-cha-ma-cation (self-imposed lunacy)."

You are the "light of the world."

> You are the light of the World—like a city
> on a hilltop that cannot be hidden. No one lights
> a lamp and then and then puts it under a bas-
> ket. Instead, a lamp is placed on a stand, where it
> gives light to everyone in the house. In the same
> way, let your good deeds shine out for all to see,
> so that everyone will praise your heavenly Father.
> (Matthew 5:14–16, NLT)

You do not have the right or permission from God to turn your "light from Christ" into a shaded resemblance of "your light," based on you.

In our world today, you are "God's lighthouse." You do not have permission nor approval to turn your light off because you do not like the approaching ship.

Don't turn your lighthouse off, because you're not familiar with or do not like the approaching ship!!!

> Don't participate in the things these people
> do. For once you were full of darkness, but now
> you have light from the Lord. So live as people
> of light! For this light within you produces only
> what is good and right and true.
> Carefully determine what pleases the Lord.
> (Ephesians 5:7–10, NLT)
> "Your word is a lamp to guide my feet and a
> light for my path.
> I've promised it once, and I'll promise it
> again: I will obey your righteous regulations."
> (Psalm 119:105 and 106, NLT)

When we start turning our "light" off and on or start getting "shady" with how much of our "light" we allow to radiate, given earthly situations, likes, dislikes, pride, opinions, etc., it is all based on the belief, "We have time to get it right."

Time on earth has a beginning and an end. All sporting events have a predetermined ending, even a process to bring the event to a conclusion, even if the predetermined ending becomes convoluted (overtime, shoot-out, tiebreakers, etc.).

This leads us to believe a lie from Satan, masquerading himself as an "angel of light" (2 Corinthians 11:14), that there is *time*, even though we know better.

We've developed all kinds of impactful statements that allow us to halt the process toward God or slow it up.

- "I'm not where I need to be with God, but I'm not what I used to be." Complete your journey to "where I need to be" *now*". Don't get happy that you're almost where you need to be with God. You might stop and look back at what you were caught up in. Your life with God is not a game of horseshoes; "almost" does not count.

> Then the men said to Lot, "Have you anyone else here? Sons-in-law, sons, daughters, or anyone you have in the city, bring them out of the place. For we are about to destroy this place, because the outcry against its people has become great before the LORD, and the LORD has sent us to destroy it." So Lot went out and said to his sons-in-law, who were to marry his daughters, "Up! Get out of this place, for the LORD is about to destroy the city." But he seemed to his sons-in-law to be jesting.
>
> As morning dawned, the angels urged Lot, saying, "Up! Take your wife and your two daughters who are here, lest you be swept away in the punishment of the city." But he lingered. So the men seized him and his wife and his two daughters by the hand, the LORD being merciful to

him, and they brought him out and set him outside the city. And as they brought them out, one said, "Escape for your life. Do not look back or stop anywhere in the valley. Escape to the hills, lest you be swept away." And Lot said to them, "Oh, no, my lords. Behold, your servant has found favor in your sight, and you have shown me great kindness in saving my life. But I cannot escape to the hills, lest disaster overtake me and I die. Behold, this city is near enough to flee to, and it is a little one. Let me escape there—is it not a little one?—and my life will be saved!" He said to him, "Behold, I grant you this favor also, that I will not overthrow the city of which you have spoken. Escape there quickly, for I can do nothing till you arrive there." Therefore the name of the city was called Zoar.

The sun had risen on the earth when Lot came to Zoar. Then the LORD rained on Sodom and Gomorrah sulfur and fire from the LORD out of heaven. And he overthrew those cities, and all the valley, and all the inhabitants of the cities, and what grew on the ground. But Lot's wife, behind him, looked back, and she became a pillar of salt.

And Abraham went early in the morning to the place where he stood before the LORD. And he looked down toward Sodom and Gomorrah and toward all the land of the valley, and he looked and, behold, the smoke of the land went up like the smoke of a furnace.

So it was that, when God destroyed the cities of the valley, God remembered Abraham and sent Lot out of the midst of the overthrow when he overthrew the cities in which Lot had lived. (Genesis 19:12–29, ESV)

It's important to get to where God wants you once you realize that's the purpose of your being. You don't have time for *change*. Become what God wants you to be. Only God controls time. All you have is this moment.

- "Only God can judge me." If you realize that God is the only one with a heaven and hell and if you realize that God is judging you right *now*, it's time right now to start preparing for that final judgment, before your actions require an early judgment from God, to get the results the Father wants from your life.

> Again the Israelites did evil in the LORD'S sight, so the LORD handed them over to the Philistines, who oppressed them for forty years.
>
> In those days a man named Manoah from the tribe of Dan lived in the town of Zorah. His wife was unable to become pregnant, and they had no children. The angel of the LORD appeared to Manoah's wife and said, "Even though you have been unable to have children, you will soon become pregnant and give birth to a son. So be careful; you must not drink wine or any alcoholic drink nor eat any forbidden food. You will become pregnant and give birth to a son, and his hair must never be cut. For he will be dedicated to God as a Nazirite from birth. He will begin to rescue Israel from the Philistines." (Judges 13:1–5, NLT)
>
> And the woman bare a son, and called his name Samson: and the child grew, and the LORD blessed him.
>
> And the Spirit of the LORD began to move him at times in the camp of Dan between Zorah and Eshtaol. (Judges 13:24 and 25, KJV)

So the Philistines captured him and gouged out his eyes. They took him to Gaza, where he was bound with bronze chains and forced to grind grain in the prison. (Judges 16:21, NLT)

Then Samson prayed to the LORD, "Sovereign LORD, remember me again. O God, please strengthen me just one more time. With one blow let me pay back the Philistines for the loss of my two eyes." Then Samson put his hands on the two center pillars that held up the temple. Pushing against them with both hands, he prayed, "Let me die with the Philistines." And the temple crashed down on the Philistine rulers and all the people. So he killed more people when he died than he had during his entire lifetime. (Judges 16:29 and 30, NLT)

You don't have time. You only have the moment. Now that you have embellished your "prayer Life," you can now understand the importance of staying in continual contact with the Holy Spirit for proper guidance. Don't let your "moment" become a "fleeting moment."

The "reveal" is to be constantly moving step by step closer to where God wants you to be, by accepting more and more guidance from the Holy Spirit.

"And now I entrust you to God and the message of his grace that is able to build you up and give you an inheritance with all those he has set apart for himself." (Acts 20:32, NLT)

"So we have not stopped praying for you since we first heard about you. We ask God to give you complete knowledge of his will and to give you spiritual wisdom and understanding. Then the way you live will always honor and please the Lord, and your lives will produce every kind of good fruit. All the while, you will grow as you learn to know God better and better." (Colossians 1:9 and 10, NLT)

"Listen, O Israel! The LORD is our God, the LORD alone. And you must love the LORD your God with all your heart, all your soul, and all your strength. And you must commit your-selves wholeheartedly to these commands that I am giving you today. Repeat them again and again to your children. Talk about them when you are at home and when you are on the road, when you are going to bed and when you are get-ting up. Tie them to your hands and wear them on your forehead as reminders. Write them on the doorposts of your house and on your gates." (Deuteronomy 6:4–9, NLT)

Then the eleven disciples left for Galilee, going to the mountain where Jesus had told them to go. When they saw him, they worshiped him—but some of them doubted!

Jesus came and told his disciples, "I have been given all authority in heaven and on earth. Therefore, go and make disciples of all the nations, baptizing them in the name of the Father and the Son and the Holy Spirit. Teach these new disciples to obey all the commands I have given you. And be sure of this: I am with you always, even to the end of the age." (Matthew 28:16–20, NLT)

"This disciple is the one who testifies to these events and has recorded them here. And we know that this account of these things is accurate.

Jesus also did many other things. If they were all written down, I suppose the whole world could not contain the books that would be writ-ten." (John 21:24 and 25, NLT)

The Spirit and the bride say, "Come." Let anyone who hears this say, "Come." Let anyone who is thirsty come. Let anyone who desires drink freely from the water of life. And I solemnly declare to everyone who hears the words of prophecy written in this book: If anyone adds anything to what is written here, God will add to that person the plagues described in this book. And if anyone removes any of the words from this book of prophecy, God will remove that person's share in the tree of life and in the holy city that are described in this book.

He who is the faithful witness to all these things says, "Yes, I am coming soon!" Amen! Come, Lord Jesus!

May the grace of the Lord Jesus be with God's holy people. (Revelation 22:17–21, NLT)

References

Scripture quotations marked (ESV) are from The ESV® Bible (The Holy Bible, English Standard Version®), copyright © 2001 by Crossway, a publishing ministry of Good News Publishers. Used by permission. All rights reserved.

Scripture taken from "THE MESSAGE (MSG). Copyright © 199 3,1994,1995,1996,2000,2001,2002. Used by permission of NavPress Publishing Group.

Scripture quotations taken from The Holy Bible, New International Version® NIV® Copyright © 1973,1978,1984,2011 by Biblica, Inc. ® Used by permission. All rights reserved worldwide.

Scripture quotations marked NLT are taken from the Holy Bible, New Living Translation, copyright © 1996, 2004. Used by permission of Tyndale House Publishers, Inc., Wheaton, Illinois 60189. All rights reserved.

Scripture taken from the New King James Version® (NKJV®). Copyright © 1982 by Thomas Nelson, Inc. Used by permission. All rights reserved.

Scripture taken from the King James Version (KJV) are in the public domain.

Scripture quotations marked CSB have been taken from the Christian Standard Bible®, Copyright © 2017 by Holman Bible Publishers. Used by permission. Christian Standard Bible® and

CSB® are federally registered trademarks of Holman Bible Publishers.

Scripture taken from the NEW AMERICAN STANDARD BIBLE® (NASB), Copyright © 1960,1962,1963,1968,1971,1972,1973,1975,1977,1995, by the Lockman Foundation. Used by permission.

Scripture taken from The Holy Bible International Standard Version® (ISV). Copyright © 1995-2014 by ISV Foundation. ALL RIGHTS RESERVED INTERNATIONALLY. Used by permission of Davidson Press, LLC.

About the Author

Ted Freeman is first and foremost a servant of the Father. He is a husband, father, grandfather, great grandfather, and a pastor for any and all who need a "word from God" to continue their journey.

CPSIA information can be obtained
at www.ICGtesting.com
Printed in the USA
FFOW02n0536180718
47461347-50709FF